RHODE ISLAND ENVIRONMENTAL LAW HANDBOOK

Third Edition

by the law firm of

Holland & Knight LLP

Editors-in-Chief

Gregory L. Benik
Robin L. Main

Contributors

William P. Devereaux
Jennifer Cervenka

Government Institutes
Rockville, Maryland

Government Institutes
4 Research Place, Rockville, Maryland 20850, USA.

06 05 04 03 5 4 3 2 1

ISBN: 0-86587-964-8

Printed in the United States of America

TABLE OF CONTENTS

PRV1 #94595 v1

About the Authors

Holland & Knight LLP

Holland & Knight clients have access to a wealth of legal resources. With more than 1,200 lawyers who practice in more than 100 areas of the law from 32 offices, we are one of the largest and legally diverse law firms in the world. We employ many methods to achieve the best possible results, evaluating a client's many needs.

The firm's services develop in response to the needs of clients requiring national and global legal representation. The firm's general business law practice is integrated; clients are served based on their need for legal services rather than their location. A state-of-the-art telecommunication system, including a networked computer system, allows us to instantaneously and electronically transmit documents from office to office, and directly to clients.

Holland & Knight's clients' businesses range in scope from local to global. Among our clientele are airlines and shipping companies; financial institutions; major utilities; insurance companies; domestic and foreign government agencies; entertainers and entertainment companies; newspapers, television broadcasters and other media enterprises; land developers; construction companies; mining and manufacturing companies; agricultural enterprises; trade associations; emerging companies; small businesses; and many individuals.

Holland & Knight's National Environmental Practice Group represents clients at the federal, regional, state, and local levels in the United States and abroad in virtually all areas of environmental law. Our experience includes: environmental requirements for siting facilities and infrastructure development, including permitting and environmental assessments; transportation and disposal requirements for hazardous waste and hazardous substances; cleanup requirements for contaminated facilities and abandoned hazardous waste; environmental compliance auditing; environmental management systems and ISO 14,000 requirements; and the development of environmental regulations. We regularly counsel national and international clients on these and many other environmental issues.

Editors-in-Chief

Gregory L. Benik

Mr. Benik is a graduate of Case Western Reserve University School of Law, and Lafayette College with honors in biology. He is Co-Chair of Holland & Knight LLP's National Environmental Practice Group. Mr. Benik is the author of numerous publications and is a regular speaker on environmental issues.

Elected to "Best Lawyers in America" in the Environmental Law category, Mr. Benik is primarily responsible for legal counsel and guidance to firm clients on all environmental matters including compliance with state and federal air and water pollution, superfund, land use, and hazardous waste regulatory programs, environmental insurance coverage issues, and representation of clients in state and federal administrative and judicial permitting, rule making, and enforcement proceedings. Mr. Benik is a member of the American Bar Association Section of Environment, Energy and Resources and serves as vice chair of the Special Committee on Solid Waste, a member and former Chair of the Rhode Island Bar Association Committee on Environmental Law, a founder and member of the Rhode Island Society of Environmental Professionals, has participated in numerous state and regional task forces and workshops created to address emerging environmental issues and has represented various trade and business groups on issues relating to environmental legislation and regulations. He is admitted to practice in Rhode Island.

Robin L. Main

Ms. Main graduated from Tulane Law School, cum laude, and from the University of New Hampshire, Phi Beta Kappa, summa cum laude. Ms. Main is a partner in the environmental practice group at Holland & Knight, LLP and is on the board of directors of the Rhode Island Society of Environmental Professionals and New England Environmental Business Council. She is a frequent speaker on environmental issues and author of a number of articles on brownsfields, superfund, and conservation easements. Her practice encompasses all areas of environmental law and complex commercial and environmental litigation. She is admitted to practice in Rhode Island and Massachusetts.

Contributors

William P. Devereaux

Mr. Devereaux graduated from Suffolk University school of Law and Wesleyan University. He served as a judge advocate in the United States Naval Reserve, as an Assistant Attorney General for the State of Rhode Island, Solicitor for the Town of Cumberland, Rhode Island, and as a Special Assistant Attorney General, Commonwealth of Massachusetts. He concentrates in general, commercial, and environmental litigation. He is a member of the Massachusetts and Rhode Island bars.

Jennifer Cervenka

Ms. Cervenka received her B.A. in Political Science, International Relations at the University of California, Santa Barbara, her J.D. at the University of Hawaii, William S. Richardson School of Law, and her L.L.M. in International Environmental and Business Law at American University, Washington College of Law. She is a member of the Hawaii, Massachusetts and Rhode Island bars.

Acknowledgements

We acknowledge with grateful thanks, Edward Southgate for his research and drafting of portions of this book. We also thank our support staff in assisting in the desktop publishing services.

Preface

In this third edition of the *Rhode Island Environmental Law Handbook,* we update the second edition's summary of Rhode Island's major environmental laws and regulations.

We must emphasize at the outset that the *Handbook* cannot be a substitute for seeking competent legal advice. Each person's or business entity's environmental responsibilities and liabilities will depend upon the unique facts of the particular matter. Nevertheless, as environmental compliance issues become more entangled with real estate acquisitions, insurance coverage, mergers and acquisitions, and financing, merely knowing where to start an inquiry or a simple discussion of the issues can often assist in a resolution of the problem. Thus, we hope that this *Handbook*, will serve as a useful reference aid to both attorneys and lay persons who may find themselves confronting environmental issues in the State of Rhode Island.

Holland & Knight, LLP

PRV1 #88793 v1

CHAPTER I:

OVERVIEW OF THE RHODE ISLAND ENVIRONMENTAL AGENCIES

A. The Rhode Island Regulatory Scheme

Rhode Island's environmental regulatory scheme, like that in the most states, follows the lead of the United State Environmental Protection Agency (the "EPA"). The EPA has delegated the administration and enforcement of many federal EPA programs in Rhode Island, such as air, water, solid waste and hazardous waste pollution, to the Rhode Island Department of Environmental Management (the "DEM"). The addresses and telephone numbers of the DEM are listed on the front inside cover of this Handbook.

B. The Department of Environmental Management

1. The Director of DEM

The DEM is headed by a director, who is appointed by the Governor, with the advice and consent of the Rhode Island Senate, and who serves at the pleasure of the Governor. The DEM also contains various branches, each headed by an associate director.

The duties of the director of the DEM include, among others:

a. The supervision and control of the protection, development, planning and utilization of the natural resources of the state;

b. The oversight and coordination of activities of the various branches of the DEM;

c. The development and adoption of all rules and regulations to carry out the functions of the DEM;

d. The issuance of rules, regulations and/or orders as may be necessary to carry out the duties assigned to the director or the associate directors of the DEM.

e. To enforce rules, regulations and orders as may be necessary to carry out his duties.

f. The regulation of public and private land trusts; and

g. The application for an accepting of any grants and bequests of funds from other states, interstate agencies and independent authorities, and private firms, individuals and foundations, for the purpose of carrying out his lawful responsibilities.[1]

2. The Divisions of the DEM

Within the DEM are the following divisions:

a. A parks and recreation division which carries out those functions relating to the operations and maintenance of parks and recreational areas;

b. A fish and wildlife division which carries out those functions relating to the administration of hunting, fishing, and shell fisheries;

c. An agriculture division which carries out those functions relating to agriculture, entomology, and the plant industry;

d. A division of coastal resources which carries out those functions relating to harbors and harbor lines, pilotage, flood control, construction of port facilities, and others;

e. A division of planning and development which carries out those functions relating to planning, programming, acquisition of land, engineering studies, public dissemination of information, public relations, and the approval and inspection of dams, reservoirs and other structures in non-tidal waters;

f. An enforcement division which enforces the laws and regulations of the department and administers the planning, enforcing, licensing, registration and inspection functions of the department;

g. A forest environment division which carries out those functions relating to the administration of forests and natural areas, including programs for utilization, conservation, forest fire protection, and improvements to those areas;

[1] *Id.* §42.17.1-2.

h. A division of boating safety which shall carry out those functions relating to the development and coordination of a safe boating program.[2]

Under the law creating the DEM, each division chief has specific powers and duties, such as supervising, controlling, and implementing the policies and regulations of the specific division for which the Chief is responsible.

3. Advisory Council on Environmental Affairs

Under the DEM, there is an Advisory Council on Environmental Affairs This Council advises the Governor and the director of the DEM on matters involving environmental management, environmental protection, natural resources, and the policies, plans and goals for the DEM. The Council must report to the Governor, the environmental standards board and the director of DEM at least once every three months. The Council must identify problems within the various functions of the department, assist the director in the exploration and development of new initiatives, review reports prepared by the director and from the Environmental Quality Study Commission, and develop alternatives for the implementation of the goals, initiatives and directives from the reports.[3]

4. Permits, Licensee, and Enforcement Proceedings

In regard to permits and licenses from the DEM, the Director has jurisdiction over the permit, license or enforcement proceeding and reviews all decisions rendered by the administrative adjudication division relative to the DEM.[4] The Director, then, may adopt, modify, or reject the findings of fact or conclusions of law of the administrative adjudication division provided, however, that any such modification or rejection of the proposed findings of fact or conclusions of law are in writing and state the reasons for the director's decision to issue or deny the permit or license.[5] The director, however, has no direct or indirect involvement in the investigation or presentation of any contested permitting, licensing, or enforcement proceeding. In addition, the director cannot have any communication, directly or indirectly, with a hearing officer relating to any issue of fact or law on any matter pending before that hearing officer.

---

[2] §42-17.1-4

[3] §42-17.1-13

[4] Administrative Rules of Practice and Procedure for the Administrative Adjudication Division for Environmental Matters §16.

[5] *Id.* §16.

In the case of notices of violation, the director of the DEM has jurisdiction to enforce an alleged violation of any law or any DEM rule or regulation.[6] The director must give a notice of the violation to the alleged violator and has authority to impose an administrative penalty for the alleged violation. If the person, who received the notice of violation, wants a hearing on the notice of violation, he or she must make a written request to the administrative adjudication division for a hearing within 10 days after service of the notice. If no written request for a hearing is made to the administrative adjudication division within 10 days of the service of notice of violation, the notice of violation automatically becomes a compliance order.[7]

When the director determines that there exists a violation of any law, rule or regulation within his or her jurisdiction, which requires immediate action to protect the environment, the director, may without prior notice of violation or hearing, issue an immediate compliance order stating the existence of the violation and the action he or she deems necessary for compliance with the law. A person who receives an immediate compliance order may not request a hearing on the order. An immediate compliance order is effective for no longer than 45 days, but may be extended, for good cause shown, for an additional period not exceeding 45 days.[8]

C. Rhode Island Department of Health

The Department of Health (the "DOH") is responsible for supervising and managing public health functions and programs. The management of infectious waste in health care facilities and laboratories, randon testing, and poison prevention packaging are some of the programs the DOH regulates. The address and telephone numbers of the DOH are listed on the inside front cover of this Handbook.

D. The Rhode Island Department of Labor and Training

The Rhode Island Department of Labor and Training (the "DLT") is responsible for administering the Employee and Community Right to Know Acts in Rhode Island. The address and telephone numbers of the DLT are listed on the inside front cover of this Handbook.

---

[6] R.I. Gen. Laws §42-17.1-2(u)(2)(A).
[7] *Id.* §42-17.1-2(u)(1).
[8] *Id.* §42-17.1-2(u)(2)(A)-(B).

E. Coastal Resources Management Council

The Coastal Resources Management Council (the "CRMC") regulates a wide range of development activities which threaten the quality of Rhode Island's coastal resources. The CRMC is responsible for developing policies and programs to establish a balance between competing uses, while protecting coastal ecosystems. The address and telephone numbers of the CRMC are listed on the front inside cover of this Handbook.

F. The DEM Division of Fish and Wildlife

The DEM Division of Fish and Wildlife regulates, among other things, commercial and recreational fishing and shell fishing. The Division of Fish and Wildlife also regulates fish traps and fishing and shell fishing licenses.

G. Municipalities and Local Agencies

In addition to the federal and state regulatory agencies, the municipalities in Rhode Island oversee various environmental issues such as recycling, open burning, waste disposal, water use, and pre-treatment regulations. The various municipal ordinances and rules in Rhode island are too numerous to include in this Handbook. Therefore, one should consult with the municipality in which he or she is located to make sure he or she is in compliance with all local environmental rules, regulations and ordinances.

H. Office of the Attorney General

The Attorney General of Rhode Island is charged with bringing all criminal and civil suits and other proceedings at law or in equity necessary to protect the rights of the State of Rhode Island. The address and telephone number of the Attorney Generals Office are listed on the back inside cover of this Handbook.

I. Environmental Protection Agency, Region I

The United States Environmental Protection Agency (the "EPA") is the federal agency responsible for administering the federal environmental laws through the promulgation and enforcement of rules and regulations. The EPA is the federal counterpart to the Rhode Island Department of Environmental Management. The EPA cooperates with and helps state agencies in implementing federally-approved state environmental programs, such as water pollution, air pollution and solid waste management programs.

EPA has 10 regional offices throughout the United States that administer its policies. EPA's Region I office is located in Boston, Massachusetts. The address and telephone numbers for the various EPA offices and divisions are listed on the inside back cover of this Handbook.

CHAPTER II:

ADMINISTRATIVE PRACTICE AND PROCEDURE

A. Rhode Island Administrative Procedures Act

Pursuant to the Administrative Procedures Act[1], the Rhode Island Department of Environmental Management (the "DEM") has adopted Rules of Practice and Procedure for Adjudicatory Proceedings (the "Rules") before the Administrative Adjudication Division for Environmental Matters (the "Division"). An "adjudicatory proceeding" is a proceeding in which the legal rights, duties or privileges of specifically named persons are determined after opportunity for an agency hearing.[2] A "Person" is defined as any individual, partnership, corporation, association, governmental subdivision, or public or private organization.[3]

B. Formal Adjudicatory Proceedings

1. Initiation of Hearings

Any person having a right to request a hearing must send the request to the Division and follow the Rules, and comply with the specific procedures set forth in the Administrative Procedures Act[4] and the applicable environmental statutes and regulations. The request for a hearing must state the specific issues in dispute, the supporting facts, the license or permit involved, if any, other information required by the specific environmental statute or regulation involved, and the relief sought.[5] All hearings take place before an administrative hearing officer (an "AHO"). Upon the motion of any party or on the initiative of the Division or an AHO, the Division or AHO may order a party to file an answer, reply, or other pleading, or amend its pleadings.[6]

A request for a hearing may be withdrawn at any time, but the withdrawal must be submitted, in writing, to the AHO or the Division and must be signed by the petitioner or his or her authorized representative. A withdrawal will be deemed a withdrawal with prejudice.[7]

---

[1] R.I. Gen. Laws § 42-35-1 *et seq.*
[2] Administrative Rules of Practice and Procedure for the Administrative Adjudication Division for Environmental Matters § 2(c)(1).
[3] *Id.* § 2(c)(14).
[4] R.I. Gen. Laws § 42-35-1 *et seq.*
[5] Rules § 7(a), (b).
[6] *Id.* § 7(c).
[7] *Id.* § 9(a).

Upon written request, the Division's Chief Hearing Officer may, for good cause, order an accelerated hearing.[8] Any other request made by a party may be ruled upon by the AHO without a hearing.

2. Filings and Timing

Pleadings, request, and other papers filed with the Division must:

a. State the particular division of the DEM involved and the file number if any;

b. State the title of the proceeding;

c. Identify the person on whose behalf the filing is made;

d. Contain the dated signature of the person on whose behalf the filing is made, or of his or her authorized representative; and

e. Include the name of the division of the DEM that is a party to the proceeding and not the names of the particular individual(s) holding office.[9]

Forms may be provided by the clerk of the Division for certain filings, and the Division or AHO may require extra copies of papers filed, in addition to the originals.[10] Upon filing the party making the filing also must send, by mail or by hand, a copy of the papers to all other parties.[11]

Any papers filed under the Rules must be filed with the clerk of the Division within a certain time limit as set forth in the Rules, other provisions of law, or as determined by the AHO. Papers filed by hand during the regular business hours[12] are deemed filed on the date of hand delivery, or on the next regular business day if delivered after hours.[13] Papers filed by mail are deemed filed either on the date stamped by the clerk of the Division, or on the date

---

[8] Id. § 9(b).
[9] *Id.* § 6(a)-(c).
[10] *Id.* § 6(d), (e).
[11] *Id.* § 6(f).
[12] The regular business hours are 8:30 a.m. to 4:00 p.m., Monday through Friday. Rules §2(c)(16).
[13] *Id.* § 5(a)(1).

postmarked if there is no stamp from the clerk affixed.[14] Papers transmitted by facsimile or telecopier are not acceptable for filing.[15] The AHO may, upon request and for good cause shown, extend any time limit not yet expired unless precluded by statute.[16]

3. Representation

The Division must inform the individual of his or her right to be represented by legal counsel.[17] Organizations not represented by legal counsel must designate a spokesperson to participate in the hearing.[18] Where the legal counsel is unavailable for a scheduled hearing because of a state or federal court appearance, the hearing officer may continue the hearing to another date under certain circumstances.[19] *Ex parte*, off the record communications between a party or its counsel and the director of the DEM or the AHO are prohibited, unless the communication relates to general procedural or scheduling matters.[20]

4. Intervention in Adjudicatory Proceedings

Any person not initially a party to a proceeding may file a petition to intervene and must be present at the pre hearing conference.[21] The petition to intervene must identify the intervenor, discuss the areas in dispute, citing each regulation where applicable, the injury alleged, and show that the petitioner is not adequately represented by the existing parties.[22] The petition must be filed not later than seven days prior to the pre hearing conference.[23] A person permitted to intervene becomes a full party to the hearing.[24]

A person also may participate in a hearing without being an intervenor.[25] Permission to participate is limited to the right to file a brief, and the participant, unlike an intervenor, is not a party.[26]

---

[14] *Id.* § 5(a)(2).
[15] *Id.* § 5(a)(3).
[16] *Id.* § 5(c).
[17] *Id.* § 4(a).
[18] *Id.* § 4(b)(4).
[19] *Id.* § 4(b)(3).
[20] *Id.* § 4(c)(1).
[21] *Id.* § 13(a).
[22] *Id.* § 13(b).
[23] *Id.* § 13(c).
[24] *Id.* § 13(d).
[25] *Id.* § 13(e).
[26] *Id.*

5. Public Participation

The hearing officer may, in his or her discretion, permit any person, not a party to the proceeding, to participate in a hearing or pre hearing conference, state his or her position on the issues, and submit questions for witnesses.[27] The rules of evidence apply to evidence admitted by the public, and any evidence not conforming to those rules must still be accepted, but marked as public comment.[28] Hearings must be held during regular business hours or at a time which provides adequate opportunity for public participation.[29]

6. Discovery

While the Rules do not require the parties in an administrative proceeding to engage in discovery, voluntary discovery, as practiced in the Superior Court of Rhode Island, is "encouraged."[30] A request for discovery may be made by motion at any time after a request for a hearing is filed.[31] The extent of discovery is at the discretion of the AHO.[32] DEM must make all discoverable records available to the parties, at a specified time, and allow the parties to make copies.[33]

7. Pre Hearing Conferences

Parties to a hearing are required to appear for a pre hearing conference before the AHO at least seven days prior to the scheduled hearing.[34] The purposes of the conference are, among other things, to simplify the issues, come to agreements on certain matters, and limit the number of expert witnesses.[35] Prior to the pre hearing conference, the parties exchange the names and addresses of prospective witnesses, a summary and time estimate of the proposed testimony of each, and resumes of expert witnesses.[36]

At the beginning of the pre hearing conference, each party must submit:

a. Any stipulations of fact;

---

[27] *Id.* § 14(a).
[28] *Id.* § 14(b).
[29] *Id.* § 12(a).
[30] *Id.* §12(a).
[31] *Id.* §12(b).
[32] *Id.*
[33] *Id.* §12(c).
[34] *Id.* §15(a)(1).
[35] *Id.* §15(a)(1) *et seq.*
[36] *Id.* §15(a)(1) *et seq.*

b. A concise summary of its position;

c. The list of exhibits and expert witnesses, including anticipated objections thereto;

d. A list of motions requiring action prior to the hearing; and

e. The names and addresses of witnesses each party intends to produce in its direct case.[37]

8. Conduct of Hearings

The Division schedules the hearing and designates its location.[38] However, a party may make a motion that the hearing be held at some other place than that designated.[39] The notice of hearing given by the Division must state the date, time, and place of the hearing and pre-hearing conference, and identify the authorized representative of the person requesting the hearing.[40] Also, the notice must present the issues involved to give the parties a reasonable opportunity to prepare and must set forth the requirements for intervention in the proceeding by any other parties.[41] If the issues cannot be fully stated in advance, they must be stated as soon as practicable.[42]

Hearings are as informal as is reasonable, but decorum must be consistent with that of any court of law.[43] The AHO has the duty of conducting the hearing, making decisions regarding evidence, and administering the oath to witnesses.[44] All parties have the right to present evidence, cross examine witnesses, and make objections, motion, and oral arguments.[45] The Rhode Island Rules of Evidence apply in adjudicatory proceedings.[46]

---

[37] *Id.* §15(a)(4) *et seq.*
[38] *Id.* §15(c).
[39] *Id.*
[40] *Id.* §15(d).
[41] *Id.*
[42] *Id.*
[43] *Id.* §15(e)(1), (2).
[44] *Id.* §15(e)(3).
[45] *Id.* §15(g).
[46] R.I. Gen. Laws §42-35-10 and Rules §15(h)(2).

A party may make a motion to the Division or the AHO, as permitted by the Rhode Island Rules of Civil Procedure, for any order or action consistent with the law.[47] Motions may be made in writing at any time before a hearing or orally during a hearing.[48] Any party opposing a written motion must file a written objection within seven days of the filing of the motion or else the objection is waived.[49] The AHO decides all motions.[50] Administrative notice may be taken of facts judicially cognizable by the courts of Rhode Island.[51] In addition, the clerk of the Division or the AHO may issue, vacate, and modify subpoenas.[52] The weight to be given to any evidence rests with the sound discretion of the AHO.[53] After the completion of the hearing, no evidence may be submitted unless ordered by the AHO or the director of DEM.[54] An electronic or stenographic transcript of the hearing is kept, and the record is available at all times for inspection by the parties.[55]

9. Final Decisions

The AHO make a recommended decision, in writing, to the director of the DEM at the conclusion of the hearing. The recommended decision must be made public when submitted to the director of the DEM for review. The director of the DEM, then, makes the final decision, which may adopt, modify, or reject the AHO's decision.[56] The final decision must be in writing and contain a statement of the reasons therefore and a determination of every issue of fact or law necessary to the decision.[57]

10. Consent Orders

At any time prior to the director of the DEM rendering a final decision, parties to a hearing may attempt to settle a matter by entering into a consent order.[58] The AHO, then, will

[47] Rules §8(a)(1).
[48] *Id.* §8(a)(2).
[49] *Id.*
[50] *Id.* §8(a)(3).
[51] *Id.* §15(j).
[52] *Id.* §15(k).
[53] *Id.* §15(o).
[54] *Id.* §15(n).
[55] *Id.* §15(l)(1), (m)
[56] *Id.* §16(b).
[57] *Id.*
[58] *Id.* §17(a).

stay the hearing to allow time for negotiations. If an agreement is not reached during the time for which the stay was approved, the AHO will promptly reschedule the hearing.[59]

If an agreement is reached, the agreement must contain an admission of all facts and an express waiver of further proceedings before the AHO. The agreement also must state that the parties waive their rights to appeal and that the agreement can be enforced by law. The agreement may state that none of the parties signing the agreement is making an admission of liability as alleged in any notice of violation.[60] Upon receiving such an agreement, the AHO may accept it and issue the order, reject it and reschedule the hearing, or take other action as he or she deems appropriate.[61]

11. Recovery of Litigation Expenses

A party may file a claim for the recovery of litigation expenses within 30 days after the conclusion of an adjudicatory proceeding before the Division.[62] An adjudicatory proceeding is deemed concluded on the date the final decision is given or a consent order is accepted.[63] The claim must conform to the general filing requirements of the Rules, as discussed above, and must contain a summary of the legal and factual basis of the claim, as well as affidavits and documentary evidence supporting the basis of the claim.[64] The Division must answer the claim in writing within 20 days of the filing.[65] A party may move for an evidentiary hearing within 10 days of the filing of the Division's answer with the AHO. A hearing will only occur if the movant convinces the AHO that affidavits are inadequate to support the claim.[66] The AHO must issue a written decision on the claim within 6 weeks of the hearing or within 7 weeks of DEM's filing of an answer if no hearing is held.[67] Litigation expenses will be awarded only if the claimant establishes by a preponderance of the evidence that:

a. The claimant is a "party" in the proceeding;

---

[59] *Id.*
[60] *Id.* §17(b).
[61] *Id.* §17(c).
[62] *Id.* §19(b).
[63] *Id.*
[64] *Id.* §19(b), (c).
[65] *Id.* §19(d).
[66] *Id.* §19(e).
[67] *Id.* §19(f)(1).

b. The claimant has prevailed against the DEM in the adjudicatory proceeding;

c. The litigation expenses are reasonable;

d. The DEM was not justified in the actions leading to the proceeding; and

e. The AHO does not deem an award of litigation expenses are unjust.[68]

C. Licenses and Permits

Persons seeking a license or permit from the DEM must consult the applicable rules or regulations of the DEM division with jurisdiction over the matter. No adjudicatory hearing on a permit or license will take place until the DEM has denied or partially denied the license or permit and the applicant has requested an adjudicatory hearing before the Division.[69]

D. Judicial Review of DEM Final Orders

1. Initiation of Judicial Review

A party who has exhausted all administrative remedies in a proceeding before the DEM, and who is aggrieved by a final order in an adjudicatory proceeding, is entitled to judicial review of the DEM decision.[70] To receive judicial review of a DEM decision, the party must file a complaint in the appropriate superior court of Rhode Island.[71] The complaint must be filed within 30 days of the mailing of notice of the final DEM order, or within 30 days of a decision if a rehearing was requested. Any person who is aggrieved by a final order concerning the assessment or determination of any tax interest or penalty made by the tax administrator must pay the amount of the tax interest or penalty to the administrator as a prerequisite to the filing of such complaint.[72] The appealing party must serve copies of the complaint upon the DEM and other parties involved in the proceeding within 10 days of filing.[73] The filing of a complaint does not stay enforcement of the DEM order; although the court or the DEM may do so.[74]

---

[68] *Id.* §19(f).
[69] *Id.* §18.
[70] R.I. Gen. Laws §42-35-15(a), 42-35-15.1(a).
[71] *Id.* §42-35-15(b).
[72] *Id.*
[73] *Id.*
[74] *Id.* §42-35-15(c).

2. The Review Proceedings

The review is conducted by the court without a jury and is confined to the record compiled during the adjudicatory proceeding.[75] The court, upon request, shall hear oral argument or receive written briefs.[76] The court may affirm the DEM order, remand the case, or reverse or modify the order if the substantial rights of the party appealing were prejudiced because the DEM order or decision was:

a. In violation of the constitution or a statute;

b. In excess of the DEM's authority;

c. Made upon unlawful procedure;

d. Affected by another error or law;

e. Clearly erroneous; or,

f. Arbitrary, capricious, or an abuse of the DEM's discretion.[77]

3. Further Review

The final judgment of the superior court may be reviewed by the supreme court of Rhode Island.[78] A petition for a writ of certiorari must be filed with the clerk of the supreme court within 20 days of the Superior Court's judgment.[79]

E. Assessment of Administrative Penalties

In 1992, the DEM adopted new rules and regulations for the assessment of administrative penalties. These regulations promote a policy of assuring the effective enforcement of all laws administered by the DEM and deterring noncompliance with the rules, regulations, permits, licenses and orders adopted pursuant to the DEM's authority by:

1. seeking any appropriate legal and equitable relief, including:

---

[75] *Id.* §45-35-15(f).
[76] *Id.*
[77] §42-35-15(g).
[78] *Id.* §42-35-15.1(b), 42-35-16.
[79] *Id.* §42-35-16.

a. the removal of any economic benefit or competitive advantage realized as a direct or indirect result of a violation; and/or

b. the restoration of any property or resources damaged as a direct or indirect result of a violation;

2. assessing administrative penalties, where appropriate, which:

a. reflect the nature and gravity of the violation and the potential for harm to the public health, safety, or environment caused by said violation;

b. reflect the length of time during which the violation was repeated or continued;

c. will deter future noncompliance by the person in violation; and

d. will encourage continued compliance by persons similarly regulated;

3. seeking from any person found to be in violation, those additional or extraordinary costs which are actually expended by the DEM during the course of the investigation of noncompliance, subsequent enforcement of the applicable regulation and resolution of an enforcement action for which the State of Rhode Island is not otherwise reimbursed other than non-overtime personnel costs; and

4. pursuing any other lawful enforcement option necessary to achieve compliance.[80]

In pursuing these objectives, the DEM may pursue any combination of the following administrative and judicial enforcement actions depending upon the circumstances and gravity of each case. Any combination of enforcement actions are not mutually exclusive and may be cumulative. These may include: (1) a Letter of Deficiency ("LOD"), Notice of Noncompliance ("NON"), Notice of Intent to Enforce ("NOI") or Notice of Responsibility

[80] The Rules and Regulations for the Assessment of Administrative Penalties §3.

("NOR") (a written warning or notification concerning a suspected or threatened violation of a legal requirement which, in the DEM's judgment, does not justify further enforcement action at that time, but may require the party cited to take such actions necessary to achieve compliance); (2) a Notice of Violation ("NOV") (a formal notice of a suspected violation issued in accordance with R.I. Gen. Laws §§42-17.1-2(u)(1) and 42-17.6-3); (3) a Cease and Desist Order (an immediate compliance order issued pursuant to R.I. Gen. Laws §2-1-24 either upon discovery of a suspected violation of the Fresh Water Wetlands Act or in combination with a notice of violation); (4) an Immediate Compliance Order (an emergency order issued in accordance with R.I. Gen. Laws §42-17.1-2(u)(2)); (5) Recordation in the Land Evidence Record (any subsequent transferee of such property shall be responsible for complying with the requirements of the recorded order or notice) and; (6) any civil or criminal court action which in the DEM's judgment is necessary to achieve compliance.[81]

Most of the above enforcement actions will state the remedies and penalties which the DEM may lawfully impose for any cited violation. The penalty may be based on the gravity of the violation. In order to determine the monetary amount that should attach to the gravity of a violation, the DEM has developed a "Penalty Matrix" for each of its regulatory programs.[82] The applicable penalty range is reached by first determining the "Type of Violation" and then the "Deviation from the Standard" of the alleged violation. The Type of Violation refers to the nature of the legal requirement allegedly violated and the Deviation from the Standard refers to the degree to which the violation is out of compliance with the legal requirement allegedly violated. Depending on the specific regulatory program that is involved, penalties may range from a Letter of Deficiency to $25,000.[83] However, any person who is assessed an administrative penalty for a violation of a law, rule, regulation, permit, license or order which is within DEM's authority and responsibility to enforce has the right to request a hearing. The request for a hearing must be filed within ten days after service of the notice assessing the penalty.[84]

The DEM's assessment of an administrative penalty will become a final order of the DEM upon the person's election to waive, or failure to timely request, an administrative

[81] *Id.* §7.
[82] *Id.* §10.
[83] *Id.* §§7, 10, Appendix.
[84] *Id.* §12(a).

hearing on the violation and/or the penalty. Each day during with the person fails to pay said penalty or otherwise fails to comply with a final order of the DEM constitutes a separate and distinct violation. An additional administrative penalty, not to exceed one thousand dollars ($1,000) for each violation of a final order, may be assessed by the DEM unless a different amount is authorized by statute as a civil penalty.[85]

[85] *Id.* §13.

CHAPTER III:

AIR POLLUTION LAWS

A. Interplay between Federal and State Air Regulations

Rhode Island's air pollution program is closely intertwined with the federal Clean Air Act. [1] Under the federal Clean Air Act, all the states are given the primary responsibility for assuring air quality within their geographic area consistent with national ambient (outside) air quality standards ("NAAQS") developed by the United States Environmental Protection Agency (the "EPA").[2] NAAQS are limitations on concentrations of certain pollutants in the ambient air. Among the pollutants regulated by NAAQS are: carbon monoxide; nitrogen oxides; sulfur oxides; hydrocarbons; ozone; lead; and total suspended particulates.

In establishing NAAQS, the EPA has developed national primary ambient air quality standards and national secondary ambient air quality standards. Primary ambient air quality standards are those, which in the judgment of the EPA, are required to protect public health.[3] Secondary ambient air quality standards are those levels of air quality, which in the judgment of the EPA, are necessary to protect the public welfare from any known or anticipated adverse effects associated with the presence of air pollutants in the ambient air.[4]

B. Rhode Island State Implementation Plan

Under §7407(a) of the federal Clean Air Act, each state must develop a plan to achieve NAAQS in its area. Thus, the State of Rhode Island has promulgated a state implementation plan ("SIP") to implement the requirements of the federal Clean Air Act. Pursuant to the Rhode Island Clean Air Act,[5] the Rhode Island Department of Environmental Management (the "DEM") has developed 39 air pollution control regulations (the "APC Regulations"), which control sources of air pollution in Rhode Island and make up most of the SIP.

Specifically, the APC Regulations regulate "air contaminants". The term "air contaminant" means soot, cinders, ashes, dust, fumes, gas, mist, smoke, vapors, odor, toxic or

---

[1] 42 U.S.C. §7401 *et seq.*
[2] *Id.* §7401(a)(3).
[3] *Id.* §7409(b)(1).
[4] *Id.* §7409(b)(2).
[5] R.I. Gen. Laws §23-23-1 *et. seq.*

radioactive materials, particulate matter, or any combination thereof.[6] The provisions of the Rhode Island SIP can be enforced by the DEM or the EPA. The following briefly describes Rhode Island's APC Regulations:

1. Visible Emissions

APC Regulation 1 controls visible emissions and makes it unlawful for any person to emit into the atmosphere any contaminant, for a period or periods aggregating more than three minutes in any one hour, which is greater than or equal to 20% opacity, unless caused by the presence of uncombined water. The term "opacity" is defined as the degree to which the air contaminants reduce the transmission of light and obscure a contrasting background.[7]

2. Hand-firing of Soft Coal

APC Regulation 2 regulates the hand firing of soft coal by making it unlawful for any person to use or consume in a hand-fired installation any solid fossil fuel, other than coke or anthracite coal. Under this APC Regulation, however, any coal, other than anthracite, may be used only in mechanically-fired installations. This Regulation does not apply to private residences.[8]

3. Particulate Emissions From Industrial Processes

APC Regulation 3 controls particulate emissions from industrial processes by making it unlawful for any person to emit into the atmosphere, during one hour, particulate matter in excess of that specifically provided for according to a certain process weight. The term "process weight" means the total weight of all materials introduced into any specific process, except liquid and gaseous fuels and combustion air, which may cause any emission of particulate matter into the atmosphere.[9]

---

[6] *Id.* §23-23-3(1).

[7] APC Regulation 1. All test to determine opacity must be done in accordance with federal regulations described I the Code of Federal Regulations, Title 40, Part 60, Appendix A, Method 9.

[8] APC Regulation 2.

[9] APC Regulation 3.

4. Open Fires

APC Regulation 4 controls open fires by making it unlawful for any person to burn any material in an open fire at a solid waste management facility and/or hazardous waste disposal facility or in connection with any salvage, industrial, commercial or institutional operation. The term "solid waste management facility" means any plant, structure, equipment or property, constructed or operated for the purpose of processing, treating, or disposing of solid wastes, but not segregated solid waste. The term "hazardous waste disposal facility" means any structure used for the disposal of hazardous waste. With the prior written approval of the DEM, the following actions are exempt from regulation under APC Regulation 4:

a. Open burning for weed abatement or pest control;

b. Bonfires of clean, untreated wood or cellulose derivatives conducted by an institution;

c. Open fires for the purpose of training fire fighters;

d. Open burning of material if no other alternative or practical method of disposal of the material is available. Alternative disposal methods include chipping, cutting, and piling for protective cover for wildlife. Burning may only be conducted during periods of good atmospheric ventilation, without causing a nuisance and with smoke minimizing starters if starters if starting aids are used.

APC Regulations 4 does not preclude a municipality from putting any other restrictions on open burning.[10]

5. Fugitive Dust

APC Regulation 5 controls fugitive dust by requiring people to take reasonable precautions to prevent particulate matter from becoming airborne. Regulated activities include: demolition/construction of structures, material stockpiles and earth moving activities, stationary sources whose activities involve handling materials which cause airborne particulate matter, secondary sources defined in the Regulations, exterior surface preparation/resurfacing

---

[10] APC Regulation 4.

operations, vehicles transporting materials which cause airborne particulate matter, commercial mining/quarrying operations, paved roads as to which earth or other material is deposited, and any other activities determined by the DEM to cause airborne particulate matter.

No person shall cause or permit any materials to be handled, transported, mined, quarried, stored, or otherwise utilized in any way so as to cause airborne particulate matter to travel beyond the property line of the emission source without taking adequate precautions (determined by the DEM, in accordance with good industrial practice) to prevent particulate matter from becoming airborne.[11]

6. Emission Monitors

APC Regulation 6 deals with continuous emission monitors. Under this Regulation, stationary sources may be required to install and operate a continuous emissions monitoring system approved by the DEM. Fossil fuel fired steam or hot water generating units burning No. 6 residual oil or solid fuel, or those units burning any other type of liquid fuels and having a heat input capacity of five million BTU per hour or more, must be equipped with an opacity monitor with an audio alarm. This Regulation does not apply to private residences.

The term "opacity monitor" means a photoelectric smoke detector that is permanently installed in breaching or a stack. The alarm must sound at 20% opacity and operate constantly during the combustion of fuel.[12]

7. Emission of Air Contaminants Detrimental to Person or Property

APC Regulation 7 makes it unlawful for any person to emit any contaminate that either alone or in connection with other contaminants, may be injurious to human, plant or animal life, or cause damage to property or may unreasonably interfere with the enjoyment of life or property.

In the issuance of any approval under APC Regulation 9 (permits), the sole determination of compliance with the above articulated standard with regard to human health shall be:

[11] APC Regulation 5.
[12] APC Regulation 6.

a. Compliance with all primary and secondary national ambient air quality standards;

b. Compliance with the applicable requirements of APC Regulation 22.3 regarding the emission of listed toxic air contaminants;

c. Compliance with a calculated ambient air level as required by sections 9.3.3(b), 9.4.2(g) and 9.5.2(e) (permit requirements); and

d. Compliance with the applicable procedures and criteria of the *Guidelines for Assessing Health Risks From Proposed Air Pollution Sources*.

In issuing a permit under APC Regulation 9, the sole criteria for compliance with the above-mentioned standard with regard to animal and plant life shall be:

a. Compliance with all secondary national ambient air quality standards; and

b. Compliance with the applicable provisions of section 9.5.2(d) (permit requirements).

In addition, compliance with the above-mentioned standard with regard to property damage will be judged by compliance with all secondary national ambient air quality standards. Furthermore, compliance with regard to interference with the enjoyment of life and property shall be judged by compliance with all of the previously mentioned criteria.[13]

8. Sulfur Content of Fuels

APC Regulation 8 regulates the sulfur content of fuels. Under this Regulation, no person can store for sale, sell, deliver, use or store for consumption high sulfur fuel except under certain circumstances. High sulfur fuel is defined as any fuel, except fuel oil, containing more than .55 pounds of sulfur per million BTU heat release potential or fuel oil containing more than 1.0% sulfur by weight. The DEM may approve the use of high sulfur fuel when, combined with an approved stack gas cleaning process, the sulfur compound emissions (expressed as sulfur dioxide) from the stack do not exceed 1.1 pounds per million BTU actual heat input.

[13] APC Regulation 7.

Also, the DEM may approve the use of high sulfur fuel if it is a part of an emissions bubble. Sulfur compound emissions from such a bubble cannot exceed 1.1 pounds per million BTU actual heat input and the sulfur content of any fuel used within the bubble cannot contain over 1.21 pounds of sulfur per million BTU heat release potential. Furthermore, particulate emissions from any single fuel burning device within the bubble cannot exceed .15 pounds per million BTU actual heat input and total particulate emissions form the bubble shall not exceed .10 pounds per million BTU actual heat input.

The applicant for emission bubble must submit an application to the DEM and include information on all fuel burning devices in the bubble, the fuels to be burned, the sulfur content of the fuel, heat input, annual fuel use and hours of operation, stack height, exit velocity and temperature of stock gas, inside diameter of stack gas, aerodynamic downwash effects, and, in certain instances, air quality modeling meeting the requirements of the Rhode Island Guideline for Air Quality Monitoring. The DEM will hold a public notice and comment period on all applications for emission bubbles. An approved bubble can be in effect for no more than three years after which time the DEM may extend the bubble. In deciding whether to extend the bubble, the DEM must consider, among other things, air quality and current air pollution control technology.

The DEM also may allow the use of high sulfur fuel oil for a period of up to 30 months in a fuel burning device with an energy input capacity of less than 250 million BTU's per hour, if the source is committed to implementing permanent energy conservation measures to converting to a fuel other than a petroleum product, such as coal, wood, or a coal-oil mixture. The owner or operator of the facility must use the savings realized during this conversion period to finance the necessary modifications or installation of pollution control equipment.

APC Regulation 8 also contains specific regulations on large fuel burning devices using coal. A large fuel burning device has a rated energy input capacity of 250 million BTU's per hour or more. The Regulation also has requirements for residual fuel oil shipments to marine terminals.[14]

[14] APC Regulation 8.

9. Approval to Construct, Modify or Operate

APC Regulation 9 makes it unlawful for anyone, without either a minor source permit or a major source permit, to construct, install, or modify a facility that releases air contaminants. Such facilities include, but are not limited to: certain fuel burning equipment; liquid petroleum storage tanks, reservoirs and containers with a capacity of 40,000 gallons or more and having a true vapor pressure greater than 1.52 psi (pounds per square inch at 69°F); any incinerator except those burning hazardous waste or used in an owner-occupied dwelling of less than three units; any source or process having the potential to emit five tons per year or more of lead; any stationary source having the potential to emit 10 tons per year or more of any hazardous air pollutant or 25 tons per year of any combination of hazardous air pollutants; any other source having the potential to emit 100 pounds or more per day, or 10 pounds or more per hour, of any air contaminant or combination of air contaminants from certain categories of sources such as surface coating, metal cleaning, textile dyeing and finishing, glass or fiberglass manufacturing, production of asphalt concrete, and the production of metal casting; and any air pollution control system.

All major sources of air contaminants having the potential to emit 100 tons or more of any air contaminant also need a permit. The term "major stationary source" means a stationary source of air pollutants which emits, or has the potential to emit 50 tons per year or more of volatile organic compounds or nitrogen oxides or 100 tons per year or more of any other regulated air pollutant.

In permitting a source of air contaminants under APC Regulation 9, the DEM requires the use of certain types of air pollution control technology. In addition, the standards for approving plans to construct, install or modify sources of air pollution regulated under APC Regulation 9 depend on whether the source is located in an area that is attainment or nonattainment for the air contaminants the source emits or will be emitting.[15]

10. Air Pollution Episodes

APC Regulation 10 and the Air Pollution Episode Act[16] regulate air pollution episodes. APC Regulation 10 takes effect when the DEM determines that air pollution in any place or area

[15] APC Regulation 9.
[16] R.I. Gen. Laws §23-23.1-1 *et seq.*

in Rhode Island constitutes an unreasonable and emergency risk to the health of those present within that area.[17] In such an instance, the director of the DEM informs the Governor of the air pollution episode.[18] The Governor, upon receiving the communication, may declare by proclamation that an air pollution episode exists as to all or any part of the area mentioned in the determination. An air pollution episode is defined as "the condition of an air pollution alert,[19] air pollution warning, [20] or an air pollution emergency."[21]

Upon declaring that an air pollution episode exists, the Governor, through the issuance of an order any prohibit, restrict, or condition the following:

a. Motor vehicle traffic in the area;

b. The operation of commercial facilities in the area;

c. The operation of incinerators in the area;

d. The burning or consumption of any type of fuel in the area;

e. The burning of any materials and open-fires in the area; and

f. Any and all other activity in the area that contributes or may contribute to the air pollution emergency.[22]

Many of the Governor's powers are incorporated into the DEM's standby plans that take effect upon the order of the Governor. Such plans contain emission reduction criteria, as well as pre-planned abatement strategies. Overall, the emission reduction plans are arranged to bring an air pollution episode under control by restricting all activating in the particular area that is contributing to the episode. The plans also detail how particular sources of air pollution are to regulate their operations during an episode. For example, many facilities are required to utilize certain fuels and to operate only at particular times.

---

[17] *Id.* §23-23.1.5.
[18] *Id.*
[19] An air pollution alert is when the concentration of pollutants triggers first state control action. APC Regulation 10.1(b).
[20] Where air quality is continuing to degrade and additional control actions are deemed necessary. APC Regulation 10.1(c).
[21] Where air quality is continuing to degrade to a level that should never be reached and the most stringent control actions are necessary. APC Regulation 10.1(d)
[22] R.I. Gen.Laws §23-23.1-5(1)-(6).

Air pollution episode orders do not require any judicial or other order or confirmation to become effective immediately upon issuance. These orders become the legal obligation of all persons, firms, corporations and other entities within Rhode Island. An order remains in effect for the duration specified in it. If no time limit is specified, it remains in effect until the Governor declares by further proclamation that the emergency has terminated. [23]

The DEM will grant to any person aggrieved by an order a public hearing. The hearing will be used to determine whether the continuance of any order, in whole or in part, is unreasonable in light of the prevailing conditions of air pollution.[24]

Upon conclusion of the hearing, if the Director of DEM determines that the order should be terminated or modified, he or she must report such findings or recommendations to the Governor. The Governor may take any action that he or she deems appropriate.[25]

The orders of the Governor will be enforced by the DEM, the State Council of Defense, State and local police, and air pollution enforcement personnel forces.[26]

Any violation of an order of the Governor or the knowing failure to comply with its directions or the knowing interference with the enforcement of an order will be punished by a fine of not more than $500, or by imprisonment for not more than 90 days, or both. Each day during which the violation continues is a separate and distinct offense.[27]

11. Petroleum Liquids Marketing and Storage

APC Regulation 11 regulates petroleum liquids marketing and storage. Under this Regulation, there are specific requirements for the storage and movement of petroleum liquids at bulk gasoline terminals, bulk gasoline plants, gasoline dispensing facilities, and large petroleum storage facilities. The purpose of the APC Regulation 11 is to prevent the escape of vapors from petroleum.[28]

---

[23] *Id* §23-23.1-7.
[24] *Id.* §23-23.1-10.
[25] *Id.*
[26] *Id.* §23-23.1-8.
[27] *Id.* §23-23.1-9.
[28] APC Regulation 11.

12. Incinerators

APC Regulation 12 applies to incinerators, except residential incinerators and those used for the degradation of hazardous materials. Under this Regulation, there are specific emission standards for small incinerators (capacity of less than 2000 pounds per hour that burn certain types of refuse), large incinerators (capacity over 2000 pounds per hour that burn certain types of refuse), pathological incinerators, sewage sludge incinerators, and special incinerators. Special incinerators burn nonhazardous gaseous, liquid, semi-liquid, or solid byproduct refuse from industrial operations.

Under this Regulation, the DEM prohibits the construction or use of a regulated incinerator unless it is approved by the DEM as being effective against air pollution. Before the construction or use of a regulated incinerator, the applicant must submit certain information to the DEM on the design of the incinerator, the waste to be incinerated, and the incinerator's air pollution control equipment.[29]

13. Participate Emissions From Fossil Fuel Fired Steam or Hot Water Generating Units

APC Regulation 13 regulates particulate emissions from fossil fuel fired steam or hot water generating units. Under this Regulation, no person can cause or permit emissions from a fossil fuel or wood residue fired steam or hot water generating unit having a maximum rated heat input capacity of one million BTU per hour or more of particulate matter in excess of .10 million actual heat input. In addition, APC Regulation 13 prohibits a person from constructing, installing, modifying or operating a fossil fuel fired steam or hot water generating unit designed to burn residual oil or wood residue, having a heat input capacity of one million BTU per hour or more, that uses a burner or burners of a design not approved by the director of the DEM. This Regulation does not apply to those generating units that are used on an emergency or standby basis or are able to maintain compliance with all applicable regulations. There are also other exemptions under this Regulation for generating units that have received approval under the provisions of APC Regulation 8.[30]

---

[29] APC Regulation 12.
[30] APC Regulation 13.

14. Record Keeping and Reporting Requirements

Under APC Regulation 14, the owner or operator of any source of air contaminants must provide data on operational processes, fuel usage, raw materials, stack dimensions, exhaust gas flow rates and temperatures, emissions or air contaminants, steam or hot water generator capacities, types of equipment producing air contaminants and air pollution control systems or other data that may be necessary to determine if the source is in compliance with the APC Regulations. Such information must be submitted at least annually to the DEM and is available for public inspection.[31]

15. Organic Solvent Emissions

APC Regulation 15 controls organic solvent emissions. "Organic solvents" are volatile organic compounds ("VOCs") that are liquids at standard conditions and that are used as dissolvers, viscosity reducers, dilutants, thinners, reagents or cleaning agents. "VOC" means any organic compound that participants in atmospheric photochemical reactions. APC Regulation 15 applies to all installations which have or have had 50 tons per year potential emissions of VOCs since January 1, 1990. This Regulation, however, does not apply to installations that are regulated by APC Regulations 11, 18, 19, 21, 22.6, 25 and 26 and does not apply to the spraying or other use of insecticides, pesticides or herbicides. In addition, APC Regulation 15 does not apply to the blending of distillate or residual fuel oils.

Emissions bubbling is provide for under APC Regulation 15 for facilities with more than one VOC emitting installation. There are, however, certain limitations on emissions bubbling under APC Regulation 15 if the State of Rhode Island is designated a nonattainment area for ozone. APC Regulation 15 also includes specific record keeping requirements and technology-based requirements for air pollution control equipment.[32]

16. Air Pollution Control Systems

APC Regulation 16 deals with the operation of air pollution control systems. Under this Regulation, any air pollution control system must be operated according to its design specifications, whenever the source on which it is installed is in operation or is emitting air

[31] APC Regulation 14.
[32] APC Regulation 15.

contaminants. In the case of the malfunction of an air pollution control system, all reasonable measures must be taken to assure resumption of the designed control efficiency as soon as possible. If the malfunction is expected or may reasonably be expected to continue for longer than 24 hours, and if the owner or operator wishes to operate the source on which it is installed at any time beyond that period, the owner or operator must petition the DEM for a variance under Rhode Island General Laws Section 23-23-15.[33]

17. Odors

APC Regulation 17 regulates odors. Under this Regulation, no person can emit or cause to be emitted into the atmosphere any air contaminant which creates an objectionable odor beyond the property line of the person's facility. Staff members of DEM will determine, by personal observation, if the odor is objectionable, taking into account its nature, concentration, location, duration, and source.[34]

18. Organic Solvent Cleaning Emissions

Suspended by Regulation No. 36.

19. Control of Volatile Organic Compounds from Surface Coating Operations

APC Regulation 19 controls volatile organic compounds ("VOCs") from surface coating operations. This Regulation applies to all surface coating facilities for which actual uncontrolled emissions from all operations in any one of the surface coating categories have been greater than 15 pounds of volatile organic compounds in any one day after December 31, 1989. APC Regulation 19 contains specific emission limitations for surface coating, compliance schedules, internal offsets for surface coating facilities, and record keeping and reporting requirements.[35]

20. Alternative Fuels

APC Regulation 20 regulates the burning of alternative fuels. The term "alternative fuels" means any materials, other than fuel oil, natural gas, coal or wood residue that is burned for the purpose of creating heat. Types of alternative fuels include, but are not limited

---

[33] APC Regulation 16.
[34] APC Regulation 17.
[35] APC Regulation 19.

to, waste oil and hazardous waste. This Regulation applies to any person burning alternative fuels and to fuel burning equipment with a heat input capacity of one million BTU per hour or more. No person may burn an alternative fuel without first obtaining written approval from the DEM. Any person burning an alternative fuel must be in compliance with all applicable rules and regulations of the DEM Division of Air and Hazardous Materials or subject to the requirements of an enforceable compliance schedule. This Regulation does not apply to a person who blends alternative fuels with primary fossil fuel, where the maximum amount of alternative fuel as a percent by volume of the primary fossil fuel is less than or equal to one. This exemption, however, does not apply to alternative fuels containing greater than fifty parts per million PCBs, nor does it exempt any person from compliance with the DEM's hazardous waste rules and regulations.[36]

21. Control of Volatile Organic Compound Emissions From Printing Operations

APC Regulation 21 regulates volatile organic compound ("VOC") emissions from printing operations. This Regulation applies to all roll, specialty, rotogravure and flexographic printing facilities whose potential to emit VOCs from printing operations is or ever has been equal to or greater than 50 tons per year. Printing operations include, but are not limited to, printing, drying, mixing and nay other functions associated with printing. Sources with potential yearly emissions of 50 tons or more of VOCs, but with actual emissions not exceeding 50 tons per year of VOC since January 1, 1990, may apply to the DEM for an exemption from this Regulation.

Under APC Regulation 21, no owner or operator of a printing facility subject to this Regulation and employing solvent-containing ink may operate, cause, allow or permit the operation of the facility unless one of the following is complied with at all times:

a. The volatile fraction of ink contains not more than 25% by volume of organic solvents and not less than 75 by volume of water;

b. The ink, as it is applied to the substrate, less water, contains not less than 60% by volume of non-volatile materials;

[36] APC Regulation 20.

c. The installation of one or more approved VOC control devices is certified to achieve at least a 90% reduction efficiency as measured across each control device; or

d. An alternative measure is employed that has been demonstrated to the satisfaction of the DEM to have a VOC emission reduction at least equivalent to an amount potentially achieved under (a) or (b) above.

In addition, a capture system must be used in conjunction with the emission control devices installed per requirement (c) above. The design and operation of a capture system must be consistent with good engineering practice, and in conjunction with the control device, must provide for an overall reduction in VOC emissions at each printing press of at least:

a. 75% where publication rotogravure printing process is employed; or

b. 65% where packaging rotogravure printing process or specialty printing process is employed, or

c. 60% where flexographic printing process is employed.

APC Regulation 21 also contains detailed information on compliance schedules, demonstration testing, internal offsets, and record keeping.[37]

22. Air Toxics

APC Regulation 22 applies to any stationary source using or generating a listed toxic substance in any process, unless exempted. The following are exempted from APC Regulation 22:

a. The application of any pesticide or herbicide regulated by either the federal insecticide, fungicide, Rodenticide Act (86 Statute 73 et. seq.) or the Rhode Island Pesticide Control Act (23-25-1 et seq), except those with ethylene oxide;

b. Gasoline filing stations; and

[37] APC Regulation.

c. Fossil fuel burning solely for producing heat.

In addition, dry cleaning facilities that use perchloroethylene as a solvent but use less than 540 pounds of perchloroethylene, 3300 pounds of trichloroethylene, and 2200 pounds of methylene chloride may be exempt from certain provisions of APC Regulation 22.

A "listed toxic substance" means any substance which has been shown to induce mutagenic, carcinogenic, fetoxic, or other acute or chronic toxic effects.

Under APC Regulation 22, no person can construct, install, modify, or operate any stationary source that has the potential to increase emissions of a listed toxic substance by greater than the minimum quantity for that contaminant without first obtaining an approved construction and operating permit from the direct of the DEM. Permits are issued in accordance with the APC Regulation 9. All permitted facilities must be designed to achieve the "lowest achievable emission rate."

APC Regulations 22 also contains specific compliance schedules and specific requirements for dry cleaning facilities.[38]

24. Removal of Lead Based Paint From Exterior Surfaces

APC Regulation 24 applies to all persons engaging in the removal of a lead based substance from the exterior surfaces of buildings and/or other structures, unless exempted. Removal of paint that is not a lead based substance from a surface shall be exempted from APC Regulation 24. To qualify for this exemption, a representative sample of any paint which is to be removed from any surface must be tested prior to the initiation of paint removal and must contain no more than .05% lead by weight calculated as lead metal in the dried solid. The person performing the paint removal operation is responsible for determining if lead paint is present on the structure. Paint removal operations which are exempt from the requirements of APC Regulation 24 must, however, comply with the requirements of APC Regulation 5 "Fugitive Dust".

APC Regulation 24 also contains specific notification and paint removal

[38] APC Regulation 22.

requirements.[39]

25. Control of Volatile Organic Compound Emissions From Cutback and Emulsified Asphalt

APC Regulation 25 applies to any person, stationary source, facility or municipality which manufactures, stores, mixes, uses or applies asphalt for road paving or repairs. However, APC Regulation 25 does not apply to the manufacture of asphalt products exclusively for use outside of the State of Rhode Island.

The Regulation prohibits the manufacture, mixing, storage, use or application of cutback and emulsified asphalt between April 1st and September 30th except under certain circumstances. In addition, the owner or operator of any facility subject to this Regulation must maintain records of the manufacture, mixing, storage, use or application of any asphalt which contains VOC between April 1st and September 30th. These records must be maintained in a readily accessible location for a minimum of three years and shall be made available to the Office of Air Resources upon request. Compliance with this regulation was required on May 1, 1994, and is required thereafter.[40]

26. Control of Organic Solvent Emissions From the Manufacture of Synthesized Pharmaceutical Products

APC Regulation 26 applies to the following sources of volatile organic compounds (VOC) at all synthesized pharmaceutical manufacturing facilities:

a. Reactors;
b. Distillation operations;
c. Crystallizers;
d. Centrifuges;
e. Vacuum dryers;
f. Air dryers;
g. Production equipment exhaust systems;
h. Rotary vacuum filters and other filters;
i. Storage tanks;
j. In-process tanks; and
k. Leaks.

[39] APC Regulation 24.
[40] APC Regulation 25.

The owner or operator of a facility subject to this Regulation must control the VOC emissions from each vent which has the potential to emit 15 pounds per day or more of VOC from reactors, distillation operations, crystallizers, centrifuges, and vacuum dryers. Any owner or operator of a facility which has sources whose emissions are below the applicability standard must comply with the certification, recordkeeping, and reporting requirements set forth in the Regulation.

In addition, APC Regulation 26 contains detailed limitation standards, compliance procedures and monitoring, recordkeeping, reporting, and certification requirements.[41]

27. Control of Nitrogen Oxides Emissions

APC Regulation applies to all stationary sources which have or ever have had, since January 1, 1990, the potential to emit 50 tons of nitrogen oxides per year form all pollutant-emitting equipment or activities. However, a stationary source with potential yearly emissions of 50 tons or more of nitrogen oxides, but with actual emissions not exceeding 50 tons per year no nitrogen oxides any time after January 1, 1990, may apply to the DEM for an exemption from certain parts of this Regulation. In addition, any emergency standby internal combustion engine which is operated less than 500 hours during any consecutive twelve (12) month period is exempt from certain parts of this Regulation.

Depending on the type of exemption obtained, if any, APC Regulation 27 requires the owner or operator of the facility to submit the appropriate Reasonably Available Control Technology (RACT) Plan to the DEM. "Reasonably Available Control Technology" means the lowest emission limitation that a particular piece of equipment or pollutant emitting activity is capable of meeting by using measures that are reasonably available in terms of technological and economic feasibility.

APC Regulation 27 also contains detailed requirements for RACT Plans, emissions monitoring, recordkeeping and reporting.[42]

---

[41] APC Regulation 26.

[42] APC Regulation 27.

28. Operating Permits Fees

APC Regulation 28 regulates operating permit fees for particular stationary sources. This Regulation applies to any of the following stationary sources as defined in the Regulations:

(a) any major source; or

(b) any affected source under Title IV of the Federal Clean Air Act; or

(c) any stationary source in a source category designed by the EPA pursuant to 40 CFR 70; or

(d) any stationary source, including an area source, subject to a standard, limitation, or other requirement under Section 111 of the Act; and

(e) any stationary source, subject to a standard or other requirement under Section 112 of the Act, except that a source is not required to pay a fee solely because it is subject to regulations or requirements under Section 112(r) of the Act.

APC Regulation 28 specifies the stationary sources that are exempt from the Regulation, and lists criteria that qualify a secondary source as a major source. It also furnishes standards for requiring payment of a fee, fee determination, payment of fees, and penalties.[43]

29. Operating Permits

APC Regulation 29 concerns Operating Permits for particular stationary sources. This Regulation applies to any of the following stationary sources, as defined in the Regulations:

(a) any major sources; or

(b) any affected source under Title IV of the Federal Clean Air Act; or

(c) any stationary source in a source category designed by the EPA pursuant to 40 CRF 70; or

[43] APC Regulation 28.

(d) any stationary source, including an area source, subject to a standard, limitation, or other requirement under Section 111 of the Act; and

(e) any stationary source, subject to a standard or other requirement under Section 112 of the Act, except that a stationary source is not required to obtain a permit solely because it is subject to regulations or requirements under Section 112(r) of the Act.

APC Regulation 29 lists the stationary sources that are exempt from obtaining a permit, and specifies criteria that qualify a secondary source as a major source. The owner or operator of a secondary source can rebut this qualification by presenting evidence to demonstrate to the satisfaction of the DEM that the potential to emit of the stationary source has been reduced by means of a physical change or change in the method of operation of the stationary source.

For the purposes of determining applicability pursuant to subsection 29.2 an owner or operator may elect to treat any part of a stationary source which part is used solely for research and development operations, as a separate stationary source If any research and development operations of a stationary source are treated separately for the purposes of determining applicability, the emissions or potential to emit of those operations may be considered separately from the emissions or potential to emit of the remainder of the stationary source. However, research and development operations may not be treated separately for purposes of determining compliance with APC Regulation 22.

Any stationary source, operating in compliance with a permit issued under this Regulation, that no longer meets any of the applicability criteria in subsection 29.2.1, may petition the DEM to terminate its permit and relieve it of its obligation to obtain and operate under a permit issued under this Regulation.

APC Regulation 29 also contains specifications for emissions caps, general requirements for application submission, applications and required information, permit content, general permits, temporary stationary sources, procedures for processing permit applications, changes at a permitted facility requiring a permit revision, changes at a permitted facility that do not require a permit revision, appeals, variances, phase II acid rain stationary sources: permitting requirements, new source view integration, compliance requirements and a list of insignificant activities.[44]

30. Control of Volatile Organic Compounds from Automobile Refinishing Operations

APC Regulation 30 applies to any person who owns, leases, operates or controls an automobile refinishing facility. This Regulation details emission limitations, equipment specifications, recordkeeping, reporting and registration requirements. All persons owning, leasing, or controlling the operation of any automobile refinishing facility shall have achieved compliance with the requirements of APC Regulation 30 no later than July 1, 1995. However, all automobile refinishing operations commencing operation after July 1, 1994 must be in compliance with the regulation upon commencing operation.[45]

31. Control of Volatile Organic Compounds From Commercial Consumer Products

APC Regulation 31 applies to any person who sells, offers for sale, or manufactures for sale within Rhode Island, any of the following commercial and consumer products:

a. Air fresheners;
b. Bathroom and tile cleaners;
c. Engine degreasers;
d. Floor polishes/waxes;
e. Furniture maintenance products;
f. General purpose cleaners;
g. Glass cleaners;
h. Hair care products;
i. Nail polish remover;
j. Oven cleaners;
k. Insecticides; and
l. Certain antiperspirants or deodorants.

With respect to these products, no person shall sell, offer for sale or manufacture for sale in Rhode Island any of these products unless the VOC content is in excess of that specified for each product in the Regulation. This APC Regulation exempts concentrated products meant for

[44] APC Regulation 29.
[45] APC Regulation 30.

dilution, with higher than specified VOC content when it can be shown that the recommended dilution yields a lower VOC content than the amount specified in the Regulation.

APC Regulation 31 also details labeling requirements, compliance schedules and compliance determination and testing.[46]

32. Control of Volatile Organic Compounds from Marine Vessel Loading Operations

APC Regulation 32 applies to any loading event in which organic liquid is loaded into marine tank vessels and to loading events in which nay liquid is loaded into a marine vessel's cargo tanks if the most recent cargo held in those tanks was an organic liquid. This regulation does not, however, apply to segregated ballasting operations.

This Regulation requires that one of the following conditions be met during any loading event:

a. Volatile organic compound emissions do not exceed 5.7 grams per cubic meter (2 pounds per 1000 barrels) of liquid loaded into the marine tank vessel, or

b. The emissions of volatile organic compounds are reduced by at least 95% by weight from uncontrolled conditions if a recovery device is used and by at least 98% by weight from uncontrolled conditions if a combustion device is used.

APC Regulation 32 contains other emission limitations, recordkeeping and recording requirements, compliance demonstration and testing requirements and compliance schedules.[47]

33. Control of Volatile Organic Compounds from Architectural Coatings and Industrial Maintenance Coatings

APC Regulation 33 applies to any person who sells, offers for sale, or applies architectural or industrial maintenance coating or who manufactures architectural or industrial maintenance coating for sale within the State of Rhode Island. Among the several exceptions to

[46] APC Regulation 31.
[47] APC Regulation 32.

this Regulation are architectural coatings supplied in containers having capacities of one quart or less, architectural coatings sold in non-refillable aerosol containers having capacities of one liter or less, architectural coatings and industrial maintenance coatings that are sold, offered for sale or manufactured in Rhode Island for shipment and use outside of Rhode Island, and architectural and industrial maintenance coatings registered with the EPA under 7 U.S.C. §136 et. seq.

This Regulation also contains detailed requirements for emission limitations, labeling and compliance demonstration and testing.[48]

34. Rhode Island Motor Vehicle Inspection/Maintenance Program

APC Regulation 34 concerns Rhode Island's Motor Vehicle Inspection/Maintenance Program. This Regulation applies to all motor vehicles subject to the inspection requirements of the Rhode Island Motor Vehicle Inspection/Maintenance Program, Safety and Emissions Control Regulation No. 1.

This Regulation furnishes standards and criteria for motor vehicles emissions inspections, and are devised to give consideration to the levels of emissions reduction necessary to achieve and maintain federal and state ambient air quality standards and the levels necessary to protect human health and the environment. The standards and criteria include, but are not limited to, a requirement to test the emissions of motor vehicles for hydrocarbons (HC), carbon monoxide (CO), and oxides of nitrogen (NOx).

Vehicles subject to the Rhode Island I/M Program shall be inspected for compliance with standards, criteria and procedures set forth in the Regulations, criteria and procedures using an exhaust emissions test, evaporative emissions test, and on-board diagnostics inspection. Vehicles subject to the Rhode Island I/M Program which cannot be inspected using a transient test because of vehicle drive system configuration such as all-wheel drive shall be inspected using a two speed idle test.

APC Regulation 34 also contains standards and guidelines for exhaust emissions standards (phase-in and final standards), inspection procedures, and audits (equipment audits and

[48] APC Regulation 33.

computer and record audits).[49]

35. Control of Volatile Organic Compounds and Volatile Hazardous Air Pollutants From Wood Products Manufacturing Operations

APC Regulation 35 applies to any wood products facility which has the potential to emit 25 tons per year of Volatile Organic Compounds (VOC) from wood products manufacturing operations or which is located at a major source of Hazardous Air Pollutants (HAP).

The owner or operator of a wood products facility which has emissions below the applicability threshold just listed but above 15 pounds VOC in any day shall comply with the record-keeping and reporting requirements contained in the Regulation, but the facility shall not be subject to any other provisions of the Regulation. If the facility becomes subject to the Regulation at a future date due to an increase in emissions of VOC or VHAP, the facility shall be subject to the applicable requirements in this Regulation on and after the date that the applicability thresholds are reached or the date that the applicability thresholds are reached or the date that the applicable requirement becomes effective, whichever is later.

APC Regulation 35 contains criteria for a facility to obtain an exemption form the VHAP emissions limitations contained in the Regulation. It also feature specifications for emission limitations for finishing operations, emissions limitations for cleaning and gluing operations, work practice standards, compliance procedures and monitoring requirements, record-keeping and reporting, and performance test methods.[50]

36. Control of Emissions from Organic Solvent Cleaning

APC Regulation 36 supersedes APC Regulation 18 and regulates emissions from organic solvent cleaning. Under this Regulation, no person may conduct organic solvent cleaning unless certain procedures are used to control emissions of VOCs. Such procedures include: storing solvent in covered containers; repairing leaks immediately; shutting the solvent cleaning unit down; and closing equipment covers when the organic solvent cleaning unit is not being used. APC Regulation 36 also contains specific equipment and operating specifications

[49] APC Regulation 34.
[50] APC Regulation 35.

for batch cold cleaning operations, batch vapor cleaning operations with and without the use of solvent/air interfaces, inline cleaning operations, compliance specifications and monitoring requirements, record-keeping and reporting requirements, and exemptions from automated parts handling system requirements.[51]

37. Rhode Island's Low Emission Vehicle Program

APC Regulation 37 concerns Rhode Island's low emission vehicle program. With this Regulation, the DEM has adopted all sections of the California Low Emission Vehicle program with the exception of Title 13 CCR 1960.1(g)(2), the zero emissions vehicle mandate and Title 13 CCR §§2220-2224, after-market parts. This Regulation applies to all 1999 model year and subsequent model year passenger cars and light duty trucks sold, leased, offered for sale or lease, imported, delivered, purchased, rented, acquired, received, or registered in the state of Rhode Island.

Notwithstanding the adoption of this program, for the duration of Rhode Island's participation in the National LEV, manufacturers may comply with National LEV, or equally stringent federal standards in lieu of compliance with this program or any other program including mandates for sales of zero emissions vehicles adopted by Rhode Island pursuant to authority provided in section 177 of the CAA, applicable to passenger cars, light-duty trucks up through 6,000 pounds GVWR, and medium-duty vehicles from 6,001 to 14,000 pounds GVWR if designed to operate on gasoline, as these categories of motor vehicles are defined in the California Code of Regulations, Title 13, Division 3, Chapter 1, Article 1, Section 1900.

The State of Rhode Island's participation in the National LEV extends until model year 2006, except as provided in 40 CFR 86.1707. If, no later than December 15, 2000, the U.S. EPA does not adopt standards at least as stringent as the National LEV standards provided in 40 CFR part 86 subpart R that apply to new motor vehicles in model years 2004, 2005, or 2006, Rhode Island's participation in the National LEV program extends only to model year 2004, except as expressly provided in 40 CFR 86.1707.

If a covered manufacturer, as defined in 40 CFR 86.1702, opts out of the National LEV program pursuant to the EPA National LEV Regulations at 40 CFR 86.1707, the transition

---

[51] APC Regulation 36.

from the requirements imposed by the National LEV program to the requirements imposed by these Regulations, or any other program adopted pursuant to the authority provided in section 177 of the CAA, applicable to passenger cars, light-duty trucks up through 6,000 pounds GVWR, and/or medium duty vehicles from 6,001 to 14,000 pounds GVWR if designed to operate on gasoline, as these categories of motor vehicles are defined in the California Code of Regulations, Title 13, Division 3, Chapter 1, Article 1, and Section 1900 and 1960.1, will proceed in accordance with EPA National LEV Regulations at 40 CFR 86.1707.

The DEM shall apply technical guidance as supplied by the California Air Resources Board (CARB) relative to the implementation of Title 13 CCR, including but not limited to Manufacturers Advisory Correspondence and Mail Outs to all vehicles subject to the Regulation.

APC Regulation 37 also provides guidelines and specifications as to emissions requirements and prohibitions, vehicle testing warranty, reporting requirements, enforcement and severability.[52]

38. Nitrogen Oxides Allowance Program

APC Regulation 38 concerns the Nitrogen Oxides Allowance Program. The NOx Allowance Program is established to limit total mass NOx emissions from budget sources (which are defined as "fossil fuel boilers or indirect heat exchangers with a maximum rated heat capacity of 250 million BTU/Hour, or more; and all electronic generating devices with a rated output of 15 MW, or more") during the control period of May 1 through September 30. Any person who applies to opt into the NOx Allowance Program shall be considered a budget source upon approval of the application.

The initial NOx budget is as follows: For 1999 and each year thereafter, through and including 2002, not to exceed 626 tons during each control period. This initial NOx budget shall be modified by the DEM to include sources who choose to opt into this program pursuant to the Regulations. Any modification of the budget after establishment of the initial budget shall be recorded and maintained by the DEM, and submitted on an annual basis, by January 1 of each

[52] APC Regulation 37.

year, to the USEPA. Modifications to the budget shall be subject to a 30-day public notice and comment period.

The NOx Allowance Program, in its entirety, applies to any owner or operator of a budget source. The requirements for an Authorized Account Representative (AAR) and account maintenance fees are applicable to the owner of a general account. Any person who owns, operates, leases, or controls a stationary source not subject to this program by definition may choose to opt into the NOx Allowance Program subject to conditions that are contained in the Regulation.

APC Regulation 38 also contains specifications on general provisions, allowance allocation, permits, allowance transfer and use, the NOx allowance tracking system (NATS), emission monitoring, record-keeping, reporting, end-of season, reconciliation, compliance certification, penalties, account maintenance fees, and program audit.[53]

39. Hospital/Medical/Infectious Waste Incinerators

APC Regulation 39 applies to the incineration of all hospital, medical, and infectious waste in Rhode Island. It supersedes APC Regulation 12 for those areas where requirements overlap. Among the several exceptions to this Regulation are incinerators burning only pathological, low-level radioactive, and/or chemotherapeutic waste, and incinerators that are co-fired, provided the operator receives a waiver of the regulation from the Office of Air Resources. Also exempt are combustor/incinerators that meet applicable federal regulations such as the Federal Solid Waste Disposal Act or 40 C.F.R. Part 60.

This Regulation contains detailed requirements for compliance, performance testing, maintenance, monitoring, reporting and recordkeeping, inspection, and operating prerequisites.[54]

41. NOx Budget Trading Program

APC Regulation 41 regulates the NOx Budget Trading Program, which is established to limit total mass NOx emissions from NOx Budget sources during the control

---

[53] APC Regulation 38.
[54] APC Regulation 39.

period of May 1 to September 30. The initial NOx budget is as follows: For 2003 and each year thereafter, through and including 2005, not to exceed 936 tons during each control period.

The following units shall be NOx Budget units, and any source that includes one or more of such units shall be a NOx Budget source, subject to the requirements of this Regulation: (1) Any unit that, any time on or after January 1, 1995, serves a generator with a nameplate capacity greater than 15 MWe and sells any amount of electricity; or (2) Any unit that is not a unit under (1) just listed and that has a maximum design heat input greater than 250 million BTU/hour.

APC Regulation 41 contains specifications for exempted units, and further specifications and criteria for NOx allowance allocations, NOx authorized account representative for NOx budget sources, permits, NOx allowance transfers, the NOx allowance tracking system, monitoring, record-keeping and reporting, compliance certification, individual opt-ins and retired unit exemption.[55]

42. Heavy-Duty Diesel Engine Standards

APC Regulation 42 adopts all sections of the California certification of model years 2005 and 2006 for heavy-duty diesel engines certifying that the engine complies with California Code of Regulations Title 13, Division 3, Chapter 1, Article 2, section 1956.8. The DEM will apply technical guidance issued by CARB relative to the implementation of Title 13, including, but not limited to, Manufactures Advisory Correspondences and Mail Outs regarding motor vehicles subject to the Regulation. APC Regulation 42 prohibits all residents of Rhode Island from selling, leasing, purchasing, renting, delivering, acquiring, or receiving any heavy-duty diesel engine or motor vehicle subject to the regulations without an Executive Order from DEM certifying that the engine or vehicle complies with section 1956.8. The DEM may require compliance documentation before it issues an Executive Order.

APC Regulation 42 provides the following exemptions:

1. A model-year 2005 or 2006 heavy-duty diesel engine manufactured by an ultra-small volume manufacturer;

[55] APC Regulation 41.

2. A heavy-duty diesel engine installed in an urban bus;
3. An engine CARB determines is exempt from section 1956.8;
4. A motor vehicle acquired as a replacement for a damaged, inoperative, or stolen vehicle, provided the replacement was acquired out of state at the time the original vehicle was stolen, damaged, or rendered inoperable;
5. A motor vehicle which predates the standards acquired through a court of competent jurisdiction;
6. A motor vehicle having a certificate of conformity issued pursuant to the Clean Air act (42 U.S.C. §7401);
7. An emergency vehicle;
8. A military vehicle or equipment; or
9. Any other motor vehicle exempted by the California Health and Safety Code, section 42656.
10. This Regulation also contains detailed requirements for compliance with California orders and voluntary recalls.[56]

C. Air Pollution Permits

The DEM Office of Air Resources reviews and issues permits for the construction, installation or modification of sources of air emissions. A permit to construct, install, or modify is required for the following minor sources, which emit or have the potential to emit less than 100 tons per year of any regulated air pollutant:

1. Fuel burning equipment designed to burn residual oil or solid fossil fuels having a heat input capacity of one million BTU or more per hour, all other liquid fuels having a heat input capacity of five million BTU or more per hour, gaseous fuel having a heat input capacity of ten million BTU or more per hour, or alternative fuels having a heat input capacity of one million BTU or more per hour;

[56] APC Regulation 42.

2. Storage tanks, reservoirs, and containers with a capacity of 40,000 gallons or more for the storage of petroleum liquids having true vapor pressure greater than 1.52 pounds per square inch at 69°F;

3. Any incinerator, except those used in owner-occupied dwellings having less than three units or incinerators used to burn or incinerate hazardous or extremely hazardous waste;

4. Any stationary source having the potential to emit five tons per year or more of lead;

5. Any stationary source that emits or has the potential to emit, in the aggregate, 10 tons per year or more of any combination of hazardous air pollutants;

6. Any stationary source which has the potential to increase emissions of a listed toxic air contaminant by greater than the minimum quantity for that contaminant;

7. Any other stationary source or process except for those requiring a major source permit which have the potential to emit at least 100 pounds per day or 10 pounds per hour of any contaminant; and

8. Any air pollution control system and appurtenances.

Permits are also required for major sources which are those sources that emit or have the potential to emit 50 tons per year or more of volatile organic compounds or nitrogen oxides ore 100 tons per year or more of any other regulated air pollutant.[57]

When applying for an air pollution permit, the applicant must provide plans, designs, specifications and any other data necessary to show the design and operation of the proposed system. Air quality modeling also is necessary to demonstrate that the project will not cause a violation of certain air quality standards. Once an applicant sends his or her application to the DEM Office of Air Resources, the Division reviews the application for compliance with all applicable state and federal standards. The DEM may hold a public hearing on the application. The Office of Air Resources, then, approves or denies the application.

[57] See APC Regulation 9.

In regard to a major source, the applicant must submit a modeling protocol, along with the application, to the Office of Air Resources. The Office of Air Resources then issues a preliminary determination and the public is afforded the opportunity to comment on the determination before final approval or denial of the application is issued.

D. Penalties

Under the Rhode Island Clean Air Act, any person who violates an order of the director of DEM or an APC Regulation will be fined not more than $10,000 for each day of violation.

The penalties under the federal Clean Air Act, however, are more severe. Civil violations are subject to a fine of up to $25,000 per day of violation. Criminal violations are subject to a fine of up to $50,000 per day of violation, imprisonment for not more than one year, or both. Penalties also may double for subsequent offenses.

CHAPTER IV:

WATER POLLUTION CONTROL AND WATER SUPPLY

A. Water Pollution Act and Permit System

The Rhode Island Department of Environmental Management (the "DEM") has been designated by the Federal Environmental Protection Agency (the "EPA") as the state water pollution control agency for all purposes of the federal Clean Water Act[1] and is authorized to take all action necessary or appropriate to secure the benefits of the federal Clean Water Act to Rhode Island. Under the Water Pollution Act[2] (the "Act"), it is unlawful for any person to place any pollutant in the waters of Rhode Island or to place a pollutant in a location where it is likely to enter the waters of Rhode Island except in compliance with a Rhode Island Pollutant Discharge Elimination System ("RIPDES") permit.[3] The term "pollutant" includes: any material or effluent which may alter the chemical, physical, biological, or radiological characteristics and/or integrity of water, including but not limited to, dredged spoil, solid waste, incinerator residue, sewage, garbage, sewage sludge, munitions, chemical wastes, biological materials, radioactive materials, heat, wrecked or discarded equipment, rock, sand, cellar dirt or industrial, municipal, agricultural, or other waste, petroleum or petroleum products, including but not limited to oil.[4] The term "waters" includes all surface water and groundwater, including all tidewaters, territorial seas, wetlands, land masses partially or wholly submerged in water, and both inter and intrastate bodies of water which are, have been or will be used in commerce, by industry, for the harvesting of fish and shellfish or for recreational purposes.[5]

The purpose of the Act is to protect Rhode Island's waters from discharges of pollutants. The discharge program regulates the types and quantity of waste material discharged into Rhode Island waters to insure compliance with all applicable effluent limitations and water quality standards. Anyone who discharges or proposes to discharge pollutants directly into the waters of Rhode Island must obtain a RIPDES permit from the DEM.[6] RIPDES permits must be renewed every five years.

---

1 33 U.S.C.S. §1251 *et seq.*
2 R.I. Gen. Laws §46-12-1 *et seq.*
3 *Id.* §46-12-5.
4 *Id.* §46-12-1(15).
5 *Id.* §46-12-1, and as promulgated in the Regulations for the Rhode Island Pollutant Discharge Elimination System.
6 There are specific RIPDES regulations that detail the application procedures for RIPDES permits.

To obtain a RIPDES permit, the applicant must submit an application form to the DEM. The application form must contain information on the identity and amount of pollutants discharged, a description of the nature of the activity generating the waste, a diagram showing waste streams, toxics used or manufactured, outfall location, location map, and any other descriptive information required by the DEM. After review by EPA and the public, the DEM, then, may issue a RIPDES permit.

The DEM also may, by regulation, order, permit, or otherwise require the holder of any RIPDES permit to:

1. Establish and maintain records on discharges;
2. Make reports on discharges;
3. Install, calibrate, use and maintain monitoring equipment or methods of discharges;
4. Sample discharges at such locations, at such intervals, and in such a manner as directed by the DEM; and
5. Provide other information relating to discharges as the DEM may reasonably require.[7]

Any person who violates the provisions of the Act or of any permit, rule, regulation or order issued pursuant to the Act, will be subject to a civil penalty of not more than $25,000 for each day during which the violation occurs.[8] In addition, any person, who is found guilty of violating, willfully or with criminal negligence, any of the provisions of the Act or of any permit, rule, or regulation issued under the Act, will be punished by a fine of not more than $25,000, or by imprisonment for not more than five years, or by both. Each day during which the violation is repeated or continued is deemed to be a separate and distinct offense.[9] Furthermore, any person who tampers with a monitoring device or who knowingly makes any false statement, representation, or certification in any document filed or required to be maintained under the Act or under any permit, rule, or regulation, will, upon conviction, be punished by a fine of not more

[7] R.I. Gen. Laws §46-12-18.
[8] *Id.* §46-12-13.
[9] *Id.* §46-12-14(a).

than $5,000 for each instance of violation, or by imprisonment for not more than 30 days, or by both.[10]

B. Certification of Water Quality Standards[11]

Water quality standards, which are regulated by the DEM Division of Water Resources, provide a system by which the waters of Rhode Island are classified by uses. The purpose of the uses is to protect the public health and welfare and to enhance the quality and provide for the optimum utilization of Rhode Island waters. Physical, chemical and biological water quality criteria are the minimum water quality parameters necessary to support these uses. The Water Quality Standards are composed of these water use classifications and water quality criteria.[12] High quality waters have strict requirements to minimize or eliminate impacts on water quality under the "anti-degradation policy." The "anti-degradation policy" prohibits the lowering of water quality.

Water quality certification may be required for approval of, and prior to the issuance of permits, involving: the U.S. Army Corps of Engineers' Section 404 program for dredging and filling in the waters of the United States; DEM freshwater wetlands; Federal Energy Regulatory Commission hydroelectric facilities; and Coastal Resources Management Council permits. The DEM also may issue a similar statement of water quality compliance as part of the RIPDES permit approval process.[13]

The DEM reviews all projects that may affect water quality in order to ensure that the proposed activities will not degrade water quality or preclude the attainment of water quality standards. The Division of Water Resources issues a water quality certificate upon a showing that the project will not affect attainment of certain water quality standards. An applicant must formally apply to the DEM Division of Water Resources.

The approval procedure commences upon application for a Section 404 permit, freshwater wetlands permit, coastal permit, or discharge permit made to the appropriate permitting agency. An application for a water quality certification must then be made directly to

---

[10] *Id.* §46-12-14(b).

[11] R.I. Gen. Laws §§42-17.1-1 et seq., 42-35-1 et seq., 42-17.6 et seq., and 46-12-1 et seq. promulgated pursuant to: Rhode Island Department of Environmental Management Water Quality Regulations.

[12] *Id.*

[13] *Id.*

the Division of Water Resources prior to commencement of the project. The application must include a site plan with the overall project proposed, a project narrative describing the scope of the work and the anticipated water quality impacts, a list of abutting property owners (with addresses), and any project specific information as required by the application. The Division of Water Resources reviews the application but will not make a final decision regarding water quality until the close of statutory comment period. The DEM may confer with the applicant and the permitting agency and require further technical documentation. The DEM may hold a public hearing on the application at its discretion or when so requested in accordance with R.I. General Laws §42-35-1 et seq. [14]

Projects which fall under the Army Corps of Engineers programmatic general permit and require a RIDEM freshwater wetlands permit are exempted from this process. In addition, projects which require an individual permit from the Army Corps of Engineers or federal energy regulatory commission and a RIDEM freshwater wetlands permit do not require direct application for a water quality certification.

In the event the water quality standards cannot be certified, the applicant has the following remedies at his or her disposal:

1. The applicant may request an adjudicatory hearing to contest the decision;
2. The applicant may request a modification of water quality standards, allowing for the downgrading of specified low quality waters to the water quality standard actually being attained; or
3. An application for a variance from the standards and limitations established in the Water Quality Regulations may be requested. It must be demonstrated that overall water quality goals and objectives can be maintained.[15]

All of these remedies require opportunity for a public hearing. The estimated time of approval for the permit is approximately one month for water quality certification not requiring a

---

[14] *Id.*

[15] In all applicable cases, the applicant *must* comply with the regulations on anti-degradation and upgrading of water quality standards.

public hearing, and up to six months or longer for complex proposals and projects involving high quality waters.[16]

C. Wellhead Protection Program[17]

Legislative authority for protecting drinking water sources was initiated with the Safe Drinking Water Act (SDWA) of 1974. Included in the SDWA is the wellhead protection program designed to protect unique underground water supplies. The focus of the program is to deal with issues concerning the protection of groundwater supplies in an effort to minimize the contamination of water resources used or with the potential to be used for human consumption.[18]

The DEM Division of Groundwater is responsible for the wellhead protection program. Under the DEM program, the designated wellhead protection area will include the surface and subsurface areas surrounding a water well or wellfield suitable for the public water supply that may be susceptible to contamination. A standardized classification system is used to develop a coordinated and comprehensive approach to groundwater protection. State and local governments may develop more stringent criteria than the federal government, delineate high priority areas, and control sources of contamination that are not federally regulated.[19]

Rhode Island's wellhead protection program establishes the guidance criteria to be used in conjunction with various municipal regulations to protect water supply areas. The protection of groundwater may be accomplished through the use of zoning restrictions, or by more stringent requirements needed on other permits (i.e. underground storage tanks, injection wells, or RIPDES permits) where certain activities are proposed in wellhead protection areas.

D. Sole Source Aquifer Program[20]

The Sole Source Aquifer Program is designed to protect unique underground water

---

[16] *Id.* §46-12-14(a).

[17] The legislative authority for this program is the Safe Drinking Water Act of 1974, 42 U.S.C.A. §§300f-j (1999 & Supp. 2001) and R.I. Gen. Laws §46-13.1-9.

[18] R.I. Gen. Laws §46-13.1 et seq.

[19] *Id.*

[20] The legislative authority for this program is the Safe Drinking Water Act of 1974, §1424(e), codified as amended at 42 U.S.C.A. §§300f-j (1999 & Supp. 2001). See the appropriate EPA regulations for a further elaboration of this program.

supplies. Under provisions of the SDWA, aquifers designated by the EPA as a sole or principal source of drinking water are afforded additional protection from contamination.[21]

Specifically, the EPA conducts a detailed review of projects which may receive federal financial assistance in their development and implementation. Projects that may result in adverse impacts on groundwater resources may be prohibited from construction by preventing a commitment of federal funding or by requiring a modification in the project design to reduce the potential risk of groundwater contamination. Projects funded by state, local, or private groups are not affected by this designation.[22]

In Rhode Island, the responsible agency for the sole source aquifer program is the EPA. The DEM Division of Groundwater, however, may provide technical assistance and coordination with the affected communities. Any individual, corporation, company, association, partnership, state, municipality, or federal agency may petition the EPA Regional Administrator to determine whether the aquifer is a sole source or principal source of drinking water.[23]

The petition should contain sufficient information to allow the EPA to verify the boundaries of the aquifer and its recharge area, and to determine whether the aquifer is the sole or principal source of drinking water.[24] Among the factors considered by the EPA as part of the review and verification process are:

1. Whether the aquifer has the capacity to supply 50% or greater of the required drinking water for a given service area;

2. Where there exists a volume of water from an alternative source which is sufficient to replace the petitioned aquifer;

---

[21] Sole Source aquifer areas are primarily located in Southern Rhode Island and have been designated under three petitions:
   a. Block Island Aquifer;
   b. Pawcatuck Basin Aquifer; and
   c. Hunt-Annaquatucket-Pettaquamscutt Aquifer Area.

[22] 42 U.S.C.A. §§300f-j (1999 and Supp. 2001).

[23] *Id.*

[24] Detailed information concerning the Sole Source Aquifer petition requirements are identified in the "Sole Source Aquifer Designation Petitioned Guidance" available from the EPA regional office.

3. Whether contamination of the aquifer would create a significant hazard to the public health; and

4. Whether the boundaries of the aquifer and its recharge area, streamflow source area(s), project designation area, and project review area are appropriate.[25]

The approval procedure commences with the preparation of a petition that includes all hydrogeological data and other information needed for designation. The EPA conducts an initial review and completeness determination of the petition, followed by a detailed review and technical verification process. Included at this time is a public hearing to obtain comments. Following the public hearing and notice period, the EPA makes a decision on a designation of a sole source aquifer area, which is published in the Federal Register.[26]

The estimated time of approval for the EPA to make a determination on the designation of a sole source aquifer is a minimum of six months from the receipt of a complete petition. Complex petitions, however, may take a longer time to process.[27]

E. Individual Sewage Disposal System Permit[28]

An ISDS permit must be obtained by anyone proposing to install, construct, alter, or repair an individual sewage disposal system or seepage pit for domestic, non-hazardous waste. The purpose of requiring an ISDS permit is to assure the proper location, design, construction and maintenance of individual disposal systems in order to protect the public health and environmental quality.[29]

The responsible agency for ISDS permits is the DEM Office of Water Resources. If the proposed ISDS construction is located within a freshwater wetland or the regulated perimeter of a freshwater wetland, an ISDS permit will not be approved until the Freshwater Wetlands Section issues a wetland permit or makes a determination that the Wetlands Act does not apply.

---

[25] 42 U.S.C.A. §300f-j (1999 & Supp. 2001).

[26] *Id.*

[27] *Id.*

[28] Promulgated pursuant to Rhode Island Department of Environmental Management, Individual Sewage Disposal System ("ISDS") Regulations.

[29] *Id.*

If a project is located in a coastal region, an applicant must obtain approval from the Coastal Resources Management Council to undertake construction following receipt of an ISDS permit.[30]

The following is a list of information required for a permit application:

1. The existing and proposed finish grades in the vicinity of the system;
2. The location of an alternate disposal area in those areas served by wells;
3. The results and location of water table test pits;
4. The results and location of the percolation tests;
5. A description of the soil profile;
6. The maximum elevation of the ground water table in the location of the proposed system;
7. The size and location of all existing and proposed buildings and the number of bedrooms, or other building features used to determine the maximum daily flow, contained therein;
8. The location of any public sewer line within 200 feet of the property lines;
9. The location of any drinking water line within 25 feet of the disposal system or alternate area;
10. The location of any watercourse, wetlands, and/or any existing proposed private wells or drains within 200 feet of the proposed disposal system and/or alternate area;
11. The location of the proposed disposal system or alternate area relative to any watershed of a public water supply or critical resource area;
12. The location of all existing or proposed public drinking water supply wells within 500 feet of the proposed disposal system or alternate area;

[30] *Id.*

13. The location of any surface waters or tributaries thereto, including storm and subsurface drains discharging thereto, within 200 feet of the proposed disposal system and/or alternate area and whether said drain discharges, directly or indirectly, into a critical resource area;

14. The location of all existing individual sewage disposal systems within 100 feet of any well to be installed on the subject property; and

15. The specifications for the disposal system.[31]

Upon application to the Office of Water Resources the following situations may arise:

1. All applications submitted in accordance w/these regulations which shall also involve freshwater wetlands shall be accompanied by all appropriate determination(s), approval(s), or permit(s) required by the DEM's division of freshwater wetlands.[32]

2. Each application relating to a sewage disposal system that will service either a proposed new building or the expansion of any existing building or system, which system will dispose of 5,000 gallons per day or more of sewage as a result of said construction or expansion, shall be accompanied by a list identifying the names and addresses of the local building official, the water supply agency whose water supply is drawn from the watershed wherein the property is located, if applicable, all property owners within 200 feet of any component of the proposed system. Systems disposing of more than 10,000 gallons per day must obtain a groundwater quality certification pursuant to DEM's Rules and Regulations on Groundwater Quality prior to ISDS approval by the Office of Water Resources.

3. If a variance is requested, a review committee evaluates the request and makes a recommendation to approve or deny the permit. Upon his/her review of the recommendation, the Director shall render a final decision approving or denying the requested variance(s), or remanding the matter back to the committee for further review and consideration of certain specified factors.

[31] *Id.*
[32] *Id.*

If the permit or variance is denied, the applicant, upon appeal, must demonstrate that the approval of the permit or variance would not be contrary to the public interest and public health. In such a case, a public hearing is required.[33]

If the permit or variance is approved, the installer of the ISDS must submit a conformance certification within 3 days after the system is installed. This certifies that the system was installed in conformance with the approved permit and plans for the system. The DEM must be notified 24 hours before an approved ISDS is to be installed to permit the DEM, if necessary, to inspect the system during or after installation and authorize the installer to cover the system.[34]

If the design is acceptable, an application for a normal residential septic system is acted on within 15 to 30 days of receipt. If the proposed system is not in conformance with the regulations, it is returned to the applicant for revisions. Processing time is longer for commercial systems, subdivisions, variances, hearings, and in cases where freshwater or coastal wetlands are involved.[35]

F. Order of approval to operate, construct, alter or repair injection wells and subsurface disposal systems for non-domestic waste[36]

The purpose of requiring approval to operate, construct, alter, or repair injection wells and subsurface disposal systems for nondomestic waste is to preserve the quality of the groundwaters of the Rhode Island by assuring the proper location, design, construction, maintenance, and operation of injection wells and other subsurface waste disposal systems. The DEM Office of Water Resources issues the approval orders and the DEM periodically reports such orders to the EPA.[37]

Any person proposing or causing to be installed, constructed, altered or repaired, any subsurface disposal system used to dispose of non-hazardous waste of a non-domestic nature must apply for approval. The rules apply to Class V injection wells, subsurface disposal systems

---

[33] *Id.*
[34] *Id.*
[35] *Id.*
[36] *Id.* §46-12-14(a).
[37] Underground Inspection Control Program Rules and Regulations.

of a non-domestic nature and multiple dwelling, community or regional systems for the injection of domestic wastes.[38] These rules do not apply to injection wells or subsurface disposal systems used to dispose of individual or single family residential domestic waste, except under specified conditions.[39] An applicant is required to provide the following general information:

1. The name and address of the facility and owner/operator;
2. The type of ownership;
3. The nature of the business;
4. The site location;
5. Any well locations;
6. The type of well and discharge constituents; and
7. The type of approval desired.

Additional information requirements vary depending on the injection well type, its existing status, the effluent characteristics, and the Rhode Island groundwater classification.[40] A pre-application meeting to inspect the site may also be required in some cases to assess the specific information to be incorporated into the application.[41]

An approval order may be obtained by providing the DEM with the plans, specifications, sample analysis for priority pollutants, and other information required to establish affirmative evidence that the facility will be in compliance with all applicable rules and regulations.[42]

---

[38] *Id.* The State Prohibits Class I-IV wells, as described by the EPA, *only* Class V wells are allowed.
[39] *Id.* Lagoons also fall within the jurisdiction of these Regulations.
[40] *Id.* Such additions may include:
a. design calculations;
b. wastewater sample analysis;
c. well construction details;
d. geologic and hydrologic conditions;
e. injection procedures;
f. testing and monitoring programs;
g. contingency plans;
h. construction procedures; or
i. plugging and abandonment plans.
[41] *Id.*
[42] *Id.*

G. Order of approval to construct, install, or modify any waste system or means of wastewater treatment[43]

The purpose of requiring such approval is to preserve and enhance the quality of the Rhode Island's waters and to protect such waters from the discharge of sewage, hazardous waste, and other waste. The approval order is required to ensure that the discharges will meet restrictions established in the Rhode Island Pollutant Discharge Elimination System ("RIPDES") permit in order to attain water quality standards. The DEM Office of Water Resources is responsible for the issuance of such orders.[44]

Anyone proposing to construct, install, add to, or modify any waste system or means of wastewater treatment, including the extension of lateral sewers to an existing sewer system, must apply for an approval order. The approval order is generally required for major industrial and publicly owned treatment works. Issuance of the order or approval does not relieve the discharger of the responsibility to obtain a RIPDES permit and state certification that the discharge will not violate water quality standards.[45]

If, at the time of application for an order of approval from the DEM, the proposed activity requires a new or revised discharge permit, applications should be made concurrently. The DEM may approve or deny an application, and may approve the system design with modifications. DEM also will make findings regarding water quality and/or certification. Applicants may appeal denials. The applicant, however, has the burden of showing that the proposed project can be constructed and operated without violating water quality criterion of receiving or downstream waters.[46]

The estimated time for approval varies depending on the complexity of the project, however, a minimum of one month is required for the approval order. A longer time will be necessary for major municipal facilities.[47]

---

[43] *Id.* §46-12-14(a).
[44] *Id.*
[45] *Id.*
[46] *Id.*
[47] *Id.*

H. Permits for the discharge of dredged material and other work in navigable water[48]

There are three different permits under this heading: A permit for the discharge or fill material (Section 404 permit); a dumping permit for dredged materials (Section 103 permit); and a permit for work in navigable waters (Section 10 permit). Section 404 and 103 permits regulate the disposal of dredged or fill material to protect human health and welfare and the integrity of the United States, inland and marine waters. Section 10 permits control activities that alter or modify navigable waters of the United States.[49]

The Army Corps of Engineers issues permits for the dredging and filling of inland and coastal waters. The DEM Office of Water Resources issues water quality certifications for all Army Corps of Engineers permits. Permits for filling in freshwater wetlands and water bodies requires a permit from the Division of Groundwater and Freshwater Wetlands. The Coastal Resources Management Council ("CRMC") issues permits for projects in the coastal zone, which require water quality certification from the DEM Division of Water Resources prior to permit approval.[50]

All persons proposing to discharge dredged or fill material in the United States' inland or ocean water, or desiring to perform work in navigable waters must apply for a permit. Generally, a description of the proposed activity and/or information regarding type and amount of material to be dredged is required. Sediment testing, the location of a DEM approved disposal site for the dredged material, other environmental data, and an impact assessment are also required.[51]

The application must be filed with the Army Corps of Engineers and state agencies where applicable. The DEM reviews the application and issues or denies water quality certification to the Corps. The DEM may be required to testify at a public hearing. The Corps then issues or denies the permit, contingent upon obtaining necessary state permit approval, most notably CRMC approval for work in coastal areas.[52]

---

[48] The legislative authority for these permit programs is the Clean Water Act, 33 U.S.C.A. §1344, 404(b)(1) Guidelines, the Ocean Dumping Act, 33 U.S.C.A. §1413, and the River and Harbors Act, 33 U.S.C.A. §404 (1986 & Supp. 1993).

[49] *Id.*

[50] *Id.*

[51] *Id.*

[52] *Id.*

I. Approval of Wastewater Pre-treatment Systems[53]

This approval requirement provides a mechanism whereby owners of pre-treatment systems installed pursuant to municipal sewer use ordinances can obtain DEM approval for providing minimum standards for wastewater entering the municipal sewer system. The approval of such pre-treatment systems by the director of the DEM allows the owner to qualify for state tax advantage provided for installation of water pollution control facilities and materials. The DEM Office of Water Resources is the responsible agency.[54]

This is non-mandatory certificate of approval provided to owners implementing pre-treatment systems installed pursuant to municipal sewer use ordinances, which function to remove contaminants and pollutants from, or alter the chemical properties of wastewater, such that they may comply with sewer use ordinance restrictions. A person seeking "Approval for State Tax Advantages" for their pre-treatment system must submit the following:

1. A brief, complete description of the pre-treatment system for which approval is sought;[55]

2. A list of supplies acquired for incorporation into or used and consumed in the operation of a pretreatment facility only, and verified by the design specifications for the facility;

3. A letter of compliance or approval from the regulatory agency with oversight on the system; and

4. Any further information requested by DEM to make its determination.

Approval is issued by the director of DEM provided that all the required information has been submitted in an acceptable form and a site inspection has been conducted by the DEM to confirm the installation and operation of the pretreatment system.[56]

---

[53] The legislative authority for this approval program is R.I. Gen. Laws §44-11-11.1(2001).

[54] *Id.*

[55] This description must include a narrative of its operation, process and instrumentation diagram, and any other schematics, shop drawings and material specifications necessary to enable the Division to determine of the pre-treatment system and its methods of operation.

[56] *Id.*

J. Storm Water Discharge

On February 9, 1993, DEM promulgated two General Permits for storm water discharge: (1) a General Permit for "storm water discharge associated with industrial activity"; and (2) a General Permit for "storm water discharge associated with construction activity" which disturbs five or more acres. Both General Permits became effective on March 19, 1993. They expire on March 19, 2003.

Consistent with EPA's guidelines and the RIPDES Regulations, these General Permits share three conditions: (1) with few exceptions, non-storm water discharge must be eliminated from all storm water systems; (2) a Storm Water Pollution Prevention Plan ("SWPPP") must be developed to minimize or even eliminate potential pollutants in industrial storm water discharges; and (3) permittees must conduct inspections of their storm water systems.

1. Storm Water Discharge Associated with Industrial Activity

a. Obtaining Coverage Under the General Permit

If a facility meets at least one of the conditions in the definition of "storm water discharge associated with industrial activity"[57] and if the storm water discharge is a point source discharging directly to a surface water body and/or a separate storm sewer system, then the facility may seek coverage under this General Permit.

For facilities operating prior to October 1, 1992, a complete Notice of Intent ("NOI") to be covered under the General Permit must have been submitted to DEM by April 19, 1993. Authorization to discharge will be immediate unless notification to the contrary is received.

For storm water discharges commencing after October 1, 1992, complete NOIs must be submitted ninety (90) days prior to discharging. Authorization is automatic at the end of a 90 day review period unless notification to the contrary is received.

b. Developing a Storm Water Pollution Prevention Plan

The General Permit for industrial activity requires that a SWPPP be developed and implemented to employ Best Management Practices ("BMPs") to reduce or eliminate

[57] *See* RIPDES Rule 31.b.15.

pollutants from storm water discharges and ensure compliance with the permit's terms and conditions. At a minimum, the plan must include a description of potential pollutant sources, storm water management control measures, and a site inspection plan. Facilities with salt storage piles and SARA Title III facilities are subject to additional requirements.

The SWPPP must be retained on-site for at least 5 years and be made readily available to DEM.

c. Monitoring the Storm Water System

The General Permit's storm water monitoring requirements adhere to a three-tiered class system, with the risk level of each class dictating parameters to be analyzed in sampling and reporting requirements. These sampling requirements range from semi-annual to no sampling at all.

Additionally, facilities of all classes are required to conduct comprehensive annual site evaluations of storm water control measures and submit their findings to DEM.

2. Storm Water Discharges Associated with Construction Activities

a. Obtaining Coverage Under the General Permit

If construction activities disturb five or more acres or land where storm water runoff is directed via a point source into a separate storm sewer system or into the waters of the State, an applicant is required to obtain a RIPDES storm water permit. As noted above, these activities fall within the parameters of the General Permit for storm water discharge associated with construction activity promulgated by DEM on February 9, 1993 and which became effective on March 19, 1993.

To gain authorization under the General Permit, an applicant must submit an NOI to DEM.

If a construction activity is already regulated by DEM's Division of Fresh Water Wetlands, the Coastal Resources Management Council or by a local Conservation District, an applicant need only send DEM a copy of its current permit or agency certification, and a complete NOI. In these circumstances an applicant's authorization to discharge under the

General Permit will be automatic after thirty days. All other construction activities will be approved after a review of the NOI and the SWPPP.

b. Developing a Storm Water Pollution Prevention Plan

The General Permit for discharge associated with construction activity requires an applicant to submit an SWPPP with its NOI and implement that plan immediately upon authorization to discharge.

This SWPPP requires the use of BMPs to reduce or eliminate the transport of pollutants (including sediment) off-site and ensure compliance with the General Permit's terms and conditions. At a minimum, the SWPPP must include: (1) a site plan with a description of potential sources of pollutants; (2) descriptions of controls for erosion and sedimentation, post-construction storm management, off-site vehicle tracking of sediments, waste disposal and response procedures, allowable non-storm water discharges, and good housekeeping practices; and (3) maintenance procedures.

The SWPPP must be retained on-site for the duration of the project and made available to DEM upon request.

c. Monitoring the Storm Water System

While there are no sampling requirements for construction activities covered under the General Permit, an applicant must inspect all storm water control measures every seven calendar days and within twenty-four hours after any storm event which produces at least .25 inches of rainfall per twenty-four hour period. An applicant must retain these records on-site for the duration of the project and make them available to DEM upon request.

3. Penalties For Noncompliance

Any unauthorized discharge or permit noncompliance constitutes a violation of Chapter 46-12 of the Rhode Island General Laws and the Federal Clean Water Act and is grounds for enforcement action which may include: (1) permit termination, revocation, reissuance or modification; (2) the denial of a permit renewal application; or (3) the imposition of civil or criminal penalties of up to $25,000 per day, imprisonment for not more than five years, or both.

K. Groundwater Quality

1. Applicability

The Groundwater Quality program applies to all groundwater in the State of Rhode Island, any individual sewage disposal system designed to treat ten thousand (10,000) gallons or more per day and any permanent monitoring well installed pursuant to the Regulations. This program is designed to protect and restore the quality of the state's groundwater resources for use as drinking water and other beneficial uses, and to assure protection of the public health and welfare and the environment.

2. Prohibitions

Groundwater shall be maintained at a quality consistent with its classification. No person shall (1) take actions that violate or cause to violate the standards established in the Regulations; (2) cause or allow a discharge of any pollutant to groundwater without the approval of the DEM; (3) take action that shall cause or allow groundwater designated non-attainment to be further degraded; (4) operate or maintain a facility in a manner that is likely to result in a discharge of any pollutant to groundwater without approval of the DEM; and (5) discharge hazardous materials to the groundwaters of the State. In addition, the establishment of new solid waste landfills and facilities for the disposal of hazardous waste: (1) are prohibited in areas where the groundwater is classified GAA and (2) shall be prohibited within areas designated by the DEM to be wellhead protection areas for community water supply wells.[58]

Owners and operators of existing solid waste landfills and facilities for the disposal of hazardous waste licensed at the date of promulgation of this rule and located within the wellhead protection area of a community water supply well, shall be prohibited from expanding the areal extent of the waste disposal area and shall obtain approval from the DEM prior to undertaking any action which constitutes a modification to an approved license, permit, operating or closure plan, issued pursuant to the Rhode Island Rules and Regulations for Solid Waste Management Facilities and to licenses or approvals issued pursuant to the Rhode Island Rules and Regulations for Hazardous Waste Generation, Transportation, Treatment, Storage and Disposal. Facility modifications which pose an increased risk of introducing pollutants to the groundwater shall be

---

[58] The Rules and Regulations for Groundwater Quality §8.

prohibited. Furthermore, disposal of solid waste is prohibited at facilities which lack a valid DEM solid waste facility license or at such facilities whose licenses have expired or lapsed, and no person shall install underground storage tanks in new locations within the wellhead protection area of community water supply wells. Any action taken in violation of the above prohibitions shall be deemed a violation of these regulations. For violations that are of a continuing nature, each and every day that the violation exists shall constitute a separate and distinct violation.[59]

3. Water Quality Standards and Preventive Action Limits

Pursuant to R.I. Gen. Laws §46-13.1-1 *et seq.* and the Regulations, the DEM shall classify the groundwaters of the State. All groundwaters in Rhode Island fall into one of four categories. Groundwater classified as "GAA" and "GA" are those resources which the DEM has designated to be suitable for public drinking water use without treatment. Groundwater classified "GB" are those groundwater resources which the DEM has designated not suitable for public or private drinking water use, and groundwater classified "GC" are those groundwater resources, which because of present or past land use or hydrogeological conditions, have been determined to be more suitable for certain waste disposal practices than for development as a drinking water supply.[60]

Those waters that have pollutant concentrations greater than the groundwater quality standards for the applicable classification shall be designated as "non-attainment" waters. For example, GAA Non-attainment (GAA-NA), GA Non-attainment (GA-NA), or GB Non-attainment (GB-NA). The goal for non-attainment areas is restoration to the groundwater quality consistent with the standards detailed in the Regulations.[61]

In addition, the DEM shall establish groundwater quality standards and preventive action limits to be used in determining compliance with the groundwater classifications, including, but not limited to, compliance of proposed discharges to groundwater, existing discharges to groundwater, groundwater remediation activities, and other facilities and activities that have an actual or potential adverse impact on groundwater quality. However, numerical groundwater quality standards and preventive action limits shall be established only for class GAA and GA.[62]

---

[59] *Id.*
[60] *Id.* §9.01.
[61] *Id.* §9.02.
[62] *Id.* §10.01.

Class GAA and class GA groundwater are suitable for drinking water use without treatment, and therefore, both classes are subject to the same groundwater quality standards and preventive action limits, which are defined below. The preventive action limit shall be set at 50% of the numerical groundwater quality standards.

a. Pollutants shall not be in groundwater classified GAA or GA, except within an approved discharge zone or residual zone, in any concentration which will adversely affect the groundwater as a source of potable water or which will adversely affect other beneficial uses of the groundwater, to include but not be limited to recreational, agricultural and industrial uses and the preservation of fish and wildlife habitat through the maintenance of surface water quality.

b. The numerical groundwater quality standards and the preventive action limits for specific substances in class GAA and class GA are listed in Table 1 of the Regulation.

c. Groundwater classified GAA and GA shall be of a quality which the DEM determines does not violate or have any reasonable potential to cause a violation of surface water quality standards established by the *Rhode Island Water Quality Regulations for Water Pollution Control*, October 1988, and amendments thereto.[63]

Furthermore, groundwater classified GB and GC shall be of a quality which the DEM determines does not:

a. Threaten public health and/or the environment;

b. Violate or have a substantial likelihood to cause a violation of surrounding groundwater quality standards; and

c. Adversely impact or have a substantial likelihood to adversely impact:

1) current or proposed uses of the facility;

[63] *Id.* §10.02.

2) current or proposed uses of groundwater and surface water at or within the facility boundaries;

3) current and future uses of surrounding property, groundwater and surface water;

d. violate or have reasonable potential to cause a violation of surface water quality standards established by the *Rhode Island Water Quality Regulations for Water Pollution Control,* and amendment thereto.[64]

In determining compliance with the groundwater quality standards for class GB and class GC at a facility, the DEM may consider the following factors, in addition to other relevant information, provided by the facility owner or operator: surrounding groundwater quality; groundwater classification surrounding the facility; surface water classification within the facility boundaries and surrounding the facility; current and proposed future uses of groundwater and surface water at or within the facility boundaries; current and proposed future uses of the facility; uses of surrounding property, groundwater and surface water; hydrogeologic characteristics of the facility and surrounding the facility, including but not limited to, groundwater flow direction, hydraulic gradient, type of subsurface materials, and depth to bedrock; actual and potential routes for human exposure and points of human exposure to the pollutant(s); man-made pathways for pollutant movement off-site, e.g., underground utility lines; and persistence and mobility of the pollutant(s) in the subsurface and the toxicity of the pollutant(s).[65]

However, any person who may be substantially and specifically affected by a groundwater classification, may petition the DEM to modify the classification assigned to particular groundwaters of the State. The petitioner must specify the precise boundary in question and prove by clear, convincing and scientifically valid evidence that a reclassification is consistent with the Regulations.[66]

4. Determination of Compliance With Groundwater Quality Standards and Preventive Action Limits

Compliance with the groundwater quality standards and preventive action limits will be determined through analytical tests of groundwater quality by the facility owner or operator.

[64] *Id.* §10.03(a).
[65] *Id.* §10.03(b).
[66] *Id.* §11.03.

Where applicable, the DEM may also require analytical test of the effluent prior to the discharge to the groundwater. In addition, the DEM may request verification of any test data or collect samples if it is deemed necessary. All groundwater samples and effluent samples must be collected, stored, transported, and analyzed in accordance with the most recent United States Environmental Protection Agency approved procedures; the most recent "Standard Methods for the Examination of Water and Wastewater" (American Public Health Association, et al.); or alternative methods approved by the DEM. Furthermore, groundwater and effluent sampling frequency and the list of parameters to test for shall be proposed to the DEM by the facility owner or operator. The DEM's determination of sampling frequency and the parameters to test for shall be made, in part, utilizing information provided by the facility owner or operator regarding the type of facility, waste generated, waste disposed of on site, materials stored or utilized on site and any site specific hydrogeologic characteristics that may be required by the DEM.[67]

All facilities that are required by the DEM to monitor groundwater quality pursuant to the Regulations and the *Underground Injection Control Program Rules and Regulations,* May 1984, and amendments thereto, shall implement a groundwater monitoring program approved by the DEM. Groundwater monitoring done in compliance with certain DEM regulations and federal programs are exempt from specific provisions of the *Rules and Regulations for Groundwater Quality.*[68] However, whether exempt from specific provisions or not, no groundwater monitoring required by the DEM may be terminated without approval from the DEM.[69]

Any point where the groundwater quality is monitored or where the groundwater is withdrawn for use, excepting points within a discharge zone or residual zone approved pursuant to the Regulations, may be used to determine compliance with groundwater quality standards for the area.[70]

---

67 *Id.* §12.01.
68 *Id.* §12.02(a).
69 *Id.* §12.03.
70 *Id.* §13.01.

5. Notification to DEM of Violations of Preventive Action Limits and Groundwater Quality Standards

Unless exempt, owners or operators of facilities that did not previously report to the DEM the discovery, prior to the effective date of these Regulations, that groundwater quality at their facility that does not comply with the groundwater quality standards in the Regulations, must notify the DEM in writing within six (6) months of the effective date of the Regulations.[71]

Furthermore, unless exempt, facility owners and/or operators that discharge to groundwater of have had a discharge or release to groundwater shall notify the DEM in writing within fifteen (15) days when it is discovered that:

a. A preventive action limit has not been met at any point of compliance at a facility that has a discharge to groundwater approved by DEM where the groundwater is classified GAA or GA;

b. A groundwater quality standard has not been met at any point of compliance at a facility in any groundwater classification;

c. An alternative notification level established under a groundwater monitoring program approved by the DEM pursuant to the Groundwater Regulations, other rules or regulations of the DEM or the federal government has not been met; or

d. The facility owner or operator has reasonable cause to believe that a discharge or release has occurred which may result in the violation of a preventive action limit and/or groundwater quality standard. Persons reporting spills of chemical and/or petroleum products to the DEM pursuant to the immediate notification requirements of other state or federal laws and regulations are exempt from this notification requirement.[72]

Any notification made to the DEM must include at least the following information:

---

[71] *Id.* §§14.02; 14.05(a). The effective date of these Regulations is August 1996.
[72] *Id.* §14.03.

a. Name, address, telephone number of person notifying the DEM and of the facility owner or operator;

b. Date and time of the discovery and the circumstances surrounding the discovery of the occurrence requiring notification;

c. Groundwater classification of the site;

d. Location of the occurrence and a legal description of the site (plat and lot);

e. Concentration of the pollutant(s) identified in the groundwater where there has been an actual detected release;

f. Identification of the pollutant(s) in the discharge or release when there is reasonable cause to believe that a discharge may violate a groundwater quality standard or preventive action limit;

g. Initial determination of the source of the pollutant(s) and an estimate of the extent of pollution; and

h. Measures taken or proposed to be taken at the time of notification.[73]

6. Responses to Violation of Preventive Action Limits and Groundwater Quality Standards

The responses the DEM may require of the facility owner or operator when a preventive action limit or groundwater quality standard is not met at a point of compliance or a discharge or release is suspected that may result in the violation of a preventive action limit or groundwater quality standard at a point of compliance include, but are not limited to, the responses listed below. The DEM may require more than one response.

a. Resample groundwater quality at a point of compliance;

[73] *Id.* §14.06.

b. Collect and submit additional data on groundwater quality on site or surrounding the site, hydrogeologic characteristics, and/or facility practices;

c. Arrange for the sampling of drinking water wells which may be adversely affected;

d. Install and sample monitoring wells: such wells shall be in compliance with the construction standards contained in the Regulations, unless otherwise approved by the DEM;

e. Require the establishment of a groundwater monitoring program pursuant to the Regulations or other groundwater monitoring program approved by the DEM pursuant to other regulations of the DEM of the federal government, or require a change in an existing groundwater monitoring program;

f. Require a revision of the operational procedures at the facility;

g. Require a change in the design or construction of the facility;

h. Require an alternate method of waste treatment or disposal;

i. Require the facility owner or operator to conduct a groundwater assessment and prepare a report pursuant to the Regulations or another report pursuant to other applicable DEM regulations, that is subject to the DEM's review and approval. Based on the results of this report, the DEM may require further investigation;

j. Require cessation of any prohibited discharges to groundwater;

k. Require prohibition of an activity;

l. Require the facility owner or operator to provide drinking water to those persons that do not have a potable water supply (for violation of groundwater quality standard only);

m. Require the facility owner or operator to conduct a groundwater investigation and prepare a report pursuant to the Regulations, to adequately assess the nature and extent of pollution. Such report shall be subject to the DEM's review and approval; and

n. Require a remedial action to restore groundwater quality to levels established by the DEM pursuant to the Regulations.[74]

---

[74] *Id.* §15.04.

7. Variances, Appeals and Penalties

A facility owner or operator may submit a written request to the DEM for a variance from any provision of the Regulations. Such a request must include at a minimum: (1) the name and address of the facility owner or operator, and the name and location of the facility for which the owner or operator seeks a variance; (2) a list of the names and addresses of the owners and tenants of all properties that abut the facility; (3) identification of the specific section of the Regulations from which a variance is requested; (4) a statement of the reasons for which the facility owner or operator seeks a variance. This statement shall specify the reasons that the facility owner or operator is unable to comply with these Regulations, why a variance is necessary, and the reasons why a hardship is alleged. The person seeking the variance should separately and by number list each reason and any other mitigating factors he believes the DEM should consider; and (5) an explanation that the alternative procedures requested are substantially equivalent to the Regulations herein in achieving protection of the public health and the environment.[75]

In addition, any person affected by a decision of the DEM pursuant to the regulations may, in accordance with the *Administrative Rules of Practice and Procedure for the Department of Environmental Management*, file a claim for an adjudicatory hearing to review the decision. The party appealing the decision bears the burden of proving that their application complies with all requirements of the Regulations.[76] Furthermore, penalties will be assessed in accordance with the DEM's *Rules and Regulations for the Assessment of Administrative Penalties* for any violation of the Regulations.[77]

---

[75] *Id.* §19.01.
[76] *Id.* §21.
[77] *Id.* §23.

CHAPTER V:

HAZARDOUS WASTE MANAGEMENT

A. Hazardous Waste Management Act

The Hazardous Waste Management Act (the "Act"),[1] and the Rules and Regulations for Hazardous Waste Management (the "Regulations") establish a regulatory program for the generation, storage, transportation, treatment, and disposal of hazardous wastes, and encourage waste recovery and recycling, as well as the development and utilization of industrial processes which generate smaller amounts of hazardous wastes. The Hazardous Waste Management Act is Rhode Island's version of the federal Resource Conservation and Recovery Act, which is the program for tracking and managing hazardous waste from "cradle to grave."[2]

B. Hazardous Waste Regulations

The Regulations define hazardous waste as any waste or combination of wastes of a solid, liquid, contained gaseous, or semisolid form which, because of its quantity, concentration, or physical or chemical characteristics, may cause or significantly contribute to an increase in mortality or serious irreversible or incapacitating reversible illness, or which poses a substantial present or potential hazard to human health or the environment.[3] The Regulations define a hazardous waste management facility as a facility for collection, source separation, storage, processing, transfer, treatment, recovery, or disposal of hazardous wastes.

1. Those Convicted of Certain Crimes Cannot Obtain a Permit

It should be noted that the Hazardous Waste Management Act prohibits anyone, who has been convicted or pled nolo contendre to a "serious"[4] crime, from obtaining a permit under the Regulations.[5]

---

[1] R.I. Gen. Laws §23-19.1-1 *et seq*.
[2] 42 U.S.C. §6901 *et seq*.
[3] Such wastes include those which are toxic, corrosive, flammable, or reactive, as well as wastes defined by the Regulations as "Rhode Island Wastes". *See* The Rules §3.25.
[4] A "serious" crime is defined as, among others, murder, kidnapping, gambling, robbery, bribery, racketeering, extortion, arson, forgery, and fraud.
[5] R.I. Gen. Laws §23-19.1-10(d).

2. Regulations for Generators[6]

The Regulations require a generator[7] who produces hazardous waste or imports hazardous waste from a foreign country to:

a. Obtain an identification number from the DEM ("EPA I.D. No.");[8]

b. Obtain a storage permit, unless hazardous waste is stored on site for less than 90 days and managed in accordance with federal and state regulations;[9]

c. Ship hazardous waste to a designated facility with an EPA I.D. No., or to a transporter of hazardous waste with an EPA I.D. No. and a valid Rhode Island Hazardous Waste Transporter Permit;[10]

d. Prepare the Rhode Island Uniform Hazardous Waste Manifest ("manifest") or other manifest approved by the EPA;[11]

e. Provide the DEM with the names and signatures of all agents authorized to sign the manifest;[12]

f. Package the waste in accordance with federal law;[13]

g. Label and mark the sides of all hazardous waste containers with the generator's name and address, generic names of the principal hazardous

---

[6] *See also* 40 C.F.R. 262 (1993) (federal regulations for generators).
[7] The Regulations do not require a generator to obtain a permit for the generation of hazardous waste, but do require permits for their hazardous waste management activities not specifically exempted by the Act or the Regulations. The Rules §5.07.
[8] *Id.* §5.01.
[9] *Id.* §5.02. *see* 40 C.F.R. §262.34(a)-(c) (1993); 40 C.F.R. §264.175(1993).
[10] *Id.* §5.03.
[11] *Id.*; *see id.* §5.03(B)-(L) (requirements for preparing a manifest). A manifest identifies the quantity, composition, type, origin, routing, and destination of hazardous waste from the point of generation to the point of treatment, storage or disposal.
[12] *Id.* §5.09.
[13] *See* 49 C.F.R. §173 (1993); 49 C.F.R. §178 (1993); 49 C.F.R. §179 (1993).

waste components, waste code, date of containerization, and the hazardous waste manifest number[14]; and

h. Maintain for at least three years all pertinent records relating to the generation of hazardous waste, including copies of each manifest, receipts for waste oil shipments, and copies of each biennial report[15], waste analysis, and any tests or other determinations made regarding the content of the waste.[16]

The Regulations also require a generator immediately notify the DEM in the event of a spill or release of hazardous waste or material on the generator's property that presents a substantial risk of injury to public health or the environment. The Regulations require the generator to takes steps to prevent, contain, and clean up the spill or release of the hazardous waste or material.[17]

3. Regulations for Transporters[18]

The Regulations prohibit any person from transporting hazardous wastes in or on the land and waters of Rhode Island without a DEM Hazardous Waste or Septage Waste Transporter Permit, unless the transporter is transporting sewage sludge produced at a publicly-owned or privately-owned treatment works, animal waste produced at a farm, household refuse that is not hazardous waste, or is using non-permitted vehicles to collect and transport, in emergency situations or as a by-product of sampling activities or in situations that satisfy 40 C.F.R. §262.20(f), hazardous wastes.[19]

In applying for a transporter permit, the applicant must include the following information:

a. The name and mailing address of the applicant;

---

[14] The Rules §5.04; *see* 49 C.F.R. §172 (1993); 40 C.F.R. §262.32 (1993); 40 C.F.R. §262.33 (1993)
[15] *See* 40 C.F.R. §262.41 (1993).
[16] The Rules §§5.05-5.06.
[17] *Id.* §5.10.
[18] *See also* 40 C.F.R. §263 (1993).
[19] *Id.* §6.01(A).

b. EPA I.D. No.;[20]

c. The name, address, and business phone number of the owner of the vehicle;

d. Year, make, vehicle identification number, capacity, and registration number of each vehicle needing a permit;

e. Storage location of permitted vehicles;

f. Location to be used for the temporary storage of hazardous waste for a period of up to 72 hours;

g. The name, address, and phone number of the applicant's personnel who may be reached in case of an emergency;[21]

h. A description of procedures for responding to spills or other emergency situations, including training and instruction measures for transporter personnel, emergency and safety equipment, and arrangements for emergency services; and

i. A description of the absorbent material to be used for the cleanup spills of liquids.[22]

All applications for a transporter permit must be submitted to the DEM along with an application fee.[23] The DEM will grant a one year permit for those vehicles which pass inspection and that are listed on the permit application.[24] Annually, transporters must have the DEM inspect each vehicle listed on the permit application prior to the receipt or renewal of the permit. An inspection must ensure confirmation of a state inspection, proper identification of the

[20] *See id.* §6.02(D) (transporters must obtain EPA I.D. No.)
[21] *Id.* §6.02(B).
[22] *Id.* §6.03(F).
[23] *Id.* §6.01(B).
[24] *Id.* §6.01(B), (D).

permit number clearly painted on the vehicle, registration, soundness of containment structures, and compliance with all safety requirements and emergency procedures.[25]

The Regulations prohibit transporters from transporting extremely hazardous waste[26] on certain roads in Rhode Island, unless the waste is generated on such a road and the DEM authorizes the transportation.[27] A list of such roads must be posted conspicuously in the cab of each vehicle registered to the permitee.[28]

The Regulations prohibit transporters from accepting hazardous waste, except sanitary septage or waste oil, unless the generator completes the generator section of the manifest, and all containers of hazardous wastes are properly labeled and tightly sealed.[29] The transporter must deliver the hazardous waste only to the facility designated in the manifest, unless otherwise instructed by the generator,[30] and must retain a copy of the manifest for three years from the date of receipt of the waste.[31]

The Regulations also require transporters of hazardous waste to maintain liability insurance coverage of one million dollars per incident,[32] and to provide adequate personnel to ensure that activities are conducted in compliance with all applicable laws and regulations.

Hazardous waste transporters must be equipped with safety equipment which minimizes the chances of spills, fire, explosion, or other emergencies, and to protect the health and safety of the public and transportation personnel.[33] Such safety equipment must include adequate communication systems, protective clothing and equipment, and first-aid supplies including an eyewash apparatus.[34] In addition, vehicles transporting hazardous waste in liquid form must be equipped with absorbent materials capable of absorbing 10% of the leak or spill of

---

[25] *Id.* §6.07.
[26] The hazardous waste manifest defines extremely hazardous waste.
[27] *Id.* §6.03(B)-(D).
[28] *Id.* §6.03(C).
[29] *Id.* §§6.03(G); 6.04(B); 6.10. Transporters accepting waste automotive oil may use the waste automotive oil manifest in lieu of the hazardous waste manifest, and must provide receipts to the generator indicating the name of the transporter, the date of the shipment, estimated quantity of waste oil, and its destination. *Id.* §§6.03(N); 6.04(A).
[30] *Id.* §6.04(H).
[31] *Id.* §§6.04(C)-(F). The transporter must complete the transporter section of the manifest, and keep the original manifest with the waste until delivery to the consignee.
[32] *Id.* §6.02(C). Transporters engaged exclusively in transporting sanitary septage need only maintain three hundred thousand dollars of coverage per incident.
[33] *Id.* §6.08(A).
[34] *Id.* §6.08(B).

hazardous waste.[35] The transporter also must prepare and conspicuously post procedures for personnel to follow in case of an emergency.[36]

A transporter immediately must notify the DEM in the event of a hazardous waste spill, and must take appropriate measures to contain and thoroughly collect the hazardous waste and soil contaminated by the spill.[37] The Regulations require that any equipment contaminated during the handling of hazardous waste be decontaminated prior to servicing or using for non hazardous waste if servicing or using the contaminated equipment would be harmful to any person.[38] Contaminated water or residues from washing or decontaminating the equipment must be collected and disposed of as hazardous waste in compliance with the Regulations.[39]

Hazardous waste in the form of powder, dust, or fine solids and hazardous waste capable of releasing hazardous gases, mists, or vapors must be handled, stored, and disposed of in covered containers.[40] Storage and transfer areas must provide spill containment structures equal to 10% of the greater of the total waste or volume of the largest container and sufficient free board to allow for containment of extensive precipitation.[41]

Temporary storage in the transporting vehicle is permissible only in locations approved by the DEM, and such temporary storage will not require a storage permit.[42] Temporary storage at the location where the transporting vehicle broke down is permissible only if the transporter notifies the DEM of the vehicle's location and estimated time for repairs.[43]

4. Regulations for Hazardous Waste Facilities[44]

a. Facility Permits

The Regulations require that all persons constructing, altering, or

---

[35] *Id.* §6.13.
[36] *Id.* §6.08(C)
[37] *Id.* §§6.03(E); 6.08(C)(2), (3).
[38] *Id.* §6.09.
[39] *Id.* §6.09.
[40] *Id.* §§6.11; 6.12.
[41] *Id.* §6.14(A).
[42] *Id.* §6.14(B), (D).
[43] *Id.* §6.14(C).
[44] *See also* 40 C.F.R. §§264-266 (1993).

operating a hazardous waste treatment, storage, or disposal facility, and all person treating, storing, or disposing of hazardous waste, obtain an operating permit or other approval from the DEM for such activities.[45] This Rule does apply to facilities that accept, treat, or store only precious metal bearing waste. Upon finding an imminent and substantial endangerment to human health or the environment, however, the DEM may issue a temporary emergency waste permit to a non-permitted facility to allow the treatment, storage, or disposal of hazardous waste subject to the requirements of 40 C.F.R. §270.61. The DEM may also provide temporary emergency permits to a permitted facility to allow for the treatment, storage, or disposal of hazardous waste not covered by an effective permit subject to the requirements of 40 C.F.R. §270.61.[46]

The owner or operator of a hazardous waste management facility must sign the application for a DEM permit or approval,[47] include a list of the direct and indirect owners of the facility,[48] and submit to the DEM plans and specification that adequately describe the facility.[49] The plans and specifications accompanying the permit application must include the following information:

1) A copy of the latest Unites States Geological Survey topographical map with the facility outlined on the survey;

2) The facility's EPA I.D. No.;

3) Photographs of the existing facility;

4) A description of the facility, including design capacities and processes;

---

[45] *Id.* §7.01. The owner or operator of a publicly-owned treatment works which accepts hazardous waste for treatment does not have to apply for a permit under this section if such owner complies with the requirements of 40 C.F.R. §270.60(c). The Rules §7.01(g).
[46] *Id.* §7.01(D).
[47] *Id.* §8.01(B).
[48] *Id.* §8.02. If the owner is a corporation the list must include all officers, directors and other persons owning ten percent or more of the corporate stock.
[49] *Id.* §§8.01(A); 8.03 (general requirements). Applicants must also comply with the provisions of 40 C.F.R. 270.11-270.21.

5) The name, address, and telephone number of the facility's operator;[50]

6) A site plan showing: all onsite structures, operational unites, and access; all property and water lines within 500 feet of the perimeter of the facility; a wind rose; north arrow; map scale; and all water courses, watersheds of public surface water supplies; public and private drinking water supply wells, barriers for drainage or flood control; land uses; contours sufficient to show patterns of surface drainage; and extent of the 100-year flood plain, if applicable, within 1,000 feet of the perimeter of the facility;[51]

7) A chemical and physical analysis of the hazardous wastes handled at the facility and a copy of the waste analysis plan;

8) A description of all security procedures, equipment, and personnel training programs;

9) A copy of the general inspection schedule, and a copy of the contingency plan;

10) The traffic pattern;

11) The facility's longitude and latitude, and

12) A copy of the closure plan and a closure cost estimate, as well as a copy of the facility's insurance policy.[52]

Facilities that store containers of hazardous waste also must provide the DEM with information on the facility's containment system,[53] including basic design parameters, dimensions, construction materials, capacity of containment systems, and provisions for

---

[50] *Id.* §8.04(A)(C)-(F).

[51] *Id.* §8.04(B). A groundwater monitoring plan capable of determining the facility's impact on the groundwater in the uppermost aquifer underlying the facility may also be required. *Id.* §8.04(G).

[52] *Id.* §8.04(H)-(T).

[53] *See* 40 C.F.R. §264.175 (requirements for containment systems).

overflow and run-off control.[54] Facilities that use tanks to store or treat hazardous waste must provide a description of the following: design standards and specifications; construction and lining materials; tank dimensions, capacity, and shell thickness; diagram of piping, instrumentation, and process flow; feed systems, safety cutoff, bypass systems, and pressure controls; procedures for handling incompatible, ignitable, or reactive wastes;[55] and flood plain operations.[56]

Permits for hazardous waste facilities are valid for five years and may be extended or renewed by the DEM for 10 years from the date upon which the original permit was effective.[57] The owner or operator of a hazardous waste facility must apply for a new permit at the end of the 10 year period, and must submit a completed application form to the DEM at least 180 days prior to the expiration date of the present permit.[58] A permit applies only to the facility in operation at the time the DEM issued the permit, and any modification of a permitted facility must be submitted to the DEM for approval.[59] Separate permits are required for facilities located in separate geographical areas, even though they are under the same management, and separate permits may be issued for distinct parts of a facility that can be identified as separate units.[60]

The DEM may issue, revoke, amend, suspend, or deny a permit.[61] If the DEM determines that a permitted hazardous waste facility is not in compliance with all of the appropriate DEM rules, regulations, and permit conditions, it may order the permitee to take whatever corrective action is needed to secure compliance, rather than revoking the facility's permit.[62]

b. Change in Facility Ownership, Location or Operation

The DEM must be notified prior to a change in the facility's ownership, location or operation.[63] A permit will be void and must be returned to the DEM immediately

---

[54] The Rules §8.04(U).
[55] *Id.* §8.04(V). *See* also 40 C.F.R. 264 and 270.16.
[56] *Id.* §8.05.
[57] *Id.* §7.12.
[58] *Id.*
[59] *Id.* §7.06.
[60] *Id.* §7.07.
[61] *Id.* §7.09. Public notice and a public hearing may be required pursuant to R.I. Gen. Laws §§23-19.1-10(b)(2)-(4). *See* the Rules §7.09(I (requirements for public notice and hearing).
[62] *Id.* §7.09(I), (C)-(F).
[63] *Id.* §7.05(A).

upon a change in location of a facility,[64] and a permit becomes voidable whenever there is a sale or change in ownership of the legal entity operating the facility.[65] A new entity, prior to commencing facility operation, must submit to the DEM information indicating the following: its technical ability to safely operate the facility; its financial ability to maintain the facility; a proposed date for the transfer of permit responsibility; insurance coverage; liability between current and new permittees; and any additional information which the DEM requests.[66] After reviewing this information, the DEM will either approve or disapprove the transfer of the permit.[67] The original permitee remains fully liable under the permit and the Regulations until the DEM transfers the operating permit to the new owner or operator.[68]

c. Incinerators and Landfills

The DEM will grant operating licenses only for hazardous waste incinerator or landfill facilities, which the applicant can show will be located, designed, constructed, and operated so as to prevent: 1) endangerment of an underground drinking water source or sole source aquifer; or 2) contamination by a discharge which violates federal or state law.[69] The DEM will not grant operating licenses for incinerator or landfill facilities which are located in a 100 year flood plain, a wetland, the direct recharge area of an existing or planned surface or groundwater community water system or a sole source aquifer, coastal high hazard area, an active fault area, or a critical wildlife habitat.[70]

The owner or operator of a hazardous waste incinerator or landfill will only receive an operating license if he or she grants an easement to the State of Rhode Island.[71] Such an easement must be recorded in the land evidence records of the city or town in which the facility is located, describe the entire facility, identify the facility as one for hazardous waste disposal, and provide the DEM access to the property for inspecting and testing purposes. An

---

[64] *Id.* §7.05(B).
[65] *Id.* §7.05(C).
[66] *Id.* §7.05(C).
[67] *Id.*
[68] *Id.* §7.05(D).
[69] *Id.* §7.05(B)(1).
[70] *Id.* §7.019B)(2). The Regulations also prohibit disposal of hazardous waste by ocean disposal and underground injection control. *Id.* §7.01(F).
[71] *Id.* §7.01(B)(3).

incinerator must also obtain from the DEM a trial burn permit prior to receiving an operating license for hazardous waste incineration.[72]

5. Land Disposal Facilities

All land disposal facilities must be designed, operated, and maintained in accordance with federal law.[73] Land disposal facilities include surface impoundments, waste piles, land treatment facilities, and landfills. A land treatment facility at which hazardous waste is applied onto or incorporated into the soil surface. A landfill is a disposal facility at which hazardous waste is placed in or on land and which is not land treatment facility, surface impoundment, or injection well.

All landfills must be designed and constructed to meet the following minimum requirements: minimum distance of 500 feet between any active portion of the facility and any surface water body or any wetland; bottom liners installed with a minimum slope of two percent and lead to collection sumps at all low points; boundaries of all active portions must be at least 500 feet from any private or livestock water supply; minimization of erosion, landslides, and slumping; separate cells for incompatible wastes; and gas collection and venting systems.[74]

6. DEM Inspection and Right of Entry

In order to enforce these Regulations, the DEM may: enter, pursuant to state law,[75] any hazardous waste management facility or any place where hazardous waste may be generated, stored, treated, or disposed of; inspect any vehicle used for the transportation of hazardous waste; obtain samples of any waste or other substances; inspect labels, containers, or samples from any hazardous waste transporter; and inspect and copy records, reports, information, or test results kept or maintained at a hazardous waste management facility.[76] Any person obstructing the DEM in the performance of these duties will be found guilty of a misdemeanor and fined up to $500.[77]

---

[72] *Id.* §7.01(c); *See* 40 C.F.R. §270.62 (1993).
[73] The Rules §10.01; *See* 40 C.F.R. §§264-267 (1993).
[74] The Rules §10.01(E)(2). In addition, a landfill must be designed as one of four classes of landfills. *See id.* §10.01(E) (requirements for Class I, Class II, Class IIIA, Class IIIB landfills).
[75] *See* R.I. Gen. Laws §23-19.1-12.
[76] The Rules§§5.11; 6.15; 7.10.
[77] *Id.* §6.15(B).

7. Penalties for Violations

Any person who violates any provision of the Act or the Regulations may be fined up to $10,000 per day.[78] In the case of a continuing violation, each day's continuance is deemed a separate offense.[79] Any person who knowingly violates any provision of the Act or the Regulations shall be guilty of a felony and imprisoned up to five years and fined up to $10,000, or both.[80] Furthermore, any person, firm, or corporation engaged in the business of collecting, and/or disposing of hazardous waste, that has been convicted of bribery, fraud, or bid-rigging in any state is prohibited from conducting business dealing in Rhode Island for a period of three years from the date of his, hers, or its conviction. Moreover, the Act requires the payment of restoration costs in any case where a court finds that the area where hazardous wastes were stored, treated or disposed of in Violation of the Act should be restored to its original state.[81]

C. Superfund Process

The federal Superfund law,[82] which was enacted in 1980, establishes a system by which facilities at which there has been a release of hazardous waste are cleaned up. Under Superfund, liability for cleanup falls on the owner(s) and/or operators of the facility, generators whose waste were disposed of at the facility, and transporters who brought waste to the facility. Liability under Superfund is strict, joint and several, and retroactive.[83] Rhode Island does not have a "state Superfund" law.

D. Hazardous Waste Management Facilities Act

The purpose of the Rhode Island Hazardous Waste Management Facilities Act (the "Act")[84] is to provide a process for locating and operating "hazardous waste management facilities"[85] within Rhode Island without compromising public health, environmental quality, or economic growth.[86] A "hazardous waste management facility" means a facility, excluding vehicles, for collection, source separation, storage, processing, treatment, recovery, or disposal of

---

[78] *Id.* §14.02 (quoting R.I. Gen. Laws §23-19.1-17) (civil penalties for violations.)
[79] *Id.*
[80] *Id.* §14.03 (quoting R.I. Gen. Laws §23-19.1-18) (criminal penalties for violations.)
[81] R.I. Gen. Laws §23-19.1-18.1.
[82] Comprehensive Environmental Response, Compensation, and Liability Act, 42 U.S.C. §9601 *et seq.*
[83] For further information on Superfund, please consult other texts on federal environmental law.
[84] R.I. Gen. Laws §§23-19.7-1 *et seq.*
[85] *Id.* §23-19.7-3(7).
[86] *Id.* §23-19.7-2.

hazardous wastes. A "hazardous waste management facility" can also be a transfer station for hazardous waste, and may include a facility at which such activities occur and where waste has been generated.

The Act regulates the site selection and operation of all new hazardous waste management facilities in Rhode Island. It does not apply to facilities already operating in compliance with the "Hazardous Waste Management Act",[87] although the Act is applicable to any existing facility which undergoes modification in its hazardous waste management practices to the extent that a new or amended permit under the Hazardous Waste Management Act is required.[88]

The Act does not apply to most "on-site"[89] generators of hazardous waste.[90] However, where changes in the management of on-site waste occur to the extent that a new permit is required under the Hazardous Waste Management Act, and where those changes are accompanied by a significant increase in the risks to public health, safety, or the environment, or where the generator imports hazardous wastes for use as a feed stock, the on-site generator must comply with the Act. Finally, the Act prohibits cities and towns from altering zoning designations so as to exclude hazardous waste facilities once an application for a permit has been submitted pursuant to the Hazardous Waste Management Act.[91] Nevertheless, local restrictions may be placed on facilities that impinge on public drinking water supplies, or on the use of landfill sites or underground wells for hazardous waste disposal.[92]

1. Requirement of Siting Agreement

Under the Act, a hazardous waste facility cannot be constructed, renovated, or operated in any community unless there is a "siting agreement" in force between the "developer" and the "host community", and an impact agreement, where necessary, between a developer and a neighboring community.[93]

---

[87] *Id.* §23-19.1-1 *et seq.*
[88] *Id.* §23-19.7-5(c).
[89] *Id.* §23-19.7-3(13).
[90] *Id.* §23-19.7-5(b).
[91] *Id.* §23-19.7-4(b).
[92] *Id.* §23-19.7-4(d).
[93] *Id.* §23.19.7-5.

2. Negotiating the Siting and Impact Agreements

After a permit to construct a hazardous waste management facility under the Hazardous Waste Management Act has been awarded, host and neighboring communities have 45 days to create local assessment committees. Each committee is composed of two local politicians, the chairman of the planning commission, and two to six public members.[94]

Each local assessment committee is given the authority to negotiate all terms and conditions of the siting or impact agreement with the developer in accordance with the best interests of the community.[95] Generally, the committee is charged with the responsibility of protecting public health, public safety, the environment, and local fiscal welfare. To help articulate and balance those interests, however, the committee also has the duty to hold public hearings for the purpose of assessing local opinion and reaction to the proposed waste management facility. The committee has the power to spend any funds received from the developer or from local, state, or federal grants to pay for costs associated with the siting process. Despite such comprehensive authority, the final agreement drafted by the assessment committee may be subject to ratification by the local legislative body.

3. Content of Siting Agreements[96]

The local siting agreement between the host community and the developer is a legally binding, comprehensive contract. Under the agreement, the host community may address areas of concern such as design, construction, maintenance, safety monitoring, host community services, tax payments, renegotiations conditions, dispute resolution, environmental protection, health and safety standards, reimbursement policy and assignment to a party other than the signatory developer. The duration of the agreement is negotiable. After 20 years, however, the agreement is subject to renegotiation at the request of either party.

4. Compensation to Host Community

Reasonable costs incurred by the host community in drawing up the siting agreement and carrying out its obligations are charged to the developer[97] in accordance with the

---

[94] *Id.* §23-19.7-6(a).
[95] *Id.* §23-19.7-6(b).
[96] *Id.* §23-19.7-8.
[97] *Id.* §23-19.7-7.

Act. The developer is required to establish an account and deposit up to 1% of the gross cost of the facility in that account for disbursement by the "host community."[98] A "host community" means a city or town of the state in which a developer proposes to construct substantially alter, or operate a hazardous waste management facility. The fund must be set up by the developer within 5 days of the time the host community appoints a "local assessment committee."[99] A "local assessment committee" means a body established by a host or neighboring community for the specific purpose of negotiating a siting or impact agreement with a hazardous waste management facility developer. Initially, the minimum deposit is $10,000 and the maximum deposit is $100,000. However, the host community can apply for additional funds if the initial amount is insufficient to meet costs incurred. Disagreement over such additional costs is subject to binding arbitration. The fund is intended to pay for such things as scientific studies, expert witnesses, negotiations, and arbitration.

5. Requirement of Impact Agreement

Under the Act, an "impact agreement"[100] is required between the developer and any "neighboring community"[101] if that community establishes the probability of experiencing a significant adverse impact from the operation of the facility. A "neighboring community" means a city or town which shares a common border with a host community, or which lies in whole or in part, within a one-mile radius of the lot on which the facility is to be built, altered, or operated.[102]

6. Content of Impact Agreement

An impact agreement is a legally binding contract between the developer and the neighboring community that may address the terms and conditions for the mitigation of or compensation for any harm to public health, safety, and the environment in the neighboring community caused by the hazardous waste facility.[103] Unlike the siting agreement with the host community, a developer is under no statutory obligation to reimburse neighboring communities for the costs involved in drawing up an impact agreement.

---

[98] *Id.* §23-19.7-3(8).
[99] *Id.* §23-19.7-3(10).
[100] *Id.* §23-19.7-3(9)(a)(2).
[101] *Id.* §23-19.7-9(c).
[102] *Id.* §23-19.7-3(12).
[103] *Id.* §23-19.7-3(9).

7. Procedural Aspects of Impact Agreement

After a developer has received a permit under the Hazardous Waste Management Act to construct or alter a hazardous waste facility, a neighboring community, absent mutual waiver, has 45 days to notify the developer that it expects a probable and significant adverse impact from such facility.[104] To establish adverse impact, the neighboring community must explain the type, nature, and extent of the impact and how the damage will be caused by the hazardous waste facility.[105] If the developer agrees that the damage is likely to occur, the parties may proceed to negotiate the impact agreement. If they fail to reach agreement on whether adverse impact will occur, the issue may be submitted to an arbitration panel.[106]

8. Provisions for Arbitration

If the developer and the local assessment committee cannot agree on the terms of the siting or impact agreements within 90 days from the date the committee was formed or the date the Hazardous Waste Management Act permit was granted, either party may invoke the binding arbitration provisions of the Act.

Within 30 days after binding arbitration has been invoked an arbitration panel must be established. The arbitration panel is composed of a developer appointee, a community appointee, and either a mutual appointee or a member chosen by the American Arbitration Association who shall act as chair person. The arbitration proceedings are limited to only those issues still in dispute. The panel has 45 days to resolve, the matter, unless the parties agree to extend the arbitration period. The arbitration panel is prohibited from adopting a siting or impact agreement unless the developer has the financial capacity to undertake the project and compensate the affected municipalities for any additional public services required. Moreover, the facility must comply with community standards for the proposed site, and it must present no greater danger to public health and safety due to fire, explosion, hazardous discharge, or pollution other than state-of-the-art industrial enterprises which are not engaged in treating, processing, or disposing of hazardous waste.

---

[104] *Id.* §23-19.7-9(a)(4).
[105] *Id.* §23-19.7-9(c).
[106] *Id.* §23-19.7-9(d).

In the event that the parties mutually resolve the issues in dispute they may, before the final arbitration decision, request that the hearings be terminated or that the settlement be included in the final arbitration award.

The arbitration decision, which may include reasonable costs incurred by the host community for assessment, negotiation, and the arbitration process itself, is final and binding.[107] Either party, however, may appeal the decision within 30 days to the superior court of Rhode Island.[108]

E. Hazardous Waste Cleanup Good Samaritan Act

The purpose of the Hazardous Waste Cleanup Good Samarian Act (the "Act")[109] is to encourage qualified or trained persons to voluntarily participate in the prevention or cleanup of a spill or release of hazardous material by shielding such persons from all civil liabilities and penalties for any acts of simple negligence. This immunity, however, does not extend to those persons who have a legal obligation to respond to the incident, or who receive reimbursement for their services.

1. Requirements for Immunity

a. Accidental or Threatened Discharge of Hazardous Material

The Act applies to an "accidental or threatened discharge of hazardous material."[110] Under the Act, "hazardous materials" are broadly defined to include all materials and substances which from 1984 on have been designated as hazardous by any state or federal law or by the regulations of any state or federal government agency.[111] Similarly, "discharge" is defined broadly and includes, but is not limited to, leakage and seepage.[112]

[107] *Id.* §23-19.7-10(b)(8).
[108] *Id.* §23-19.7-10(c)(1).
[109] *Id.* §23-19.8 et seq.
[110] *Id.* §23-19.8-3(4).
[111] *Id.* §23-19.8-2(2).
[112] *Id.* §23-19.8-2(3).

b. Qualified or Trained Persons

To received immunity from civil liability or penalties for negligence under the Act, a person must be "qualified or trained."[113] The statute does not define the terms "qualified" or "trained", although the spirit of the statute would seem to warrant an interpretation broad enough to shield most individuals, corporations, or other entities with knowledge, skill, or experience in dealing with the hazardous materials and the procedures at the request of a person or agent responsible for causing, preventing, or cleaning up the hazardous waste discharge.[114] The protected activity under this section includes advice, assistance, prevention, cleanup, and disposal.

2. Explanation of Exemptions

The Hazardous Waste Cleanup Good Samaritan Act does not extend immunity from civil liability or penalties to any party who is legally obligated to respond to the incident or who receives compensation, other than reimbursement for out-of-pocket expenses, for services in rendering assistance or advice.[115] Nor does the Act protect any party who is legally obligated to render assistance.[116] Finally, the Act will not affect the liability of any person for damages resulting from gross negligence or reckless, wanton, or intentional misconduct.[117]

F. Hazardous Waste Reduction, Recycling, and Treatment Research and Demonstration Act of 1986

1. Description

Under the Hazardous Waste Reduction, Recycling, and Treatment Research and Demonstration Act of 1986,[118] the Rhode Island General Assembly declared that the generation of hazardous waste must be reduced or eliminated as expeditiously as possible. To this end, every generator of hazardous waste must submit a report to the Rhode Island Department of Environmental Management ("DEM") at least once every two years, on changes in the volume

[113] *Id.* §23-19.8-3.
[114] *Id.*
[115] *Id.* §23-19.8-4.
[116] *Id.* §23-19.8-5.
[117] *Id.* §23-19.8-6.
[118] *Id.* §23-19.10 et seq.

and toxicity of hazardous waste achieved through waste reduction during the period for which the report is issued.[119]

To promote the reduction, recycling, and treatment of hazardous waste and to encourage private sector participation in these efforts, the DEM has established a hazardous waste technology, research, development and demonstration program.[120] The program consists of contracting with and providing grants to universities, governmental agencies, and private organizations for the research and development of hazardous waste reduction, recycling, and treatment technologies. The program also provides grants under specified conditions to cities, towns, and private organizations for the commercial demonstration of hazardous waste reduction, recycling, or treatment technologies.[121] Hazardous waste reduction, recycling and treatment technologies are technologies that have as their primary purpose the reduction, recycling, or conversion of hazardous waste into a less hazardous form.[122] The technologies do not include solidification or treatment occurring directly in, or on, the land, such as techniques using evaporation, surface impoundments or land farming.[123]

2. Projection Selection and Funding

a. Criteria

To evaluate a proposed project for the possibility of funding, DEM has adopted criteria that considers the feasibility of the project's particular technology, the research and, technical spin-offs likely to be generated by the project, the degree to which the findings of the project can be disseminated and evaluated for replication elsewhere, and the consistency of, and contributions of, the project to the state's hazardous waste management program.[124] Projects selected also must meet one of the following requirements:

1) The project has on-site, as well as offsite, potential for the reduction, recycling or treatment of hazardous waste;

[119] *Id.* §23-19.10-5.
[120] *Id.* §23-19.10-2(4), 23-19.10-6.
[121] *Id.* §23-19.10-6(1), (2).
[122] *Id.* §23-19.10-3(2).
[123] *Id.*
[124] *Id.* §23-19.10-7(2).

2) The project has the potential to benefit, or be utilized by, small businesses; or

3) The project is applicable to range of industries.[125]

b. Grants

Grant funding for the construction of equipment necessary to a demonstration project is provided in four consecutive steps:

1) Step I grants are made to study the feasibility of a proposed project with an emphasis on cost-effectiveness;[126]

2) Step II grants are made for project design. In activities funded by Step II grants, the applicant prepares detailed plans and specifications for the selected facilities, establishes schedules for implementation and obtains necessary permits;[127]

3) Step III grants are made for the construction of the facilities;[128] and

4) Step IV grants are made to evaluate the effectiveness of grant-funded facilities, develop information on compliance with regulatory permits, and assess the applicability of the selected approach to other generators of similar hazardous wastes.[129]

c. Evaluations

DEM will evaluate all projects funded by grants and make such evaluations available to interested parties as expeditiously as possible.[130] DEM must notify any interested party of the availability of project evaluations.[131]

---

[125] *Id.* §23-19.10-7(3)(i)-(ii).
[126] *Id.* §23-19.10-8(2)(i).
[127] *Id.* §23-19.10-8(2)(ii).
[128] *Id.* §23-19.10-8(2)(iii).
[129] *Id.* §23-19.10-8(2)(iv).
[130] *Id.* §23-19.10-9.
[131] *Id.*

d. Research Grants

DEM also may issue grants to and enter into contracts with universities, governmental agencies, and private organizations for the research and development of hazardous waste reduction, recycling and treatment technologies.[132] These grants may be applied to personnel, equipment, and administrative costs and, to extent possible, will be used to augment other sources of research and development funding, including federal and private funds.[133]

G. Hazardous Substances Act

1. Definition of Hazardous Substance

Under the Hazardous Substances Act (the "Act"),[134] the term "hazardous substance" includes any substance or mixture of substances which is toxic, corrosive, an irritant, a strong sensitizer, flammable, combustible, or radioactive. The term also includes any substance that generates pressure through decomposition, heat or other means if such substance may cause substantial personal injury or substantial illness during, or as a proximate result of, any customary or reasonably foreseeable handling.[135] Any toy or other article intended for use by children that presents an electrical, mechanical or thermal hazard is also a "hazardous substance."[136] The term "hazardous substance" however, does not apply to substances subject to the State Pesticide Control Act or the State Food, Drug and Cosmetic Act.[137]

Substances intended for use as fuels when stored in containers and used in the heating, cooking or refrigeration system of a house are not hazardous substances, nor are manufactured goods in process, or waste in transit for proper disposal.[138] In addition, under the Act, the Rhode Island Consumer's Council (the "Council") has no authority to restrict the manufacture or sale of firearms or ammunition.[139] However, any article which is not an economic poison itself, but is a hazardous substance under the Act by reason of bearing or containing an economic poison will be regulated.

[132] *Id.* §23-19.10-10(a).
[133] *Id.* §23-19.10-10(b).
[134] *Id.* §23-24-1 et seq.
[135] *Id.* §23-24-2(6)(i).
[136] *Id.* §23-24-2(6)(i)(D).
[137] *Id.* §23-24-2(6)(ii).
[138] *Id.*
[139] *Id.* §23-24-2(6)(iii).

2. Prohibited Acts

The Act prohibits the introduction or delivery in intrastate commerce[140] of any "misbranded hazardous substance" or "banned hazardous substance."[141] A "misbranded hazardous substance" is a hazardous substance intended, or packaged in a form suitable for use in the household or by children which is packaged or labeled in violation of the state Poison Prevention Packaging Act or fails to bear a label stating conspicuously:

a. The name and place of business of the manufacturer, packer, distributor or seller;

b. The common or usual name, or the chemical name, if any;

c. the word "DANGER" on substances which are extremely flammable, corrosive or highly toxic;

d. The word "WARNING" or "CAUTION" on all other hazardous substances;

e. An affirmative statement of the principal hazard(s) of the substance, such as "flammable", "vapor harmful", "combustible", "causes burns", or similar wording descriptive of the hazard;

f. Precautionary measures describing actions to be followed or avoided;

g. Instruction for first-aid treatment when necessary or appropriate;

h. The word "poison" for any "highly toxic" substance;[142]

i. Instructions for the handling and storage of packages that require special care;

[140] "Intrastate commerce" means commerce within the State of Rhode Island. *Id.* §23-24-2(q).

[141] *Id.* §23-24-4(1) and (3).

[142] *Id.* §23-24-2(12)(i).

j. The statement "Keep out of reach of children" or its practical equivalent or, if the article is intended for the use by children and is not a banned hazardous substance, adequate directions for the protection of children from the hazard.[143]

All required statements and instructions must be in English, be located prominently on the label, and be in conspicuous and legible type.[144]

The term "banned hazardous substance" includes any toy or other article intended for use by children that is a hazardous substance or any article intended or packaged for use in the household which is classified by the Council as a "banned hazardous substance" because of the article's inherent hazardous qualities.[145] Chemistry sets and common fireworks are specifically exempted, provided adequate labeling exists to protect the purchasers and users.[146]

Under the Act, it is unlawful to alter, mutilate, destroy, obliterate, remove the whole or any part of the label of, or do any other act with respect to a hazardous substance, if that act is done while the substance is in intrastate commerce or held for sale in Rhode Island and results in the substance being misbranded or banned.[147] It also is unlawful to give a false guarantee that a hazardous substance is not misbranded or banned.[148] A person who in good faith relies upon such a guarantee has not committed an unlawful act.[149]

The Act further prohibits the reuse of food, drug or cosmetic container as a container for a hazardous substance, which results in the hazardous substance being a misbranded hazardous substance.[150]

3. Enforcement

The Council may conduct examinations, inspections and investigations at reasonable times, of any factory, warehouse, establishment or vehicle in which hazardous

143 *Id.* §23-24-2(12)(J).
144 *Id.* §23-24-2(12)(J)(II)(ii).
145 *Id.* §23-24-2(1).
146 *Id.* §23-24-2(1)(B)(I), (II).
147 *Id.* §23-24-4(2).
148 *Id.* §23-24-4(4).
149 *Id. See also id.* §23-24-5(B)(2).
150 *Id.* §23-24-4(6).

substances are manufactured, processed, packed, or held in intrastate commerce. It is unlawful to prevent such an inspection.[151] If the inspector obtains any sample, prior to leaving the premises, he or she must give to the person in charge a receipt describing the samples obtained.[152] If an analysis is made of the sample, a copy of the results of such analysis must be furnished promptly to the person in charge of the facility inspected.[153]

Upon the request of the Council, carriers engaged in intrastate commerce and persons receiving hazardous substances in intrastate commerce must permit the Council, at reasonable times, to have access to and to copy all records showing the movement in intrastate commerce of any hazardous substance or the holding of any hazardous substance before or after this movement, and the quantity, shipper, and consignee of the hazardous substance.[154] It is unlawful for the carrier to prohibit access to or the copying of any requested records, when the request is accompanied by a statement, in writing, specifying the nature or kind of hazardous substance to which the request relates.[155] Evidence obtained from records may not be used in a criminal prosecution of the person from whom it was obtained.[156]

a. Embargoed Articles

Whenever the Rhode Island Department of Environmental Management (the "DEM") finds, or has probable cause to believe, that any article is misbranded, banned or presents an electrical, mechanical or thermal hazard, the DEM will order a tag or other appropriate marking to be affixed to the article.[157] The tag will give notice that the article is suspect and has been detained or embargoed, and will warn all persons not to remove, sell, or dispose of such article until the DEM or a court gives permission to do so.[158] When the DEM determines that an article detained or embargoed is misbranded, banned or an electrical, thermal or mechanical hazard, the DEM will ask the appropriate court, in whose jurisdiction the article is detained or embargoed, for a condemnation of the article.

[151] *Id.* §23-24-4(5).
[152] *Id.* §23-24-11(c).
[153] *Id.*
[154] *Id.* §23-24-12.
[155] *Id. See also id.* §23-24-4(5).
[156] *Id.*
[157] *Id.* §23-24-6(a).
[158] *Id.*

If the court finds that an article is misbranded, banned or presents some other hazard, the article will be destroyed at the expense of the claimant and all court costs, fees, storage and other expenses must be paid by the claimant of the article.[159] If the misbranding or electrical, mechanical, or thermal hazard can be corrected, the court may direct that the article be delivered to the claimant for correction under the supervision of the DEM.[160]

b. Repurchase Requirement

The manufacturer, distributor, or dealer of any article or substance that is a banned hazardous substance must repurchase the banned hazardous substance from the person to whom he or she sold it and refund the purchase price paid and any reasonable and necessary expenses incurred.[161]

c. Civil and Criminal Penalties

Any person who violates the Act is guilty of a misdemeanor and, upon conviction, is subject to a fine of not more than $500, or to imprisonment for not more than 90 days, or both.[162] For actions committed with an intent to defraud or mislead, or for second and subsequent offenses, the penalty is imprisonment for not more than one year, or a fine of not more than $3,000, or both.[163] A person is not subject to the foregoing for having received, delivered or proffered delivery of a misbranded or banned hazardous substance in good faith, unless that person refuses to furnish, on request, the name and address of the person from whom he or she purchased or received the hazardous substance and copies of all documents pertaining to the delivery of the hazardous substance.[164]

---

[159] *Id.* §23-24-6(c).
[160] *Id.*
[161] *Id.* §23-24-14(a)(1)(i)-(ii).
[162] *Id.* §23-24-5(a).
[163] *Id.*
[164] *Id.* §23-24-5(b)(1).

CHAPTER VI:

SOLID WASTE MANAGEMENT

A. Solid Waste Management Corporation

1. Overview

The Rhode Island General Assembly, realizing that solid waste poses a serious environmental problem for many municipalities,[1] passed the Rhode Island Resource Recovery Corporation Act (the "Act"), which created the Rhode Island Resource Recovery Corporation (the "Corporation"). "Waste management" involves the receipt, storage, transportation, and processing of solid waste for resource recovery, recycling, or disposal.[2] The term "solid waste" is defined as, among other things, garbage, sludge from a waste treatment plant, or discarded materials, including solid, liquid, semisolid, or contained-gaseous materials generated by residential, institutional, commercial, industrial, or agricultural sources.[3]

The Corporation is a public agency, separate and distinct from the state, but exercising governmental functions of the state.[4] The Corporation's powers are vested in its nine commissioners, consisting of the director of administration, or the director's designee, four public members to be appointed by the governor, one resident from the town of Johnson to be appointed by the governor, two members from the house of representatives to be appointed by the speaker of the house, and one member from the senate to be appointed by the senate majority leader.[5] The Governor may remove any member for misfeasance, malfeasance, or willful neglect of duty.[6] All meetings of the Corporation are open to the public and the minutes are a matter of public record.[7]

2. Purposes

The Corporation is involved with all aspects of solid waste management, including the planning and developing of solid waste management facilities. The term "solid waste management facility" includes any plant, structure, equipment, and other property used for

---

[1] R.I. Gen. Laws §23-19-2(1,2).
[2] *Id.* §23-19-5(21).
[3] *Id.* §23-19-5(18).
[4] *Id.* §23-19-6(a).
[5] *Id.* §23-19-6(c).
[6] *Id.* §23-19-6(f).
[7] *Id.* §23-19-6(i).

the receipt, storage, treatment, utilization, processing, transporting, final disposition, or recovery of, resources from solid waste other than segregated solid waste.[8] The term "solid waste management facility" also includes any facility which disposes of solid waste by reconstituting, converting, or otherwise recycling the solid waste into material that is not waste.[9] At its solid waste management facilities, the Corporation accepts solid waste for resource recovery and disposal. The term "resource recovery" means the processing of solid waste to produce materials or energy which may be used in manufacturing, agriculture, and other processes.[10] The Corporation also provides recycling at or near all of its solid waste management facilities.[11] The Corporation contracts with private businesses in its recycling and resource recovery efforts, and the Corporation will assist in developing commercial enterprises for recycling and resource recovery.[12]

3. Powers and Duties

The Act enumerates an extensive but not exclusive list of the Corporation's powers, including: the authority to buy, sell, or lease land; acquire land through eminent domain; borrow money and issue bonds; hire staff and professional consultants; design and construct solid waste management facilities; and control the transportation, storage, and final disposal of solid waste. The Corporation promotes and conducts research in source reduction and separation techniques, as well as produces marketable energy and materials from its own recycling and resource recovery activities. The Corporation also provides consulting and technical advice to persons or institutions on solid waste management issues.[13]

4. Solid Waste Facilities Siting Board

Under the Act, a solid waste Facilities Siting Board (the "Board") has been established to work with the Corporations in developing solid waste facilities. The Board is comprised of five members, who represent a broad range of interests and who are designated by the Governor. The Corporation submits a written report to the Board when the Corporation desires to acquire land by purchase or by eminent domain. After public notice, the Board holds a

[8] *Id.* §23-19-5(19).
[9] *Id.* §23-19-5(19).
[10] *Id.* §23-19-5(12).
[11] *Id.* §23-19-9(6).
[12] *Id.* §23-19-9(3), (5).
[13] *Id.* §23-19-10.

hearing on the acquisition of the desired property. Within thirty days of the hearing, the Board submits a transcript of the meeting to the Governor and an advisory opinion as to the need to acquire the land. The Governor, in his or her discretion, has the ultimate authority to allow the Corporation to acquire land for solid waste disposal facility.[14]

5. Municipal Participation in The Corporation

All municipalities that treat, store or transfer solid waste must use a facility approved by the Corporation. The Act allows transfer stations in operation as of December 1, 1986, to continue under existing permits as long as they maintain the appropriate permit to continue their operations. The Act does not affect municipal contracts for waste disposal entered into prior to March 1, 1985 until the terms of their expiration. Municipalities cannot engage in any activity or enter into any contracts that compete with the Corporation, but they may contract with the Corporation for solid waste disposal. Municipalities also can contract with licensed private facilities if the Corporation approves the contract. The Corporation also may allow municipalities to contract among themselves for waste disposal. If other state or local laws conflict with the ability of municipalities to enter into a long-term contracts, the Act controls.[15] No municipal ordinance, however, may prevent a public waste disposal facility from being located in the municipality.[16]

All municipalities must establish written plans addressing their arrangements for the separation and collection of solid waste and inform the Rhode Island Department of Environmental Management (the "DEM") and the Corporation of such plans. Municipalities must begin a separation and recycling program within one year of the time that the resource recovery facility they utilize becomes operational.[17]

Municipalities must pay the Corporation for the disposal of solid waste at Corporate facilities according to a fee per ton schedule.[18] There is no charge for recyclable materials delivered to a Corporate recycling facility.[19]

---

[14] *Id.* §23-19-10.2(2).
[15] *Id.* §23-19-13(a), (b).
[16] *Id.* §23-19-10.2(3)(c)(l).
[17] *Id.* §23-19-13(d).
[18] *Id.* §23-19-13(g)(l).
[19] *Id.*

6. Enforcement and Prohibited Activities

The Act may be enforced by both the State of Rhode Island and the Corporation. The attorney general may bring suit in the name of the State of Rhode Island, and the Corporation may bring suit on its own behalf through its legal counsel. The Corporation or the State may bring an action in court for restraining orders or other injunctive relief to prevent violations or threatened violations of the Act or to demand specific performance of obligations.[20] The Corporation also may impose administrative penalties under the Act.

No person or municipality may dispose of wastes generated or collected out-of-state at the Corporation's central landfill. Violators of this provision are subject to a fine of up to $5,000 and imprisonment up to three years for each unauthorized deposit.[21]

No Corporate resource recovery system or facility may accept any infectious or pathological waste. This includes pathological waste from a hospital, clinic, medical laboratory, nursing home, teaching hospital, or medical examiner. Any facility violating this provision must pay a fine of no less than $2,500 and no more than $5,000 to the town or city in which it is located. Any person who knowingly violates any aspect of this provision will be personally fined no less than $2,5000 and no more than $5,000.[22]

B. Refuse Disposal Act

The Refuse Disposal Act[23] prohibits the disposal of solid waste at any place other than a solid waste management facility licensed by the Rhode Island Department of Environmental Management (the "DEM"). Under the Refuse Disposal Act, the term "solid waste management facility" means any plant, structure, equipment, real and personal property, except mobile equipment or incinerators with a capacity of less than 1,000 pounds per hour, operated for the purpose of processing, treating or disposing of solid waste, but not segregated solid waste.[24] The phrase "dispose of solid waste", as prohibited in the Refuse Disposal Act, refers to the depositing, casting, throwing, leaving, or abandoning of a quantity greater than three cubic yards of solid waste. The term "solid waste", as used in the Refuse Disposal Act, means garbage,

---

[20] *Id.* §23-19-28.
[21] *Id.* §23-19-13.1.
[22] *Id.* §23-19-13.2.
[23] R.I. Gen. Laws § 23-18.9-1 *et seq.*
[24] *Id.* §23-18.9-7(11).

refuse, and other discarded solid materials generated by residential, institutional, commercial, industrial, or agricultural sources, but does not include solids or dissolved materials, and domestic sewage or sewage sludge, nor does it include hazardous waste.[25] Used asphalt, concrete, Portland concrete cement, and tree stumps also are not considered solid waste under the Refuse Disposal Act.

C. Specific DEM Regulations on Solid Waste Management

1. Licensing

a. General

Under the Refuse Disposal Act, no person may construct, develop, establish, manage, own, or maintain a solid waste management facility without first having obtained approval from the DEM.[26] A license for a solid waste management facility is issued for a period of three years, unless sooner suspended or revoked. Furthermore, all solid waste management facilities, must comply with all applicable water and air pollution laws and regulations.[27]

The application for a solid waste management facility must be submitted at least nine months prior to the planned opening date for the facility. An application for a license renewal must be submitted three months prior to the expiration date of the license.

Applications for licenses must be include the following information:

1) Documentation of ownership;

2) Certification;

3) A general plan stamped by a professional engineer, land surveyor, or landscape architect as appropriate who is registered with the State of Rhode Island;

4) Groundwater quality certification. In order to determine compliance with groundwater classification, groundwater

---

[25] *Id.* §23-18.9-7(10).
[26] *Id.* §23-18.9-8(a).
[27] Solid Waste Regulations Number 1: General Requirements, § 1.4.00(1997) as amended (2001).

certification in accordance with and pursuant to Section 17 of the Rules and Regulations for Groundwater Quality is required for the issuance of a solid waste disposal facility license;

5) A general closure plan. This plan must estimate the cost of closure and provide some suitable form of financial assurance.

The granting of a license, license renewal or permission for an equipment addition at a solid waste management facility in no way affects the applicant's responsibility to meet all zoning and other local ordinances, nor the applicant's responsibility to obtain any local permits.[28]

b. Sanitary Landfills

In addition to the general requirements outlined above, any person who desires to construct, develop, establish, manage, own, or maintain a sanitary landfill must submit with his application the following:

1) Engineering plans, including a locus map, radius plan and a site plan, detailing the proposed location of the property boundaries, adjacent land uses and complete construction plans;[29]

2) Operating the plans which comply with the sanitary landfill construction standards and the sanitary landfill operating standards and indicate the cost to the affected communities, vector, litter, odor and dust control;[30]

3) A sedimentation and erosion control plan which shall be drawn to an appropriate scale adjusted to fit on a standard size sheet.[31]

4) An engineering report containing a description of the existing site conditions and an analysis of the proposed landfill in accordance

[28] *Id.* §1.5.00 *et seq.*
[29] Solid Waste Regulation Number 2: Solid Waste Landfills, § 2.1.01(2)(1997).
[30] *Id.* §2.1.01(b).
[31] *Id.* §2.1.01(c).

with the sanitary landfill construction standards;[32]

5) A quality assurance / quality control report;[33]

6) A contingency plan which discusses an organized, planned and coordinated, technically and financially feasible course of action to be taken in responding to contingencies during the construction and operation of the landfill;[34]

7) A hydrogeological report which defines the landfill site geology and hydrology and relates these factors to regional and local hydrogeologic patterns. The report must also provide a three-dimensional understanding of groundwater and surface water flow at the site sufficient to determine the ultimate suitability of the site for landfilling. Furthermore, the report must establish an environmental monitoring system capable of readily detecting a contaminant release from the facility and determining whether the site is contaminating surface or subsurface waters; and form the basis for design of the facility and contingency plans relating to ground or surface water contamination or gas migration; [35]

8) A legal document certifying acceptance of leachate by the operator of a waste water treatment facility for the discharge of leachate to that facility, if applicable, or a RIPDES system permit;[36] and

9) A closure and post closure plan prepared by pursuant to the regulations.[37]

In addition, prior to and as a condition of granting a license for a solid waste management facility, the owner of the land on which the facility is to be located must grant

---

[32] *Id.* §2.1.01(d).
[33] *Id.* §2.1.01(e).
[34] *Id.* §2.1.01(f).
[35] *Id.* §2.1.01(g).
[36] *Id.* §2.1.01(h).
[37] *Id.* §2.1.01(i).

to Rhode Island a perpetual conservation easement. This easement must be recorded in the land evidence records of the city or town in which the land is located and must describe the permanent facility and activities to be conducted on this facility. Under the easement, DEM must have a perpetual right to enter the land at reasonable times for the purpose of inspecting the facility or conducting test at the facility. Such easement shall include a prohibition on any excavation or other disturbances or construction of the facility site without prior written approval from the DEM.[38]

Furthermore, at the time of the engineering survey, the following areas shall be marked with stakes which must be visible and maintained at all times:

1) Area enclosed by legal boundaries;

2) Areas to be filled as indicated in operating plan;

3) Areas to be used for leachate treatment, storage or disposal;

4) Areas to be used for storing salvaged materials; and

5) Areas to be used for special waste as listed in the regulations.[39]

c. Incinerators and Resource Recovery Facilities and Transfer and Collection Station

In addition to the general requirements outlined above, the following plans and specifications are needed:

1) A radius plan which must be drawn to a minimum scale of one inch to two hundred feet (1" = 200'), adjusted to fit on standard 24 x 36 inch sheet(s) and include all areas within one quarter (1/4) mile radius from all property lines of the site. A radius plan must include the zoning area, legal boundaries of the site and licensed area, all roads, all buildings and dwellings, all water supplies, all surface water courses, a north arrow, a locus plan, and, where applicable, extent of 100 year flood plan.[40]

---

[38] *Id.* §2.1.11

[39] *Id.* §2.1.10.

[40] *Id.* §4.1.02.

2) A site plan which must be drawn to a minimum scale of one inch to one hundred feet (1"-100'), adjusted to fit on standard 24 x 36 inch sheet(s). A site plan must include all information pertaining to the site as required by regulation;[41]

3) The construction and engineering plans and specifications relating to all buildings, equipment and key features of the facility must be submitted to the Department. This set must be in sufficient detail to allow for a comprehensive application review;[42] and

4) A detailed operating plan.[43]

In addition to the preceding requirements, applicants for incinerators and resource recovery facilities must submit additional information. These applicants must submit a description of the proposed facility.[44] They must also list and describe all environmentally related authorizations and approvals that are required for this facility including, but not limited to, those from other Divisions of RIDEM, other state agencies, federal agencies, local government, agricultural districts, fire equipment insurance underwriters, and the appropriate electric utility.[45]

It should be noted that any person who desires to construct and/or operate a private solid waste disposal facility must submit to the DEM, simultaneously with the application, a certificate of final determination from the municipality in which the site is proposed. The certificate must state that the site conforms with all applicable local land use and control ordinances. If there is a dispute between the municipality and the owner or operator of the facility in regard to the certificate, then the applicant must obtain a final judgment stating that the proposed site for the facility conforms with all applicable land use and control ordinances of the municipality. The applicant also must submit, simultaneously with the application, a certificate of approval of the proposed site issued by the state planning council.[46]

---

41 *Id.* §4.1.03.
42 *Id.* §4.1.04.
43 *Id.* §4.1.06.
44 *Id.* §4.1.05.
45 *Id.* §4.1.08.
46 *Id.* §R.I. Gen. Laws § 23-18.9-9(a).

Prior to a change in ownership, location or discontinuance of services of the solid waste management facility, the DEM must be notified. A license for a solid waste management facility is void and must be returned to the DEM upon a change in the location of any facility, or upon the sale, lease or change in ownership of the legal entity, conducting, maintaining or operating the facility.[47] Separate licenses are required for solid waste management facilities that are located in separate geographical areas, even if they are under the same management.[48] A separate license may also be required for a distinct part of a facility if it can be identified as a separate unit.

The DEM, after notice and opportunity for hearing for the applicant or licensee, is authorized to deny, suspend, or revoke a license where it finds there has been failure to comply with the regulations established by the DEM. The DEM, however, in lieu of or in addition to the suspension or revocation of the facility's license, may order the licensee to take whatever corrective action necessary to comply with the regulations established by the DEM.[49]

The application for a license or a license renewal for a solid waste management facility may include a request for a variance from the provisions of the regulations for solid waste management facilities. Such request for a variance shall be in writing and signed by both the owner and operator of the facility and a registered professional engineer. The DEM will evaluate each request for a variance.[50] Variances may be granted provided that DEM finds that the variance will not be contrary to the purposes or policies of the Regulations and that the alternative methods proposed by the operator of the solid waste management facility will fulfill the purposes of the regulations. The DEM may require a public hearing prior to approving a variance where a substantial question exists as to the environmental or public health impacts of such a variance. The applicant may appeal DEM's denial of the variance.[51]

Any person whose application for a license renewal, other approval, or a variance has been denied by DEM, may appeal the decision to the Administrative Adjudication Division of the DEM.[52] In addition, any person who has been issued a notice of violation of any

---

[47] Solid Waste Regulation Number 1: General Requirements § 1.6.03.
[48] *Id.* §1.6.05.
[49] *Id.* §1.6.07(a), (b).
[50] *Id.* §1.10.00 *et seq.*
[51] *Id.* §1.10.02.
[52] *Id.* §1.11.01.

of the provisions of the Regulations may request a hearing to show compliance.[53] All hearings and administrative procedures must conform to the "Administrative Rules of Practice and Procedure for the Department of Environmental Management, Administrative Adjudication Division for Environmental Matters."[54]

Any person who constructs a solid waste management facility or installs equipment in such a facility without first obtaining approval of the plans and specifications for the facility, or any person who operates such a facility without obtaining a license to do so from the DEM will be punished by a administrative penalty up to $25,000. Each day the violation continues is considered to be a separate offense.[55] Furthermore, any person who disposes of solid waste at other than a licensed solid waste facility will be assessed an administrative penalty of up to $5,000 for each day during which the violation is repeated or continues.[56] The criminal penalty for either violation may add up to five year jail sentence.

2. General Operating Requirements for All Solid Waste Management Facilities

Although access to a solid waste management facility is limited to those times in which authorized personnel are on duty, time will be allowed for personnel to attend "Housekeeping Chores", such as the application of cover material at sanitary landfills and wind-blown refuse control at all facilities.[57] Public access to the facility during these times is prohibited.[58] Gates are required to prevent unauthorized entry to the solid waste management facility and must be locked at all times in which the facility is unsupervised.[59] The DEM also requires fences to be erected around the solid waste management facility to prevent further unauthorized entry.[60] The DEM, however, may inspect a facility at any reasonable time.[61]

Materials to be salvaged at a facility must be stored separately from the solid waste that is unloaded and compacted.[62] The salvage of refuse must never interfere with the safe

[53] *Id.* §1.11.02.
[54] *Id.* §1.11.09.
[55] R.I. Gen Laws §23-18.9-10(a)(i).
[56] *Id.* §23-18.9.10(a)(z).
[57] Solid Waste Regulations Number / General Requirements §1.7.02(a).
[58] *Id.*
[59] *Id.* §1.7.02(b).
[60] *Id.*
[61] *Id.* §1.6.08.
[62] *Id.* §1.7.03.

and efficient operation of the facility nor endanger the health and safety facility personnel.[63] Operation of the facility must comply with the guidelines of the Rhode Island Pollution Act[64] and the Federal Water Pollution Control Act and not pollute the waters of the state.[65]

Every effort must be made to control rodent and insect pollution at the facility.[66] The use of professional exterminators is required to insure sanitary conditions at all times.[67]

A sign must be erected at the entrance of the facility which must list the name and operator of the facility, an emergency phone number, any restricted materials, if applicable; and the hours of operation.[68] In addition, signs should be placed within the facility to facilitate the efficient flow of traffic while trucks are unloading refuse.[69] A means of communication must be made available at every solid waste management facility, such as a telephone or two-way radio.[70]

All facilities are subject to state and federal laws on air standards.[71] The open burning of any substance is strictly prohibited.[72] Also, appropriate measures should be taken to control odors at the facility such as immediate processing odorous materials or transporting the materials to another facility.

The operation of the facility must not cause or contribute to the taking of any endangered or threatened species or critical habitat.[73] The operator of the facility must control the production of dust and monitor roadway access to the facility and all other areas related to the facility's operation.[74] Also, refuse and litter must be controlled by routine maintenance of the facility grounds.[75]

---

63 *Id.*
64 R.I. Gen Laws §46-12-1 *et seq.*
65 Solid Waste Regulation Number 1: General Requirements §1.4.02
66 *Id.* §1.7.05(b).
67 *Id.*
68 *Id.* §1.7.06(a).
69 *Id.* §1.7.06(b).
70 *Id.* §1.7.07.
71 Solid Waste Regulation Number 4: Incinerators and Resource Recovery Facilities §4.3.16.
72 *Id.* §4.3.11.
73 Solid Waste Regulation Number 1: General Requirements §1.7.09.
74 *Id.* §1.7.10.
75 *Id.* §1.7.11.

Once operating and engineering plans for the facility are approved, variances from the plans may be obtained upon written request to the DEM.[76] In order for an owner or operator to close a facility, he or she must submit a plan to DEM for approval at least three months prior to the anticipated date that closure operations are to begin.[77] Once DEM approves the plan, the owner or operator is authorized to implement it.[78] A professional engineer registered with the State of Rhode Island must certify that the facility is properly closed in accordance with the approved closure plan.[79] Upon full compliance with the closure procedures, the director of DEM is authorized to issue a certificate of closure.

3. Additional Requirements for Specific Types of Solid Waste Management Facilities

a. Sanitary Landfills

Sanitary landfill facilities must maintain a "working face" no larger than 150 feet in width.[80] The term "working face" refers to the portion of the landfill site which solid waste is discharged and compacted prior to the application of cover material. No "lift"[81] should exceed 12 feet in height unless an approved engineering plan provides otherwise.[82] Six inches of cover material should be applied at the conclusion of each day, and an additional layer of six inches should be applied within one week where an additional layer of refuse is not to begin for another six months.[83] A final cover of 24 inches must be maintained when: (1) the final proposed site elevation has been reached; (2) the facility has begun closure proceedings; or (3) no lift is scheduled to begin within a year.[84] The facility must keep a four day supply of cover material on the premises on all times.[85] The final cover must be able to support vegetative growth, which the operator shall plant and maintain on all completed areas.[86]

---

[76] *Id.* §1.10.01.
[77] *Id.* §1.7.14(a).
[78] *Id.* §1.7.14(b).
[79] *Id.* §1.7.14(c).
[80] Solid Waste Regulation Number 2: Solid Waste Landfills §2.3.03.
[81] "Lift" shall mean a compacted layer of solid waste plus its overlying material in a sanitary landfill. Solid Waste regulation Number 2: Solid Landfills §1.3.108.
[82] Solid Waste Regulation Number 2: Solid Waste Landfills §2.3.03.
[83] *Id.* §2.3.04(a), (b).
[84] *Id.* §2.3.04(c).
[85] *Id.* §2.3.04(d).
[86] *Id.* §2.3.04(g).

The operation facility should never cause pollution of the groundwaters or surface waters within or beyond the borders of the landfill.[87] Monitoring wells must be installed throughout the facility to determine if the facility is impacting the groundwater.[88] In determining whether the operation of a sanitary landfill is causing or is likely to cause pollution of the groundwaters or the surface waters of the State, the Director may consider the following factors:

1) Whether groundwater monitoring results from the licensed area of the sanitary landfill show significant statistical increases in excess of any one or more of the parameters set by law;

2) Whether groundwater monitoring results from the facility show detection of one or more of the parameters set by law;

3) Whether topography, hydrology and geology of the area encompassing the sanitary landfill indicates a likelihood of contamination of a surface water body or groundwater;

4) Whether the groundwater leaving the licensed area is likely to impact private or public drinking wells down gradient from the facility;

5) Whether groundwater leaving the licensed area is likely to impact groundwater used for commercial or industrial processes down gradient from the facility;

6) Whether the facility violated a groundwater standard; and

7) Whether there exists an actual or potential discharge into any surface water.[89]

The DEM is authorized to require such measures as may be necessary to avoid, abate or eliminate contamination of groundwater or surface water bodies such as:

---

[87] *Id.* §2.3.05(a)(1).
[88] *Id* §2.3.11.
[89] *Id.* §2.3.05(a)(2).

1) Groundwater removal treatment;

2) Encapsulation of the contaminated groundwater;

3) Provision of alternative sources of drinking water to affected individuals;

4) Control of the surface water percolating into the refuse filled areas.

5) Identification and closure of a particular cell or portion of the facility that is causing the pollution; and

6) Closing of the facility.[90]

A landfill must not be operated within the watershed of any surface public water supply and cannot be located on the drainage areas of any surface public water supplies. In addition, no refuse at a landfill can be deposited within 200 feet of any surface water or within 1200 feet on any river.[91] No landfill may be located where solid waste may be in direct contact with groundwater. There must be at least five feet between the highest water table and the lowest level of deposited refuse at the landfill. Also, landfills cannot be located within 400 feet of any public water supply well.[92]

In those municipality where an existing or planned public drinking source is located and the municipality has enacted an ordinance to protect such public drinking source, solid waste cannot be disposed of on or in ground overlying the groundwater reservoirs or groundwater recharge areas.[93] The DEM is also authorized to order the closure of a facility if:

1) After notice of a public hearing, the municipality has requested the DEM to determine if the operation of the landfill presents a hazard to the designated public drinking water source; and

2) Once the DEM has completed an investigation, notice has been sent to the landfill, and a hearing has been held, the DEM

---

[90] *Id.* §2.3.05(a)(3).
[91] *Id.* §2.3.05(b)(1).
[92] *Id.* §2.3.05(c).
[93] *Id.* §2.3.05(d)(1).

determines operation of the facility is a risk to the public drinking water source.[94]

The regulations also outline other measures for handling specific types of waste:

1) Bulky Waste must be stored in a separate area approved by the DEM or the purpose of salvaging these items. Any salvageable materials must be stored in a closed top container for a period approved by the DEM;

2) Demolition and construction waste must be covered daily;

3) Brush must be stored no less than 200 feet from the working face or, in the alternative, buried. If the brush is not buried, it must be chipped within one week, and then can be stored indefinitely;

4) In order for a facility to accept nonhazardous liquid waste, special provisions must be made for such disposal and be approved by the DEM. Furthermore, any non-hazardous liquid waste accepted for disposal shall be covered immediately after it is dumped at any sanitary landfill. No uncovered pools of these materials will be allowed at any time;

5) Non-containerized liquid waste cannot be landfilled unless it is a household waste other than septic waste or the waste is leachate or gas condensate derived from the SWLF unit. Containerized liquid waste can only be placed in landfills if it is household waste or if the container is small or similar in size to that normally used for containing household waste;

6) For oil spill cleanup debris, disposal can only occur in a sanitary landfill constructed with a liner system, pursuant to these regulations or in a facility approved by DEM;

---

[94] *Id.* §2.3.05(d)(2).

7) Asbestos material may not be accepted without the express approval of the DEM. The approval will be based on but not necessarily limited to, the amount of refuse accepted at the landfill, the equipment and personnel available, and the need for asbestos disposal facilities. The director of the DEM, however, may revoke approval at any time. Friable asbestos materials must be treated with water or otherwise processed into a non-friable form before it may be accepted for disposal. The asbestos material must be placed at the bottom of the working face and immediately covered with two feet of refuse or six inches of clean fill.[95]

The regulations outline the general requirements for the use of equipment landfill.[96] All equipment used shall meet the performance specifications necessary for operating the landfill in accordance with the operating requirements in the regulations. Each piece of equipment must have a minimum basic weight without accessories, of 17,000 pounds . The types and quantities of vehicles must be sufficient to meet the requirements in the regulations. In addition, arrangements should be made to have emergency equipment on site within a 24 hour period in the event of equipment breakdown.[97] All landfills must make arrangements with the local fire department to provide emergency service whenever necessary. Also, within 1,000 feet of the working face, there must be a high pressured water supply or the equivalent of four days cover material for the exclusive use of fighting fires. Finally, all equipment must be supplied with a fire extinguisher.[98] At a landfill, no refuse should be disposed of within 600 feet of any property line.[99] At no time shall any refuse be deposited in the one hundred (100) year flood plan.[100]

In addition, the concentration of methane gas generated by the facility may not exceed 25 percent of the lower explosive limit for methane[101] in facility structures (excluding

---

[95] *Id.* §2.3.06(d)(1)-(6).
[96] *Id.* §2.3.07.
[97] *Id.* §2.3.07(c).
[98] *Id.* §2.3.09
[99] *Id.* §2.3.12.
[100] *Id.* §2.3.14(a).
[101] The lower explosive limit means the lowest percent of volume of a mixture of explosive gases in air that will propagate a flame at 25 degrees Celsius and atmospheric pressure.

gas control or recovery system components).[102] The concentration of methane gas also may not exceed 25 percent of the lower explosive limit for methane at the facility property boundary.[103] In order to ensure compliance with these regulations, all sanitary landfills must implement a routine methane monitoring program. The type and frequency of monitoring be determined on base soil conditions, the hydrogeologic conditions surrounding the facility, the hydraulic conditions surrounding the facility, and the location of facility structures and property boundaries.[104] Monitoring must, however, be conducted a minimum of four times per year.

If methane gas levels exceeding the limits established above are detected, the facility must immediately take all necessary steps to ensure protection of human health and notify the DEM. Also, within 7 days of detection, the facility must detail in the operating plan the methane gas levels detected and the steps taken to protect human health. Furthermore, within 60 days of detection, the facility must implement a remediation plan for the methane gas releases, place a copy of the plan in the operating plan, and notify the DEM that the plan has been implemented. The plan shall describe the nature and extent of the problem and the proposed remedy.[105]

The Regulations also outline certain restrictions as to the notation and recordation of the deed for the landfill. Each deed must include information on the type of waste at the site, the exact location of the waste and notice that previously filled areas will not be excavated without the express approval of the DEM.[106] Finally, an annual survey must be conducted to monitor the elevation of the landfill. Once elevation has reached 80% of its proposed final site elevation, the DEM may require surveys to be conducted more frequently to avoid exceeding the proposed final site elevation.[107]

b. Incinerator, Transfer Station, Collection Station, and Resource Recovery Facility Operating Standards

In general, incinerators, transfer stations, collection stations, and resource recovery facilities must meet the same general operating standards that sanitary landfills must

---

[102] *Id.* §2.3.08(a).
[103] *Id.* §2.3.08(b).
[104] *Id.* §2.3.08(c)(1).
[105] *Id.* §2.3.08(d).
[106] *Id.* §2.3.15.
[107] *Id.* §2.3.16.

meet, as discussed above. Incinerators, transfer stations, collection stations, and resource recovery facilities, however, must comply with additional operating standards. For example, they must have an alternate method of disposal, approved in writing, with another solid waste facility for use in the event of equipment failure or shutdown.[108]

For incinerators, transfer stations, collection stations and resource recovery facilities, waste storage must comply with the following requirements:

1) All unprocessed, incoming solid waste to be incinerated must be stored in pits, bunkers, or similar containment vessels, and shall be kept at all times at levels that prevent spillage or overflow;

2) All combustible and/or putrescible waste storage shall be conducted within the confines of a protective structure;

3) The capacity of the storage pit must be equal to at least the rated capacity of the incinerator/combustion chamber for one and one-half (1 1/2) days of operation; and

4) No combustible solid waste shall be stored for more than forty-eight (48) hours at the facility, except for three (3) day holiday weekends.

In addition , all such waste must be disposed of in a manner that will not pollute any source of private or public water supply, any waters of Rhode Island, or any groundwaters.[109]

A comprehensive training program covering normal job responsibilities and procedures, emergency situations, and procedures and safety issues, must be provided to facility employees. Employees that are involved with the operation and maintenance of the facility must receive training at least annually. These employees include the chief of facility operator, shift supervisors, control room operators, ash handlers, maintenance personnel, and crane/load handlers. These employees shall receive specific training and operating manuals to assist in their training. Furthermore, the chief facility operator and the shift supervisor for each

---

[108] *Id.* §4.3.08.
[109] *Id.* §3.07, 4.3.12, 4.3.18.

operating shift shall obtain and keep current ASME operator certification or an equivalent certification approved by the DEM. Also, the facility shall not operate at any time without the presence of a certified shift supervisor or other certified operator.[110]

The penalties for violating any operating standards for an incinerator, transfer station, collection station, or resource recovery facility are the same as those for sanitary landfills, discussed above.

In January 1997, DEM further modified its Solid Waste Regulations as follows:

Solid Waste Regulation No. 1 – General Requirements

These Solid Waste Rules and Regulations are intended to minimize environmental hazards associated with the operation of solid waste landfills, transfer stations and collection stations, incinerators and resource recovery facilities, waste tire storage recycling facilities, petroleum-contained soil processing facilities, facilities that process construction and demolition debris, and composting facilities.

The DEM shall adopt, amend, promulgate and enforce such rules and regulations and standards with respect to all solid waste management facilities, composting facilities, and projects to be licensed or registered to further the accomplishment of the purposes of the applicable Rhode Island General Laws.

Applications for licenses and registrations must include plans and specifications. All applicants, regardless of facility type, must demonstrate their ability to comply with all applicants, regardless of facility type, must demonstrate their ability to comply with all General Operating Standards set forth in these Rules and Regulations, as well as the general requirements in this rule. Each applicant must also submit all plans and specifications required for the particular type of facility, as enumerated in Regulations Numbers 2 through 8.

Included in Solid Waste Regulation No. 1 are guidelines and regulations as to the Organized and Method of Operation of the Office of Waste Management; Prohibitions; General Requirements and Procedures; Issuance, Renewal, and Conditions of Licenses and Registrations; General Operating Standards; Existing Composting Facilities and Solid Waste Management

[110] *Id.* §4.3.31.

Facilities; New Composting Facilities or Waste Management Facilities; Procedures for Approval or Denial of Variances; Opportunity for Hearing; Effective Dates; and Fees.[111]

Solid Waste Regulation No. 2 – Landfills

Solid Waste Regulation No. 2 sets guidelines for the construction and operation of landfills in Rhode Island. For Solid Waste Landfills, there are Regulations pertaining to Applications, Engineering Plans, Operating Plans, Sedimentation and Erosion Control Plans, Engineering Reports, Quality Insurance/Quality Control Reports, Contingency Plans, Hydrogeological Reports, Closure and Post-Closure Plans and Financial Assurance, Site Engineering, Conservation Easements, and Landfill Gas Recovery Facilities.

As for the Solid Waste Landfill Construction Standards, regulation No. 2 sets guidelines for Horizontal and Vertical Control; Liner Systems; Leachate Collection and Removal Systems; Landfill Subgrades; Soil Components of the Liner System; Geomembrane Liners; Soil Drainage Layers; Leachate Collection Pipes; Geosynthetic Drainage Layers; Filter Layer Criteria, Final Cover Systems; Construction Certification Reports; and Equivalent Design.

Finally, Solid Waste Operating Standards, Regulation No. 2 contains regulations on Working Faces; Lift Height; Cover Material; Water Pollution; Waste Handling; Equipment Requirements; Gas Controls; Fire Protection; Surface Drainage; Monitoring Wells; Distance to Property Lines; Limited Access; and Flood Plain, Wetlands, and Costal Restrictions.[112]

Solid Waste Regulation No. 3 – Transfer Stations and Collection Stations

Solid Waste Regulation No. 3 regulates Transfer Stations and Collection Stations. These requirements are related to the facility and its site only. All information relating to other types of facilities used in the final disposal or intermediate processing of the refuse must be submitted as required in the rules relating to the particular type of operations, and also must meet the general requirements of these Regulations.

For transfer stations and collection stations, Regulation No. 3 sets guidelines for Radius Plan; Site Plans; Construction and Engineering Plans; Operating Plans; and Closure Plans.

---

[111] Solid Waste Regulation No. 1.
[112] Solid Waste Regulation No. 2.

For transfer station and collection stations operating standards, Regulation No. 3 has regulations for Waste Storage, Wastewater and Leachate; Fire Protection; Structures; Equipment failure and Shutdown Provisions; and Brush Handling.[113]

Solid Waste Regulation No. 4 – Incinerators and Resource Recovery Facilities

Solid Waste Regulation No. 4 sets guidelines and criteria for incinerators and resource recovery facilities. These requirements are related to the incinerator or resource recovery site and buildings. All information relating to the residue disposal site required in these Rules must also be submitted. For these facilities, Regulation No. 4 features detailed specifications for Radius Plan, Site Plans, Construction and Engineering Plans and Specifications, Descriptions of Proposed Facilities, Operating Plans, Closure Plans, and a Permit Section.

Regulation No. 4 also contains detailed regulations on Incinerators and Resource Recovery Design Standards and Operating Standards.[114]

Solid Waste Regulation No. 5 – Waste Tire Storage and Recycling Facility

Solid waste Regulation No. 5 regulates Waste Tire Storage and Recovery Facilities. In addition to the General Requirements set forth elsewhere in these Regulations, each applicant for a license to construct and operate a Waste Tire Storage and Recovery Facility subject to this rule must meet detailed criteria listed as to Site Plan, Construction and Engineering Plans, Operating Plans, Contingency Plans, and Closure Plans.

Regulation No. 5 also contains requirements as to Waste Tire Storage and Recycling Facility Operating Standards, particularly Applicability, Waste Tire Storage, Sorting of Waste Tires, Processing of Waste Tires, Fire Prevention and Control, Vector Control, and Security Plans.[115]

Solid Waste Regulation No. 6 – Petroleum Contaminated Soil Processing Facility

Solid Waste Regulation No. 6 regulates the design, construction, and operation of facilities that process virgin petroleum contaminated soil that has been generated from

---

[113] Solid Waste Regulation No. 3.
[114] Solid Waste Regulation No. 4.
[115] Solid Waste Regulation No. 5.

aboveground or underground petroleum leaks or spills. For Petroleum Contaminated Soil Processing Facilities, all general requirements set forth elsewhere in these Regulations must be submitted, and regulations must be considered pertaining to Radius Plan; Site Plans; Construction Engineering Plans and Specifications; Operating Plans; and Closure Plans.

For Petroleum Contaminated Soil Processing Facility Operating Standards, Regulation No. 6 contains guidelines for Field sampling to Provide Analytical Data for evaluation of Candidate Soil; Laboratory Tests of Field Site Samples; Fingerprint Analysis and Testing; Sampling of Incoming Loads at Processing Facility for Fingerprint Analysis; Transportation Practices; Acceptable Uses of Processed Soil; Limits of Parameters in the Processed Soil; Sampling of Processed Soil at Processor's Facility.

Finally, for Petroleum Contaminated Soil Processing Facility Design Standards, Regulation No. 6 features criteria for Process Equipment; Design of Storage Chamber for Incoming Contaminated Soil; and Design Holding Area for Processed Soil at Process Facility Site.[116]

Solid Waste Regulation No. 7 – Facilities That Process Construction and Demolition Debris

Solid Waste Regulation No. 7 contains guidelines and regulates Facilities That Process Construction and Demolition Debris. Pursuant to R.I. Gen. Laws §23-18.9-8, any person who desires to construct, develop, manage, operate, own, or maintain a construction and demolition debris processing facility, as defined in this Regulation, must obtain a solid waste management facility license from the DEM in accordance with these Regulations. Detailed criteria on Exemptions, Radius Plans, Site Plans, Construction and Engineering Plans, Operating Plans are contained in Regulation No. 7.

Regulation No. 7 also regulates operating standards for Facilities that Process Construction and Demolition Debris, including guidelines for Wastewater and Leachate; Groundwater Monitoring Wells; Buffers; Fire Protection; Equipment Failure and Shutdown Provisions; and Closure Fund Agreement or Closure Bond.

[116] Solid Waste Regulation No. 6.

Lastly, Regulation No. 7 contains criteria for reuse, sampling, and testing requirements for construction and demolition debris, particularly in the areas of Screenings – Reuse, Sampling and Testing Requirements, and wood chips – Reuse, Sampling and Testing Requirements.[117]

Solid Waste Regulation No. 8 – Rhode Island Solid Waste Composting Facility

Solid Waste Regulation No. 8 regulates Leaf and Yard Waste Composting Facilities, Putrescible Waste Composting Facilities, and Mixed Solid Waste Composting Facilities, and Compost Products.

For Leaf and Yard Composting Facilities, Regulation No. 8 contains both specific Registration Requirements and Operating Standards. Before constructing a composting facility and commencing leaf and yard waste composting, an owner or operator of a new leaf and yard waste composting facility shall register such facility with in the office of Waste Management (DEM) and obtain from the DEM a written approval that such registration is complete. An owner or operator of an existing leaf and yard waste composting facility shall register such facility within 90 days after the effective date of this section of the "Rules and Regulations for Solid Waste Management Facilities". Lastly, all leaf and yard waste facilities shall meet all requirements set forth in this Rule as to General Operating Standards contained in these Regulations.

Regulation No. 8 also contains detailed Registration Requirements and Operating Standards for Putrescible Waste Composting Facilities. Before constructing a composting, an owner or operator of a putrescible waste composting facility shall register such facility with the Office of Waste Management of the DEM, and obtain from the DEM a written approval that such registration is complete. An owner or operator of an existing putrescible waste composting facility shall register such facility after the effective date of this section of the "Rules and Regulations for Solid Waste Management Facilities." Also again, all putrescible waste composting facilities shall met all requirements set forth in this Rule in addition to he General Operating Standards contained in these Regulations.

License Requirements, Design Standards, and Operating Standards for Mixed solid Waste Facilities are also contained in Regulation No. 8. A mixed solid waste facility is not

[117] Solid Waste Regulation No. 7.

eligible for a registration. No person shall construct or operate a mixed solid waste compost facility unless said person has received a license approved by the DEM to construct and operate a mixed solid waste composting facility. In addition to meeting the general requirements set forth in these Regulations, each applicant for a license to construct and operate a mixed solid waste facility must contain particular plans, narratives, and information that are outlined in this Rule. Also, all mixed solid waste composting facilities shall meet all the requirements set forth in this Rule in addition to the General contained in these Regulations . Lastly, for General Operating Standards, any such facility must meet all regulations set forth in these Rules and shall comply with the limitations of all other pertinent regulations of the DEM, including the General Operating Standards contained elsewhere in these Regulations.

Finally, Solid Waste Regulation No. 8 contains specific guidelines for Compost Product Requirements and Distribution. This Rule applies to compost produced in all types of composting facilities subject to these Regulations. The parameter limits for three classes of compost, Class 'A", Class "B", and Class "C" are established in this section. The allowed limit uses of these three classes of compost are also provided. Any finished compost which does not meet the limits established for Class "A", Class "B", shall be considered Class "C" where specific Class "C" limits for heavy metals are omitted.[118]

[118] Solid Waste Regulation No. 8.

CHAPTER VII:

STORAGE TANK REGULATIONS

A. Underground Storage Tanks

1. Applicability

The Rhode Island Department of Environmental Management's (the "DEM") Regulations for Underground Storage Facilities Used for Petroleum Products and Hazardous Materials (the "Regulations"), which became effective on July 1, 2002,[1] apply to proposed, new and existing storage tank facilities, at which petroleum products or hazardous materials are or have been stored underground in a tank or tank systems for industrial, institutional, commercial, educational, agricultural, residential or governmental operations.[2] The Regulations define an "underground storage tank system" as any one or more underground tanks and their associated components, including piping, used to contain an accumulation of petroleum product(s) or hazardous material, and the volume of which is 10% or more beneath the surface of the ground. The term "hazardous materials" includes any material defined as a hazardous substance under §101(14) of the Comprehensive Environmental Response, Compensation, and Liability Act of 1980[3] or any material defined as a "hazardous waste" pursuant to the Rhode Island Hazardous Waste Management Act of 1978,[4] as well as any of the following materials: acetone, ethanol, ethylene oxide, methanol, methylene chloride, and perchloroethylene.

The Regulations, with certain exceptions[5], do not apply to the following: hydraulic lift tanks; storage tanks located entirely within structures such as a basement or cellar provided that a) the structure allows for physical access to the tank, b) the structure is <u>not</u> part of a secondary enclosure, and c) the tank is situated upon or above the surface of a concrete floor; septic tanks; pipeline facilities; flow through process tanks; underground storage tanks storing propane or liquefied natural gas; underground storage tanks used for the temporary storage of raw materials and products by industry; emergency spill protection and overflow tanks; underground storage tanks connected to floor drains or other piping outlets which serve residential structures of one, two, or three dwelling units; residential tanks holding less than or equal to 1,100 gallons used for

---

[1] Regulations for Underground Storage Facilities Used for Petroleum Products and Hazardous Materials (the "Regulations").
[2] *Id.* §5.
[3] 42 U.S.C. §9605.
[4] R.I. Gen. Laws §23-19.1-1 *et seq.*
[5] Regulations §11.02(A) and (B) (prohibition of new installations, §14.00 (Leak and Spill Response))

storing No. 2 heating oil and serving a one, two, or three family dwelling; farm tanks holding less than or equal to 1,100 gallons used for storing No. 2 heating oil for non-commercial purposes.[6]

2. Existing and New Facility Requirements

a. Existing Facilities

All UST's must be maintained and operated by trained personnel in compliance with the applicable national codes of practice for the handling and storage of petroleum or hazardous materials.[7] In addition, anyone wishing to upgrade a UST may upgrade the tank system once, provided that the Director receives a written description of the proposed upgrade method at least 30 days prior to the upgrade, and the upgrade is properly conducted in accordance with national codes of practice.[8] In approving the upgrade, the Director will require the tank to be precision tested once the upgrade is complete. Upon completion, the owner or operator must submit a verification to the Director within 15 days which documents that the method of upgrade is compatible with the product being stored and that the tank system is structurally sound in a manner that will prevent releases due to structural failure or corrosion during its operating life.[9] Furthermore, all USTs are required to permanently mark the fill pipe so that the product inside the tank is identified.[10]

All existing facilities except those which store heating oil of any grade that is consumed on-site must comply with the following additional requirements. The owners or operators of existing UST facilities must provide for corrosion protection of all steel tanks and steel piping no later than December 22, 1998. This entails either closing all tank systems which do not meet corrosion protection standards or upgrading existing tanks and piping to provide for corrosion protection through interior lining and/or cathodic protection.[11]

The owners or operators of these existing tanks must also satisfy all leak detection requirements. Owner/operators may opt for either a continuous monitoring system or a precision testing system. A continuous monitoring system would require double-walled USTs to

---

[6] Regulations §5.03
[7] *Id.* §10.02(A). *See* Appendix B of the Regulations.
[8] *Id.* §10.04(A), (B). *See* Appendix B of the Regulations.
[9] *Id.* §10.04.
[10] *Id.* §10.11.
[11] *Id.* §10.03.

install interstitial continuous monitoring devices. Single-walled tanks would be required to install and operate an approved continuous monitoring system compatible with the product and tank material and perform a precision test of the tank at five year intervals following installation of monitoring devices, until the tank has been installed for a period of twenty years. After the twenty year mark, precision tests must be conducted once every two years.[12]

Owner/operators who choose the precision testing method and who know and can verify the date on which their USTs were installed must perform a precision test annually if the tanks were installed prior to January 1, 1965. If the tanks were installed subsequent to January 1, 1965 then a precision test must be performed 5, 8, 11, and 13 years after installation and annually thereafter.

Each precision test result submitted to the DEM must include the following information:

1. Date the test was performed;
2. Facility name and address;
3. Facility owner name and address;
4. Identification of the USTs tested, including volume, stored material and DEM's tank identification number;
5. Brand name and type of precision test equipment used for the test;[13]
6. Identification of the UST system components tested; e.g., UST and lines, tank only;

[12] *Id.* §10.06(A).

[13] The equipment used must be capable of detecting a 0.1 gallon per hour leak rate from the full tank system, accounting for the effects of thermal expansion or contraction of product, vapor pockets, tank deformation, evaporation, condensation, and the location of the water table. The probability of detection must be no less than 95% and the probability of a false alarm shall be no more than 5%. *Id.* §10.06(b)(8).

7. Identification of who performed the test, including the names of any person assisting in the test;

8. Data sheets with the test readings recorded;

9. Calculations pertaining to the test method and test results;

10. Location of monitoring or observation well, if used in the test procedure;

11. Description of the method used to measure the water table if required, and the result;

12. Signature of a licensed tester attesting to the accuracy of the information submitted in the test result;

13. DEM facility ID number; and

14. A site plan identifying all tanks on site with tank numbers on cover sheet corresponding to tank numbers on the site plan.[14]

In addition to providing for tank leak detection, the owner/operator is also responsible for detecting leaks in any piping that is associated with the UST facility. If double walled piping is used then interstitial or annular space monitoring is required. If single walled piping is used the owner/operators must comply with the following requirements:

1) All tank systems equipped with pressurized piping must perform a tightness test upon installation and every year thereafter;

2) All tank systems equipped with suction piping shall have a line tightness test performed upon installation, 5, 8, 11, and 13 years following installation and annually thereafter; and

3) Piping pressure tightness tests shall have a detection limit of .1 gallon per hour at 1.5 times normal operating pressure.[15]

---

[14] *Id.* §10.06(B)(6).
[15] *Id.* §10.07(B)(1)-(3).

Alternative leak detection methods for piping that are equivalent in accuracy and reliability to the methods listed may be approved by the DEM.[16]

b. New Facilities

No new USTs may be installed where the groundwater has been designated as a wellhead protection area for a community well. However, facilities registered prior to June 11, 2002 may upgrade in accordance with the applicable provisions of these regulations.[17] Furthermore, the installation of bare steel or metal USTs for storage of petroleum products or hazardous materials is prohibited.[18] Also, no person shall commence construction of a new facility or replacement tank system, and no substantial modification (including product piping replacement) may be made to any underground storage tank facility for which an application for a certificate of registration is required, without prior written notification to and approval by the DEM.[19]

In addition, all new or replacement tanks or piping systems must be made of or lined with materials that are compatible with the substance(s) stored.[20] The owner/operator shall not introduce, or allow to be introduced, any material into an underground storage tank that is incompatible with the UST system.[21] The tanks and associated piping must also provide for secondary containment and must be constructed in accordance with one of several national codes, and the specific requirements set out in section 11.05 of the Regulations. Approved spill and overfill prevention equipment must be used to prevent spilling and overfilling during product transfers to the tank.[22] This includes placing steel wear plates under all openings with minimum 8" x 8" area and installing submerged fill tubes.[23] Prior to installation, however, all new and replacement USTs must be factory tested at a minimum of five pounds per square inch gauge and must be guaranteed tight by the manufacturer. This guarantee must be filed with the DEM at the time of installation application.[24]

---

[16] *Id.* §10.07(C).
[17] *Id.* §11.02(A).
[18] *Id.* §11.02(B).
[19] *Id.* §11.02(C)
[20] *Id.* §11.04.
[21] *Id.*
[22] *Id.* §11.05; *Id.* §11.12
[23] *Id.* §§11.06-11.07.
[24] *Id.* §11.08.

Once all tanks and piping have been installed, a precision test must be performed. This test must be performed when installation is complete but before regular UST operations are commenced. This test must be capable of detecting a 0.1 gallon per hour leak rate from the full tank system, and the margin of error may not exceed 5%. The results of this test must be reported to the DEM within 15 calendar days of test completion.[25]

c. Facility Modifications

The Regulations prohibit any substantial modification of an existing or new underground storage tank facility without prior written notification to and approval by the DEM.[26] Modifications include any addition to an existing facility or replacement, restoration, refurbishment, or renovation which: increases or decreases the in-place storage capacity of the facility; alters the physical configuration of the facility; alters the design or specifications of the facility's components; or impairs or affects the physical integrity of the facility or its monitoring systems.[27]

All modifications to or replacement of existing or new facility components must comply with the requirements for new facilities.[28] Any facility may install used tanks which meet the specifications for new facilities that: (1) the owner/operator makes a written request for and receives approval from the DEM for the proposed modifications; (2) the manufacturer inspects and tests the used tanks; and (3) the manufacturer certifies that the tanks are reusable for the material being stored, and gives the same warranty as a new tank.[29] In addition, a facility may repair or reline an underground storage tank once so long as the repair or upgrade is properly conducted, DEM approves the repairing and relining method, the method is compatible with the material stored, and the tank is precision tested within 30 days of repairing and relining and such test does not detect any leaks.[30] Results of the precision test must be submitted to the director within 15 days of the test's completion. All metal pipe sections that have released material as a result of corrosion or other damage must be replaced.

---

[25] *Id.* §11.10.
[26] *Id.* §12.01
[27] *Id.* §7.38
[28] *Id.* §12.02.
[29] *Id.* §12.03
[30] *Id.* §12.04.

d. Monitoring and Recordkeeping

All owners or operators of new and existing facilities, with the exception of facilities that store heating oils that are consumed on-site, must maintain records of the following on the facility's premises or at an alternate site approved by the DEM: all data used to complete the application for the certificate of registration; all records of repairs, modifications or upgrades to any element of the UST system; monitoring and testing results; records of closure activities; records of leaks, spills, overfills, site investigations and remedial response activities taken; precision test results; and certificate of installation.[31] In addition, records of maintenance and calibration, continuing monitoring data, monthly tests of instrumentation, records pertaining to the operation and maintenance of approved corrosion protection method, and a daily written inventory showing all out flows and in flows of the product or material stored must be maintained.[32] The facility owner or operator must maintain the records for at least three years from the date of recording or for the life of the facility, whichever is greater, and must provide the DEM with all pertinent records upon request.[33] Some records may be required to be maintained for longer mandates.

3. Closure Requirements

The Regulations prohibit the abandonment of underground storage tanks but permit temporary or permanent closure. Closure means removing an underground storage tank from service consistent with the regulations.

a. Temporary Closure

The term "temporary closure" means taking an underground storage tank out of service for more than 90 days but less than 180 days. An owner or operator who closes any underground storage tank for this period of time must cap and secure all fill lines against tampering, secure manways, pumps and other components, including pump out suction lines, but must keep vent lines open.[34] In addition, the owner must maintain records regarding the location and size of any underground storage tanks, the date on which the facility temporarily closed the tank, and the procedures which the facility uses to maintain safe operating

---

[31] *Id.* §13.02(A).
[32] *Id.* §13.02(B).
[33] *Id.* §13.02.
[34] *Id.* §15.03(A)-(B).

conditions.[35] The owner/operator must continue to comply with all general operating requirements and he must comply with release detection requirements if regulated substances are stored in the UST or if greater than 1 inch of residue is measured in the tank bottom after all liquids have been evacuated.[36] The DEM may extend the period of temporary closure beyond 180 days for an additional 180 days provided that the owner or operator files a petition for extension within 150 days after temporary closure and that such petition demonstrates good cause for the extension.[37] An extension request for a period greater than 12 months must be accompanied by a closure assessment consistent with the regulations to be granted.

b. Permanent Closure

An owner or operator seeking to permanently remove an underground storage tank from service must apply to the DEM for a certificate of closure at least 10 days prior to the date the UST is to be permanently removed from service.[38] The closure application must contain the following information: the date the tank is to be permanently closed; the age of the tank; the type of material stored in the tank; the facility's closure procedures; the size, type, and location of the tank if it will remain in the ground; the date of excavation if the tank will be removed from the ground; any appropriate documentation substantiating compliance with the Regulations' closure procedures and appropriate documentation demonstrating notification of local fire officials.[39]

The owner or operator must notify the DEM at least 3 working days prior to the proposed date of excavation or closure of the USTs. Upon notification, arrangements must be made to have the DEM inspect the closed tanks or the excavation zone during the closure process.[40] Furthermore, the owner or operator must retain consultants to be present on the site during the tank removal process in order to ensure that an adequate closure assessment is performed.[41]

---

[35] *Id.* §15.03(E).
[36] *Id.* §15.03(F)-(G).
[37] *Id.* §15.04.
[38] *Id.* §15.06.
[39] *Id.* §15.06 (A)-(H).
[40] *Id.* §15.08 (A), (B).
[41] *Id.* §15.08 (C).

The owner or operator may then permanently close underground storage tanks by removing the tanks and related facility components, provided: (1) all material is removed from the tank and its connecting lines; (2) the tank is free from any residue; (3) the closure and removal operations are conducted in accordance with applicable federal, state, local, and industry standards; and (4) the tank is permanently rendered unfit for further use.[42] In addition, the facility must dispose of any excavated, contaminated soil or debris according to appropriate federal and state laws.[43] The owner or operator of the facility and the person responsible for transporting any residues or contaminated soil generated by the closure must maintain records indicating the final destination for all such materials, the date(s) of such shipment(s), and the person or company responsible for the transportation. In the case of material that qualifies as "hazardous waste" the manifest required by the DEM's Regulations for Hazardous Waste Management will suffice for this requirement.[44]

Upon permanently closing an underground storage tank, the facility owner may leave the tank or its components underground so long as a precision test is conducted on the tank and its associated piping. The results must be reported to the DEM, and the test must not reveal any leaks.[45] If the precision test reveals a leak in the tank, the DEM will determine which, if any, of the facility's components will be removed to investigate the extent of environmental damage. An owner leaving a permanently closed tank in the ground also must ensure that all product is removed from the tank and connecting lines;[46] the tank is free from any residue;[47] all lines are disconnected; all associated piping is capped or plugged;[48] and the tank is filled with an inert, solid material.[49]

4. Leak and Spill Response

A leak is a loss or gain to an underground storage tank of .05 gallons per hour. A spill is a loss of petroleum product or hazardous material in a manner other than a leak occurring

---

[42] *Id.* §15.11.
[43] *Id.* §15.11(F).
[44] *Id.* §15.11(G).
[45] *Id.* §15.12(A).
[46] *Id.* §15.12(B).
[47] *Id.* §15.12(C).
[48] *Id.* §15.12(D).
[49] *Id.* §15.12(E).

at the facility and in such a way that the underground storage tank's product or material is likely to enter ground or surface water.

Any owner or operator who knows or has reason to know of a leak or spill from any underground storage tank must report such information immediately to the local fire chief, the DEM, and if the leak or spill occurs in a public supply watershed or in a wellhead protection area for community water supply wells, then the local public water supplier must be notified.[50] Precision test results that indicate a leak in the system shall be reported to the DEM within two hours of the test. Persons reporting leaks or spills to such officials must provide the following information: the name and phone number of the person reporting the release; the location of the release and the name of the facility; the date and time of the release; the type, and to the extent known – the amount of material released and; the name and phone number of the potentially responsible party if know.[51]

When a confirmed release occurs the owner/operator shall take the following actions, unless instructed by DEM to do otherwise: arrange for, and, within 24 hours or as soon as possible, complete removal of the contents of the UST system; contain all discharged oil, oil contaminated debris and hazardous waste; assess safety risks and take steps to mitigate them; take steps to prevent the migration of any released substance; investigate and remove free product; and carry out other actions as directed by DEM.[52]

In addition, the owner or operator must file a Release Characterization Report with the DEM within seven days of the time the leak or spill was discovered. This report must include the following information: date on the nature and estimated quantity of the release; date from available sources and site investigations concerning surrounding populations, water quality, locations of wells potentially affected by the release; subsurface soil conditions; locations of subsurface sanitary sewers and stormwater lines; climatological conditions (where pertinent); land uses; the names, addresses and plat and lot numbers of the owners of all properties that abut the facility; and all pertinent data obtained from Initial Abatement Actions.[53] Upon completion of an initial Release Characterization Report, the owner or operator must conduct a full

---

[50] *Id.* §14.04(A).
[51] *Id.* §14.04(B).
[52] *Id.* §14.05.
[53] *Id.* §14.07.

investigation of the release and the on-site and off-site areas known or potentially affected by the release.[54]

The DEM may also require that a site investigation be conducted at any UST facility where one or more of the following conditions exists:

a. The facility has closed USTs storing hazardous materials;

b. Groundwater or surface waters adjacent to the facility have been affected by a release of petroleum product or hazardous material;

c. An inspection of a tank closure reveals soil or groundwater contamination; or

d. Other evidence of a release exists.[55]

The DEM may also require that the site investigation be conducted, and a Site Investigation Report prepared, under the supervision of a professional engineer, certified professional geologist or any other person with appropriate qualifications and relevant professional experience.[56] The results of the site investigation should be reported to the DEM within 60 days or within an alternate deadline pre-approved by the DEM.[57]

Based upon the site investigation or other data, the DEM may require the owner or operator to develop a Corrective Action Plan, within a time frame specified by the DEM, to address contaminated soils or groundwater or other related environmental or public health impact.[58] When a Corrective Action Plan is required it should contain the following: a summary of the findings from the Site Investigation Report and any additional information the DEM may require; a description of the proposed remediation method; a proposed schedule for implementation of the Corrective Action Plan; and a proposed groundwater monitoring

[54] *Id.* §14.08(A).
[55] *Id.* §14.08(B).
[56] *Id.* §14.08(C).
[57] *Id.* §14.08(D).
[58] *Id.* §14.11(A).

program.[59] Furthermore, the DEM will provide public notice to the town or municipality concerning the releases and any remedial action.[60]

5. Facility Registration Requirements

a. New Facilities

The Regulations require an owner or operator of a new facility to obtain a certificate of registration from the DEM before commencing construction.[61] An application for a certificate of registration must contain a set of detailed engineering plans and specification for the project, including a description of any storage tanks, the size and composition of the tanks, and the types of materials to be stored in the tanks.[62]

In addition, the application must include a site plan showing: the proposed location of all tanks, piping, and dispensing pumps and of any on-site observation wells; water table elevation; the location of all public water supply wells or reservoirs within 400 feet of the facility; the location of all facilities served by private wells within 200 feet of the facility; proposed building locations; legal boundaries; and a North Arrow.[63]

b. Existing Facilities

To be in compliance with the Regulations, the owner or operator of an existing facility that stores No. 4, No. 5 or No. 6 fuel oils must have applied for a certificate of registration by January 1, 1993. Tanks that store 1,100 gallons of motor fuels or less at residential properties and farm tanks that store 1,100 gallons or less of motor fuel must also have applied for a certificate of registration by January 1, 1993. Tanks that serve floor drains must apply by July 1, 1994, and all other tanks subject to regulation must store petroleum products or hazardous materials must have applied for a certificate of registration by April 9, 1985.[64] An application for a certificate of registration must contain a description of the size, and construction material of the storage tanks, the types of material stored therein, and any tank, piping and corrosion and spill/overflow protection methods, all existing and proposed leak monitoring

---

[59] *Id.* §14.12(A).
[60] *Id.* §14.15.
[61] *Id.* §8.03(A).
[62] *Id.* §8.04(A). All plans for new facilities must be stamped by a registered professional engineer.
[63] *Id.* §8.04(A)(3).
[64] *Id.* §8.03(B).

programs, as well as the results of any tests conducted on all tanks and associated piping, if available, and a description of all spills and leaks that have occurred at the site on or after October, 1984.[65] A description of all repairs performed on the tank system, if applicable, should be included. The application for an existing facility must also include a site plan showing the location of all tanks, piping, and dispensing pumps; any existing on-site monitoring wells; a description of water service to the facility and properties within 200 feet of the facility; legal boundaries; and a North Arrow.[66]

c. Renewal

All owners or operators must renew their registration of underground storage tanks annually.[67] The DEM will revoke the registration of any person who fails to comply with the procedures for underground storage tank registration renewal.[68] In addition, failing to obtain a certificate of registration constitutes a violation of the Regulations and may subject the owner or operator to certain penalties.[69] A facility owner or operator who has failed to comply with these Regulations must immediately implement facility closure procedures[70] and obtain a certificate of closure.[71]

d. Revocation

The DEM may deny, modify, or revoke a certificate of registration for cause, including but not limited to, the following: when the information on the registration application was incomplete, false, or misleading; or circumstances forming the basis of the DEM's decision to grant the certificate have materially or substantially changed since issuance; failure to pay registration fees; or noncompliance with these regulations.[72] Immediately upon the denial or revocation of a registration certificate, the owner or operator must implement facility closure procedures pursuant to the Regulations.[73]

---

[65] *Id.* §8.04(B).
[66] *Id.* §8.04(B).
[67] *Id.* §8.09.
[68] *Id.* §8.18(D).
[69] *Id.* §8.16(A).
[70] *Id.* §8.19.
[71] *Id.* §15.13.
[72] *Id.* §8.18.
[73] *Id.* §15.

e. Transfer of Certificates of Registration and Closure

The Regulations permit an owner or operator of a facility to transfer certificates of registration or closure if the new certificate holder notifies the DEM in writing, by certified mail, of the proposed transfer at least 30 days prior to the transfer date. This notification must include: the name, address and registration number of the current facility; the name and address of the current owners and operators; the name and address of the new owners and operators and person upon whom legal process can be served; and the proposed transfer date on which the new owner will receive the certificate and assume all accompanying responsibilities.[74] The notice also must include a notarized statement signed by a duly authorized officer or agent of the new owner or operator stating that such officer or agent has read the original certificate application and believes there has been no substantial modification in the facility since the certificate was issued or describes any such changes.[75]

6. Penalties

The DEM will assess penalties for noncompliance with the Regulations. Depending upon the nature of the leak or spill and the type of product or material involved, the DEM may assess penalties pursuant to the "Rhode Island Water Pollution Act," the "Department of Environmental Management Act," or the "Solid Waste Management Corporation Act," the "Hazardous Waste Management Act," and the "Rules and Regulations for Assessment of Administrative Penalties."[76]

B. Oil Pollution Control Regulations

1. Applicability

The Oil Pollution Control Regulations ("Regulations") apply to activities conducted in or on the waters of the State of Rhode Island, as well as to those activities conducted at a location where oil or other pollutants, such as garbage, sewage, or chemical wastes, are likely to enter the waters of Rhode Island.[77] The term "waters of Rhode Island" means all surface waters and groundwater, including the territorial sea, tidewaters, all inland

---

[74] *Id.* §§18.02(A)(1)-(4), (6).
[75] *Id.* §18.02(A)(5).
[76] *Id. See* R.I. Gen. Laws §§46-12, 42-17.1, 42-17.6 and 23-19.1.
[77] Id. Note that persons and activities subject to these Regulations may also be subject to other DEM and federal Regulations. §4(a).

waters by any river, stream, brook, pond or lake, wetlands and all underground waters of whatever nature.[78] Any person, including but not limited to, an individual, trust, firm, joint stock company, corporation, partnership, association, syndicate, municipality, or non-profit agency, who engages in the storage or transportation of oil, and to a limited extent, residential homeowners, may be subject to these Regulations.

2. Prohibited Activities

The Regulations generally prohibit the placing of oil or pollutants into the waters of Rhode Island or in a location where they are likely to enter the waters of Rhode Island. Such placing is only allowed where the action is in compliance with the terms of a permit or an order issued by the DEM.[79]

The activities specifically prohibited by the Regulations include, but not limited to, releases, discharges or the placement of pollutants from:

a. Stormwater runoff from an oil refinery, oil storage tank farm, or oil manufacturing facility;

b. Boat or ship repair and maintenance;

c. Bilge or ballast water from any vessel;

d. Exhaust storm from any coil or other device used to heat oil;

e. Drainage from an underground pipe gallery used as a conduit for oil pipes;

f. Drainage from the floors of a boiler room;

g. Drainage from dike areas around oil storage tanks;

h. Drainage from unauthorized underground injection wells or lagoons; or

i. Drainage from automobile repair, maintenance or wrecking operations.[80]

The Regulations do not, however, prohibit the discharge into any public sewer system, provided that the local public sewer authority approves the discharge and the discharge

---

[78] *Id.* §5.
[79] *Id.* §6(a).
[80] *Id.*

complies with all local, state and federal pretreatment requirements. Also, the Regulations do not prohibit the discharge of oil waste, chemical waste or bilge waste from an oceangoing ship into a certified "reception facility".[81]

3. Requirements for Oil and Waste Transfers and Oil Storage Tanks and Boilers

The Regulations require owners and operators of oil carrying vessels, whether self-propelled or not, and the owners and operators of terminals[82] for the transfer or handling of oil to follow numerous precautionary acts prior to and during the transfer of oil and wastes. For example, the Regulations state that hoses used in the transfer of oil and wastes must be pressure-tested, drip pans must be placed under hose connections, and trained personnel must be stationed at appropriate places to check for equipment malfunctions.[83]

In addition, owners and operators of boiler rooms and remote fill tanks are required to install various drains and traps on such equipment. Any above ground and underground storage tanks with a remote fill must be equipped with a high level warning alarm system. Also, all facilities are required to install spill containment around their fill areas.[84]

4. Above Ground Storage Facilities

The Regulations contain detailed specifications for above ground storage facilities with a combined storage capacity of over 500 gallons. The Regulations specify in detail the procedures to be taken to prevent the overfill of such a storage facility. For example, the Regulations specify which party is responsible for activities involving the transfer of petroleum product and also provide detailed sections on the appropriate valves and gauges to be used when petroleum is transferred to an above ground storage facility.[85]

---

[81] Reception facility is defined as "a facility that has obtained a certificate of adequacy, from the Coast Guard and means anything capable of receiving shipboard oil or chemical wastes that include, but is not limited to: (a) fixed piping that conveys wastes from the vessel to a storage or treatment system; (b) tank barges, railroad cars, or tank trucks and other mobile facilities; and (c) any combination of fixed and mobile facilities." *Id.* §5.

[82] *Id.* §7.

[83] *Id.* §7.

[84] *Id.* §9.

[85] *Id.* §10.

Furthermore, the Regulations require secondary containment systems for above ground tanks to prevent spills of petroleum from entering the groundwater or surface waters of Rhode Island before cleanup can occur. The minimum capacity of a secondary containment system must be 110% of the volume of the tank or 110% of the largest tank in a multiple tank containment system.[86]

Inspections of above ground storage facilities are required on a monthly basis and basically consist of an overall visual inspection. The Regulations require 10 year inspections for above ground tanks with a capacity of 10,000 gallons or more, or for any tank with a capacity of less than 10,000 gallons that could reasonably be expected to discharge petroleum into the waters of Rhode Island. Ten year inspections, however, are not required for: (1) tanks that are entirely above ground, such as those resting on racks or stilts; (2) tanks storing No. 5 or No. 6 fuel oil or asphalt products; and (3) tanks installed in conformance with the standards for new tank construction.[87] Reports for both monthly and ten year inspections must be kept on file at the facility and made available for review upon request for at least 10 years. If any facility or any portion of a facility is not inspected as required, the DEM will require it to be removed from service.[88] The Regulations also require certain facilities, such as those with a combined capacity greater than or equal to 50,000 gallons, or any facility with a combined storage capacity greater than or equal to 5,000 gallons located in an environmentally sensitive area, to be equipped with groundwater monitoring programs approved by the DEM.[89] The monitoring programs must consist of a sufficient number of wells to detect the release of hydrocarbon products from storage tanks, pumping facilities, manifolds and other appurtenances. For the monitoring program, the Regulations outline the well construction standards, the site monitoring requirements, and the reporting requirements for the wells.[90]

The Regulations specify requirements for the construction of new storage facilities, the modification of existing facilities, and the repairing and reconditioning of above ground storage tanks. For new and substantially modified above ground petroleum storage

---

[86] *Id.* §10(c).
[87] *Id.* §10(d)(2).
[88] *Id.* §10(d)(5).
[89] *Id.* §10(h). An environmentally sensitive area is an area with a groundwater classification of GA (a classification of groundwater suitable for public or private drinking water without treatment pursuant to R.I. Gen. Laws §46-13.1-4 and corresponding rules and regulations) or GAA (a classification of groundwater suitable for public drinking water use without treatment pursuant to R.I. Gen. Laws §46-13.1-4 and the corresponding rules and regulations).
[90] *Id.* §10(h).

facilities, the following apply: (1) tanks must be constructed of steel and be built in accordance with certain design and manufacturing standards, unless prior DEM approval is obtained; (2) tank bottoms must have cathodic protection; (3) impermeable barriers must be placed on tank bottoms; (4) the painting of the exterior of the tanks must be done according to specific requirements; new above ground tanks must have secondary containment; must not be exposed to traffic; have a well designed and stable foundation; be tested for tightness; and (5) tank monitoring systems must follow specific requirements.[91] For the repairing and reconditioning of above ground storage tanks, there also are certain requirements. For example, all repairs must be permanent in nature and equal to or better than the standards of original construction, all tank welds must be tested before the tank is returned to service, and all tanks must be cleaned prior to repair. Furthermore, there are very specific regulations on the coating of existing tanks.[92]

5. Closure

When above ground tanks are closed, either temporarily or permanently, certain procedures must be followed. If it is a temporary closure for 30 days or more, all the product must be removed from the tank and the piping systems, and all the tank openings must be either plugged, locked or capped. If a tank is closed for 180 days or more, it is considered permanently closed. For permanent closure, the tank must be completely drained of all product, including being rendered free of petroleum vapors, all connecting lines must be disconnected or blanked, manways must be securely fastened, and the tank must be stenciled with the date of permanent closure.[93]

6. Release Response and the Handling of Oil Spill

The Regulations' oil and waste release response provisions are applicable to any person engaged in the transfer or storage of oil.[94] This includes, but is not limited to, owners and operators of oil-carrying vessels, terminals, reception facilities, oceangoing vessels, oil storage

[91] *Id.* §10(i).
[92] *Id.* §11.
[93] *Id.* §10(e).
[94] *Id.* §5.

tanks, and property at which an oil tank is located, as well as owners and operators of oil tanker trucks.[95]

The Regulations list the actions that must be taken when a release of oil occurs. For example, the oil transfer operation must immediately cease, containment and removal plans must be put into effect, and the incident must be reported to the appropriate authorities. Notification must be made to the DEM Division of Groundwater and Freshwater Wetlands or to the DEM Division of Enforcement, and to other appropriate local, state, and federal officials. Such officials may include the local fire chief, the Coast Guard, the Environmental Protection Agency, the Coastal Resources Management Council, and the National Response Center.[96] Within ten days following the incident, a written report must be made to the DEM that includes information such as the type of material released, the containment operations, and a description of the circumstances causing the release. The Regulations also prevent the use of chemical agents, dispersants, surface collecting agents,[97] biological additives,[98] burning agents,[99] or sinking agents[100] without the prior consent of the Chief of the DEM Division of Groundwater and Freshwater Wetlands.[101]

The Regulations outline the actions to be taken for the storage and removal of oil spill cleanup debris. Oil spill cleanup debris is defined as "waste resulting from the cleanup of oil debris caused by spilling, depositing, releasing or placing of oil onto the land or waters of the State of Rhode Island and, includes but is not limited to, soil, absorbent material, or any other material contaminated with oil."[102] The Regulations state that debris may only be stored when it meets particular storage restrictions, may only be removed from the site when it is in secured

[95] *Id.* §12(a).
[96] *Id.* §12(b).
[97] Surface collecting agents are defined as "those chemical agents that form a surface film to control the layer thickness of oil." *Id.* §5.
[98] Biological additives are defined as "microbiological cultures, enzymes, or nutrient additives that are deliberately introduced into an oil discharge for the specific purpose of encouraging biodegradation to mitigate the effects of the discharge." *Id.*
[99] Burning agents are defined as "those additives that, through physical or chemical means, improve the combustibility of the materials to which they are applied." *Id.*
[100] Sinking agents are defined as "those additives applied to oil discharges to sink floating pollutants below the water surface." *Id.*
[101] *Id.* §12(d).
[102] *Id.* §5.

drums or canisters or in a vehicle which is covered, and may only removed to certain facilities.[103] Within ten days of such removal, the owner or operator of the site must submit to the DEM documentation showing when the material was removed and to where it was removed. In the event of an oil release or if the DEM has reason to believe that a release has occurred, the DEM may require any person subject to these Regulations to initiate monitoring, remediation, and cleanup actions. These actions must continue until the oil release been remedied or mitigated. Discontinuance of actions is subject to the approval of the DEM.[104]

7. Spill Prevention and Emergency Plans

The requirements for the formulation of spill prevention and emergency plans are applicable to owners and operators of reception facilities, outdoor storage tanks and terminals. They are not applicable to tanks with a capacity of 500 gallons or less that store heating oil. Each facility subject to this provision must have readily available, on the premises, an emergency plan containing at least the following:

a. Up-to-date schematic diagrams showing the location of all outdoor tanks and piping used for the storage and conveyance of oil, including the location of all emergency shutoff valves;

b. A description of on-site emergency containment and cleanup equipment;

c. Description of off-site auxiliary emergency equipment that can be readily obtained, including a list of cleanup contractors to contact for such equipment;

d. Emergency telephone numbers of local, state and federal officials who should be contacted in case of an oil spill.

Upon the request of the DEM, the owner or operator of the facility must make these plans available for inspection and copying. Emergency plans or other similar spill

---

[103] These facilities are as follows: a. special facilities constructed within a licensed sanitary landfill; b. asphalt manufacturers or others that are licensed as solid waste management facilities and approved by DEM to accept Oil Spill Debris; or c. any out-of-state facility that will agree to take the material and that is allowed to accept the material by the state in which it is located. *Id.* §13.

[104] *Id.* §12(e).

prevention control plans required under federal or state requirements may be substituted for the plan required here, provided the plan contains, at a minimum, the four items listed above.[105]

8. Discharge to Reception Facilities

The Regulations require any owner or operator of a vessel which intends to transfer or discharge any shipboard oil to a reception facility to file with the DEM evidence of financial responsibility.[106] Evidence of financial responsibility includes a surety bond, letter of credit, certificate of insurance or corporate guarantee in the amount of at least $50,000 payable to the State of Rhode Island. The owner or operator of a reception facility must require the owner or operator of the vessel to produce such evidence of financial responsibility before accepting any shipboard oil. The money will be used to cover costs incurred by Rhode Island to rectify and clean up any damage to the environment and natural resources and any fines and penalties imposed by the State. The owner or operator still remains liable for any costs or fines exceeding the $50,000 amount. An amount greater than $50,000 may be required depending on the volume, location, and composition of the discharge, history of spills or noncompliance by the owner or operator, and other factors that may pose a threat to the environment.[107]

The owner or operator of a vessel also may be considered a generator of hazardous waste and, therefore, may be subject to Rhode Island hazardous waste regulations.[108]

9. Variances

An owner or operator of a facility may submit a written request to the DEM for a variance from some or all of the Regulations. The owner or operator must show by clear and convincing evidence that a variance should be granted because alternative design or operating standards are substantially equivalent to the Regulations and will have no adverse effect on the public health and/or the environment. The DEM may schedule a public hearing to solicit public comment prior to rendering a decision on the variance request. The DEM's decision on the variance request must be in writing and may impose appropriate requirements necessary to

[105] *Id.* §14.
[106] *Id.* §15.
[107] *Id.* §15(f).
[108] *Id.* §15(g). *See*, *infra*, Chapter V for discussion of Rhode Island hazardous waste regulations.

protect the public health and the environment. Any person affected by the grant or denial of a variance may petition for an adjudicatory hearing to review the initial decision.[109]

10. Penalties

Any person who violates the Regulations will be fined $25,000.00 for each day the violation occurs. Any person who is found guilty of violating, willfully or with criminal negligence, any Regulation will be punished by a fine of not more than $25,000.00, or by imprisonment for not more than five years, or both. A person is liable for a separate and distinct offense for each day during which the violation is repeated or continued.[110]

[109] *Id.* §16.
[110] *Id.* §18.

CHAPTER VIII:

REMEDIATION REGULATIONS

A. Operation and Enforcement

Pursuant to the Rules and Regulations for the Investigation and Remediation of Hazardous Material Releases (the "Regulations"), the Department of Environmental Management ("DEM") is responsible for the investigation and remediation of contamination resulting from releases of hazardous materials; the granting, denial, suspension or revocation of approvals and permits for remediation of that contamination; and the granting, denial, suspension, revocation or approval of the plans and specifications for the installation of any equipment for such remediation.[1]

The DEM Division of Site Remediation is the lead Division for reviewing and accepting information submitted pursuant to the Remediation Regulations. When the Division of Site Remediation becomes aware of an actual or potential release, the Division may inspect and/or investigate the subject area in order to determine its compliance and the necessity for response actions. The Division may inform known responsible parties of their obligations under the Regulations through the issuance of a Letter of Responsibility. Failure to meet the obligations imposed by the Regulations may result in the issuance of enforcement actions including Notices of Violation and Immediate Compliance Orders or the filing of a civil action. Furthermore, these enforcement actions are not exclusive remedies and may also include the assessment of administrative penalties or criminal sanctions.[2]

At the point in the process when the DEM determines that no further action is necessary, the site will be determined to be compliant and a Letter of Compliance will be issued.[3]

B. Prohibitions

No person may release any hazardous material in any manner which may impact the classification or uses of the land, ground water or surface water without complying with all applicable rules and regulations.[4]

---

[1] Rules and Regulations for the Investigation and Remediation of Hazardous Material Releases. §1.03.
[2] *Id.* §2.02
[3] *Id.*
[4] *Id.* §4.01.

Any responsible party[5] who discovers or is notified of the potential unpermitted disposal, release or presence of hazardous materials released from, present on, or originating from its operating or property must immediately initiate investigations and actions as specified by the Regulations.[6]

In addition, for purposes of enforcing the Regulations, the DEM may:

1. Enter any place the DEM has reason to believe hazardous materials are generated, used, stored, treated, or disposed of, and which may have contributed to a release;

2. Inspect any site, material, vessel or transport vehicle that the DEM has reason to believe is associated with a release of hazardous material;

3. Obtain samples of any material, from any vessel or transport vehicle or site, which the DEM has reason to believe was released, is or was contaminated by a release, or is otherwise associated with a release, of hazardous material; and

4. Inspect and copy records, reports, information, or test results kept or maintained at any place, on any vessel or transport vehicle that the DEM has reason to believe is associated with a release of hazardous material.[7]

C. Notification

The responsible party must notify the DEM, in writing, of all releases of hazardous materials not previously reported by any responsible party. Notifications must be submitted no later than 15 days after the discovery of the release, including any release of hazardous material from a source area discovered subsequent to the promulgation of the Regulations.[8]

---

[5] Responsible party is defined as: a) the owner or operator of a vessel, transport vehicle, or a site at which there is a known or suspected release; b) any person who, at the time of storage or disposal of any hazardous material, owned or operated a site at which there is a known or suspected release; c) any person who, by contract, agreement, or otherwise directly or indirectly, arranged for the disposal of hazardous material at a site at which there has been a known or suspected release; d) any person who, directly or indirectly, transported any hazardous waste to a storage, disposal or treatment facility, vessel, transport vehicle or site at which there is a known or suspected release; e) any person who otherwise caused or is legally responsible of a release of hazardous material from vessel, transport vehicle, or operation at a site; f) the person or legal entity controlling a site, transport vehicle or activity that contains or led to a known or suspected release; g) is now listed under those who are not responsible parties and shall not be held liable for losses or damages associated with a release of hazardous chemicals; h) "Responsible party" also means any and all combinations of the above mentioned person(s). *Id.* §3.60.

[6] *Id.* §4.02.

[7] *Id.* §4.04.

[8] *Id.* §5.01. The Regulations were promulgated on March 31, 1993 and were amended in 1996.

In addition, upon discovery or identification of a release of hazardous material on the site or directly resulting from activities at the site, the responsible party must immediately evaluate the release and determine if it poses an Imminent Hazard.[9] If the release is determined to be an Imminent Hazard, the responsible party must immediately notify the DEM. Notification may be made by telephone with written notification following no later than forty-eight hours after the time of the discovery of the release.[10]

In cases where notification is required, the written notification of a source area and/or release of hazardous material must include, but not necessarily be limited to, the following information:

1. The names, addresses, and telephone numbers of: the person notifying the DEM of the release; the owner(s) and operator(s) of any properties impacted by the release of the vessel where the release has occurred; any other responsible parties; and the contact person at the impacted area or vessel where the release has occurred;

2. The city/town, street address, legal description (plat and lot) and the general location of the area impacted by the release;

3. The date of and the circumstances leading to and surrounding the discovery of the release;

4. An identification of the hazardous material released, the approximate concentrations of hazardous substances in the released material and the approximate quantity of the hazardous material released;

[9] Imminent Hazard means a release of hazardous material that meets any of the following criteria: a) the release poses an immediate and substantial threat or risk of acute or chronic adverse affect on human health; b) the release poses a threat or risk of harm which could cause immediate destruction or significant adverse impact on an environmentally sensitive area or the contamination of a wellhead protection area or other drinking water source; c) the release poses an immediate threat of fire or explosion. Further factors to consider when evaluating releases resulting in a threat of fire and explosion shall include: i) the ignitability of the hazardous material, and the mixture resulting from the release of the hazardous material; ii) the reactivity of the hazardous material, and the mixture resulting from the release of the hazardous material; iii) the potential compatibility of the hazardous material, and the mixture resulting from the release of the hazardous material, with other materials which can be reasonably be expected to be stored or handled in the area of the release; and iv) the potential impacts of a fire and/or explosion; and d) the release may be influenced by site-specific factors which have the potential to lead to an imminent threat to human health and the environment. The Regulations *Id.* §3.31.

[10] *Id.* §6.04.

5. An initial estimate of the source of the release and the extent of the contamination resulting from the release;

6. Measures taken or proposed to be taken in response to the release as of the time of notification;

7. Any other relevant information relating to the potential for environmental impacts and other factors evaluated in determining whether or not the release presents an imminent hazard including, but not limited to: (1) whether the release of hazardous material has the potential to adversely impact any wetland or surface water; and (2) whether the extent of hazardous material contamination in soil or groundwater is within 500 feet of a surface water or wetland;

8. A determination as to whether the release impacts an area utilized for residential activity, industrial commercial activity, or both;

9. An identification of the underlying groundwater classification, and if the classification is GB, the distance to the nearest GA/GAA area; and

10. An indication of whether the background consistent with Rule 8.06 (Background Concentrations for Soil) will be performed and submitted subsequent to notification.[11]

D. Emergency Response

In the case of a hazardous material release, the responsible party must immediately take appropriate action to stop or minimize a release posing an imminent hazard and/or any ongoing spill of hazardous material at the time of discovery. However, all Emergency Response Actions undertaken by the responsible party must be conducted in a manner which is protective of human health and the environment. Furthermore, no Emergency Response Action undertaken by the responsible party may be conducted in a manner which increases the potential for harm, either short term or long term, to human health or the environment.[12]

[11] *Id.* §5.02.
[12] *Id.* §6.01.

All Emergency Response Actions which include the treatment of hazardous material or of substances contaminated by a release of hazardous material must be approved by the DEM prior to initiation.[13] In addition, the duration of Emergency Response Actions involving the treatment of hazardous material will be determined on an incident-specific basis by the DEM. However, the duration of any portion of an approved Emergency Response Action involving hazardous waste treatment is limited to less than twenty four (24) hours from the time of discovery of the release.[14]

In cases where onsite treatment of hazardous waste is necessary to remove the imminent hazard, and it is anticipated to take longer than twenty four hours, responsible parties must obtain an Emergency Permit prior to initiating the treatment actions proposed as part of that response. Application for an Emergency Permit may be made orally with written application following no later than forty eight (48) hours after the discovery of the release. Emergency Permit applications must include the manner and location of all proposed treatment operations. Emergency Permits may be granted orally with a written permit subsequently issued.[15]

Emergency Permits shall not exceed ninety (90) days in duration,[16] and all Emergency Permits will be accompanied by a public notice published in a local newspaper of largest regional circulation. The responsible party will write that notice in a block ad format and be responsible for its publication. A final copy of the public notice must be submitted and approved by the DEM prior to publication. The notice must be published within ten (10) days of the release. The notice must contain, at a minimum, the following information:

1. The name and address of the responsible party receiving the permit;
2. A brief description of the wastes involved;
3. A brief description of the treatment action and/or other actions authorized by the permit;
4. The name and address of the permitting agency; and
5. The duration and effective dates of the permit.[17]

---

[13] *Id.* §6.02.
[14] *Id.* §6.03.
[15] *Id.* §6.04.
[16] *Id.* §6.05.
[17] *Id.* §6.06.

Also, the DEM may order, via an Immediate Compliance Order or Order to Cease and Desist, the immediate cessation of any Emergency or Short Term Response Action without process if the DEM has reason to believe that the termination of that response action is necessary to protect human health or the environment. An order may also be issued if the DEM finds that the responsible party has not yet complied with the terms and conditions of an Emergency Permit or if the imminent hazard has not been removed.[18]

In all cases where an Emergency Response Action is initiated, the responsible party must, throughout the implementation of that action, monitor and evaluate the performance, effectiveness and completeness of the action in abating, preventing or eliminating contamination and, more specifically, the imminent hazard identified at the site. The DEM may require the submittal of progress reports on a specified schedule throughout the Emergency Response Action.[19]

Following the completion of any Emergency Response Action, the responsible party undertaking the action must prepare an Emergency Response Report providing a detailed summary of all investigations and activities taken in response to the release. This report must be submitted to the DEM within thirty (30) days of completion of the Emergency Response Action. The Emergency Response Report must contain, where applicable, at least the following information:

1. The basis for the determination that the release presented an imminent hazard;

2. The design specifications of any physical structures built or installed as part of the response;

3. A site plan showing the areal extent of the release and noting all treatment units, pertinent structures, areas, and/or other aspects of the release and Emergency Response Action;

[18] *Id*. §6.07.
[19] *Id*. §6.08.

4. Documentation of any off site migration of released material including notation of any factors, such as weather conditions, which may have caused or aggravated this migration;

5. The location of all samples, including those from monitoring activities, taken and the results of the analysis of those samples;

6. The manifests, receipts and/or bills of lading for any hazardous material or material contaminated by the release;

7. The nature, concentrations and extent of residual contamination. In cases where the responsible party considers the Emergency Response Action as the final remedy, it must demonstrate compliance with Section 8 (Risk Management); and

8. In cases where an Emergency Permit was issued, evidence that Public Notice was issued pursuant to the Regulations.[20]

The Emergency Response Report and all associated progress reports must include the following statements signed by an authorized representative of the party specified:

1. A statement signed by an authorized representative of the person who prepared the Emergency Response Report certifying the accuracy of the information contained in that report to the best of their knowledge; and

2. A statement signed by the party responsible for the submittal of the Emergency Response Report certifying that the report is a complete and accurate representation of the circumstances known about the release and the subsequent response activities to the best of their knowledge.[21]

E. Site Investigation

The DEM may require a performing party for any contaminated site to conduct, in a specified amount of time, an investigation of the contaminated site to adequately assess the

---

[20] *Id.* §6.09.
[21] *Id.* §6.10.

nature and extent of contamination, and to evaluate and design a proposed remedy. The DEM shall base the decision to require the investigation on the available information regarding the mobility, toxicity, and volume of the hazardous material released and the resultant potential for harm to human health or the environment.

The Site Investigation must determine the nature and extent of the contaminated site and the actual and potential impacts of the release. Remedial alternatives shall be considered and date generated during the Site Investigation must be in such a form and substance as to aid in the selection of a remedy for the contaminated site that is protective of both human health and the environment.

The scope of the Site Investigation shall be tailored to specific conditions and circumstances at the site under investigation using professional judgment. A later Remedial Investigation may be conducted in phases which may focus on specific releases, source areas, or exposure pathways.[22]

Upon formal written notification from the DEM that a Site Investigation is necessary, the performing party may develop, and submit to the DEM for review, guidance, and approval a Site Investigation Work Plan detailing the specific objectives of the Site Investigation, the date that is necessary to meet those objectives, and the methods which will be used to collect the data. Unless otherwise specified by the DEM, the submittal of the Site Investigation Work Plan is voluntary.[23]

The Regulations detail at length the information that must be contained in the Site Investigation Report.[24] Details on the requirements of periodic Progress Reports and for Public Notice are contained as well. [25] Upon completion of the Site Investigation Report, the Director shall issue a Remedial Decision Letter, identifying the preferred remedial alternative.[26]

F. Risk Management

---

[22] *Id.* §7.01 *et. seq.*
[23] *Id.* §7.02.
[24] *Id.* §§7.03-7.05, 7.08.
[25] *Id.* §§7.06, 7.07.
[26] *Id.* §7.09.

The appropriate remedial objectives for all hazardous substances in all impacted media at a contamination site shall be consistent with the Regulations[27] so as to manage the actual or potential risks to human health and the environment by ensuring that the requirements contained therein are met. These include Soil Objectives, Groundwater Objectives and Method 3 Remedial Objectives.[28]

Also, based on information provided in the Notification, Site Investigation, or any other source, if a release of hazardous materials has the potential to adversely impact an environmentally sensitive area, then the DEM may require the following, including but not limited to:

1. An Ecological Risk Assessment, conducted in accordance with EPA/630/R-92/001, February 1992, Framework for Ecological Risk Assessment, or functional equivalent. The Ecological Risk Assessment shall be conducted only after DEM review and approval of an Ecological Risk Assessment Workplan, and

2. An Ecological Risk Assessment Report, which proposes remedial objectives demonstrated to mitigate any risks to the impacted media identified in the Ecological Risk Assessment. Soil objectives which result from the Ecological Risk Assessment Report shall be considered Method 3 Soil Objectives.[29]

Requirements concerning Background Concentrations for Soil and Upper Concentration Limits in soil and groundwater are contained in the Regulations.[30]

Also, performing parties must institute environmental land usage restrictions for all properties subject to final decisions which result in levels of hazardous substances greater than those protective against direct exposure associated with residential land usage; or are subject to final decisions under a variance pursuant to the Regulations (Variances) relating to a remedial objective pursuant to these Regulations; or are subject to any final decisions based solely or in part on the limitation of reasonably foreseeable exposures to hazardous substances in any media.

---

[27] *Id.* §8.00 *et. seq.*
[28] *Id.* §§8.02-8.04.
[29] *Id.* §8.05.
[30] *Id.* §§8.06-8.07.

The owner(s) of a contaminated site shall document their concurrence with this restriction by entering an Environmental Land Usage Agreement with the DEM. This agreement, and the associated restrictions and controls shall be subject to approval by the DEM and shall include provisions to accomplish objectives contained in the Regulations.[31]

Finally, a contaminated site shall be considered by the DEM to be compliant with the Remediation Regulations when it is demonstrated that the appropriate remedial objectives have been met at all source areas within the contaminated site. The Regulations specify procedures for determining compliance with the appropriate soil and groundwater objectives applied to the contaminated site. Compliance procedures with all other remedial objectives shall be considered on a site specific basis.[32] All remedial objectives must be approved by the Director at one of two points in the site management process. These are: (1) Rule 7.04 (Development of Remedial Alternatives); or (2) Rule 9.02 (Remedial Objectives).[33]

G. Remedial Action Work Plan

The performing party for a site where remedial action is found to be necessary under the Regulations must prepare and submit to the DEM for review and approval a Remedial Action Work Plan documenting how the proposed remedial action will be implemented. The DEM shall base the decision to require remedial action on the information available on the mobility, toxicity and volume of the hazardous material released and the resulting potential for harm to human health and the environment.

The performing party may prepare and submit a limited Remedial Action Work Plan for interim or partial remedial actions. Limited or partial Remedial Action Work Plans must contain appropriate assurances that a more complete scope of activities will be evaluated as the contaminated site is investigated and characterized.[34]

The Remedial Action Work Plan must address the remedial objectives for <u>all</u> impacted media at the contaminated site including, as appropriate, the following:

---

[31] *Id.* §8.09.
[32] *Id.* §8.10.
[33] *Id.* §8.11.
[34] *Id.* §9.01.

a. Groundwater Objectives: The responsible party must propose a remedial objective for all hazardous materials found to have actual or potential impacts on groundwater. The groundwater objectives must meet the requirements of Rule 16.04 of the Groundwater Quality Regulations;

b. Surface Water and Sediment Objectives: The responsible party must propose a remedial objective for all hazardous materials found to have actual or potential impacts on surface water and/or sediments, that is consistent with the actual and potential uses of the surface water and/or sediment in the impacted area, and the policies and regulations of the Office of Water Resources;

c. Soil Objectives: The responsible party must propose a remedial objective for all hazardous materials found to have actual or potential impacts on soil, that is consistent with actual and potential uses of the land in the impacted area. The soil remedial objective must also take into account the potential for hazardous constituents to leach into groundwater and/or surface water from these impacted soils and, subsequently, should be consistent with the actual and potential uses of the groundwater and/or surface water in the impacted area and the policies and regulations of the appropriate regulatory authority for that resource;

d. Air Objectives: The responsible party must propose a remedial objective for all hazardous materials found to have actual or potential impacts on air quality, whether the impact is from gaseous or particulate emissions and/or entrainment on soil. The air remedial objective must be consistent with the requirements of the Rhode Island Clean Air Act and the rules and regulations promulgated pursuant thereto.[35]

The remedial objectives for each media should be expressed, wherever possible or appropriate, as a residual concentration of hazardous material or hazardous substance. Furthermore, the responsible party must estimate the time period necessary to meet all appropriate groundwater, surface water, sediment, soil and air objectives. In every case, a remedial action should be

[35] *Id.* §9.02.

designed, whenever practicable, as a permanent solution to meet the remedial objectives for hazardous substances in all affected media in the shortest time frame feasible.[36]

The Remedial Action Work Plan must clearly explain the proposed remedy and justify the ability of the remedy to meet the remedial objectives. For Remedial Plans that include on site treatment and/or containment of contaminated media, the performing party must demonstrate that best management practices will be followed to: (1) prevent the infiltration/migration of contaminants at levels harmful to human health or the environment; (2) prevent direct contact with hazardous substances at levels harmful to human health or the environment; (3) eliminate volatilization and entrainment of hazardous substances; (4) minimize and manage surface runoff from the area during the remedial action.[37]

Requirements for Remediation of Impacted Groundwater, Limited Design Investigation, Points of Compliance, Proposed Schedules for Remediation, Contractors and/or Consultants, Site Plans, Design Standards and Technical Specifications, Set-up Plans, Effluent Disposals, Contingency Plans, Operating Logs, Security Procedures, Shut Down, Closure, and Post-closure Requirements, Institutional Controls and Notices, and Compliance Determinations are contained in the Regulations.[38]

Finally, the Remedial Action Work Plan and all associated progress reports must include the following statements signed by an authorized representative of the party specified:

1. A statement signed by an authorized representative of the person who prepared the Remedial Action Work Plan certifying the accuracy of the information contained in that report to the best of their knowledge; and

2. A statement signed by an authorized representative of the performing party responsible for the submittal of the Remedial Action Work Plan certifying that the report is a complete and accurate representation of the contaminated site and the release and contains all known facts surrounding the release to the best of their knowledge.[39]

---

[36] *Id.*
[37] *Id.* §9.03.
[38] *Id.* §§9.04-9.18.
[39] *Id.* §9.19.

H. Remedial Action Approvals

The performing party must receive approval of the Remedial Action Work Plan from the DEM prior to initiating any activities contained therein. Remedial Action Approvals which include the treatment of hazardous waste at the site will be in the form of a Temporary Remedial Action Permit subject to the requirements and conditions of R.I. Gen. Laws §23-19.1-10.3, *Emergency and Temporary Permits*. The performing party must have a Temporary Remedial Action Permit throughout the period that hazardous waste is being treated.[40] In addition, approvals for Remedial Actions which include the remediation of impacted groundwater must obtain a Groundwater Quality Certification pursuant to the requirements of Section 17 of the *Groundwater Quality Regulations*.[41] The application and renewal fee for Remedial Action Approvals is one thousand ($1,000.00) dollars.[42]

The DEM may issue conditions to the Remedial Action Approval when the DEM finds that those conditions are necessary to protect human health and the environment. Conditions may include, but not necessarily be limited to, requirements that the responsible party provide financial assurances that the Remedial Action will continue.[43]

In addition, at least thirty (30) days prior to any change in ownership of the contaminated site or a change in operator of the Remedial Action, the responsible party must notify the DEM of the proposed change. Remedial Action Approvals will be voidable whenever there is a change in ownership of the contaminated site or a change in operator of the Remedial Action.[44]

The performing party must also apply to the DEM for approval of any modifications that the performing party finds necessary during the design, construction or implementation of the remedy. The DEM may require modification of a permit or approval if there is a reason to believe that the remedy is not working as anticipated or the DEM may require a new Remedial Action Work Plan in cases where the DEM determines that the proposed modifications substantially alter any process or the results of the remedy.[45]

---

[40] *Id.* §10.01.
[41] *Id.*
[42] *Id.* §10.02.
[43] *Id.* §10.01.
[44] *Id.* §10.03.
[45] *Id.* §10.04.

The DEM may order the immediate cessation of any remedial action whenever the DEM determines that a responsible party is not in compliance with all of the appropriate rules and regulations established by the DEM, or that the responsible party is not performing the remedial action in conformance with approved plans or conditions of a permit or approval. However, the DEM may, in lieu of revocation or suspension of the permit or approval issued to the performing party, order that performing party to take whatever corrective action is needed to secure compliance with the rules and regulations established by the DEM.[46]

These operational Requirements apply to performing parties conducting any remedial action activities.[47] The performing party must operate and maintain all portions, activities, and/or operations in accordance with all the terms and conditions of its Remedial Action Approval, and all other applicable laws and regulations.[48] The performing party must notify DEM immediately if it has any reason to believe any of the remedial objectives will not be met. Operating Records, Personnel Training programs, and Progress Reports all must be provided according to the Regulations.[49] Also, the performing party must dispose of all treated effluent, products, and/or byproducts from the proposed remedial action in the manner specified in the Remedial Action Approval and in compliance with any other applicable rules and regulations.[50]

The performing party must comply with all applicable Rules of the Rules and Regulations for Hazardous Waste Management for all hazardous waste shipments that they generate, and with the requirements of the Rules and Regulations for Solid Waste Management Facilities for all solid waste shipments that they initiate.[51] The performing party must maintain a contaminated site security program equivalent to that specified in the Remedial Action Approval.[52] Finally, the performing party must close the remedial action and maintain all post closure requirements as specified in the Remedial Action Approval.[53]

I. Variances and Extensions

---

[46] *Id.* §10.05.
[47] *Id.* §11.00 *et seq.*
[48] *Id.* §11.02.
[49] *Id.* §§11.03-11.05.
[50] *Id.* §11.06.
[51] *Id.* §11.07.
[52] *Id.* §11.08.
[53] *Id.* §11.09.

An applicant may apply to the DEM for a variance from or extension to any of the Regulations. The DEM may upon application issue a variance or an extension if the applicant presents substantial evidence which indicated that a variance or extension is needed to avoid undue hardship. The applicant must also, however, present substantial evidence that the issuance of a variance or extension:

1. Will provide protection to human health and the environment equivalent to that which is provided by the Regulations;

2. Will not endanger the public health and safety;

3. Will not result in exceedances of applicable remedial objectives as described in Section 8 (Risk Management) beyond the control of the performing party;

4. Will not significantly interfere with the public use and enjoyment of any recreational resource;

5. Will not significantly adversely impact any surface water or any groundwater, or cause contamination of any drinking water supply or tributary thereto; and

6. Will not violate any provisions of any pertinent federal or state statutes, rules or regulations regarding air, land or water resources.[54]

The DEM may also consider background conditions including, but not limited to, groundwater classification, contaminant migration pathways, mobility and toxicity of constituents of concern, volume of contamination, institutional controls and the resulting risk to human health and the environment. The Director reserves the right to limit the effective time period for a variance.[55]

J. Penalties and Appeals

Administrative penalties may be assessed for any violation of the Regulations. These penalties will be calculated based on the methodology specified in the DEM's *Rules and Regulations for the Assessment of Administrative Penalties*.[56]

[54] *Id.* §12.03.
[55] *Id.*
[56] *See infra* Chapter II.

In addition, any person affected by a decision of the DEM pursuant to the Regulations may, in accordance with the *Administrative Rules of Practice and Procedure* for the DEM, file a claim for an adjudicatory hearing to review the decision. The party appealing a DEM decision bears the burden of proving that they comply with the Regulations and that the denial by DEM was arbitrary and capricious or characterized by an abuse of discretion.[57]

[57] *Id.* §13.02.

CHAPTER IX:

WASTE RECYCLING

A. Rhode Island Recycling Act

Under the Rhode Island Recycling Act,[1] upon full implementation of the recycling program in Rhode Island, all solid waste from cities and towns and commercial establishments be separated into recyclable and non-recyclable components.[2]

B. Commercial and Non-Municipal Residential Solid Waste Reduction and Recycling Regulations

The Rules and Regulations for Reduction and Recycling of Commercial and Non-Municipal Residential Solid Waste (the "Regulations") apply to certain businesses that generate commercial solid waste and to managers of multi-unit housing facilities in which non-municipal residential solid waste is generated. A multi-unit housing facility is defined as a facility that has been designated "multi-unit" by the governing body of the municipality wherein it is located. The term "commercial solid waste" is defined as all solid waste, except hazardous waste and solid waste that is generated by residents of a municipality in the course of their daily living.[3] The Rhode Island Department of Environmental Management ("DEM"), in cooperation with the Solid Waste Management Corporation, is responsible for the administration of the commercial solid waste reduction and recycling program.

The Regulations require businesses employing 50 or more people, or any property owner or property manager employing 50 or more people, to complete a commercial solid waste reduction and recycling plan (a "Plan"). The Plan shall be consistent with DEM requirements, submitted to the DEM within 60 days of registering with the Rhode Island Department of Employment and Training.

In preparing a Plan, a business is required to include a waste audit, a description of the process by which recyclable materials are to be segregated, and a plan for the reduction of solid waste and recyclables generated.

---

[1] R.I. Gen. Laws §23-18.8-1 *et seq.*
[2] *Id.* §23-18.8-2.
[3] Rules and Regulations for Reduction and Recycling of Commercial and Non-Municipal Residential Solid Waste (the "Regulations") §§5(B), (1), (2).

The business shall be in compliance with an approved source reduction and recycling plan no later than 60 days after notice of Plan approval is issued by the DEM, unless the DEM shall specify a later time for compliance. Finally, by March 1 of each year, the business shall submit a report of recycling activity, covering the previous calendar year, to the DEM. Business or property owners/managers employing less than 50 employees will not be required to submit a plan or an annual report but shall be required to source separate recyclable materials pursuant to the Regulations.[4] All government agencies who generate commercial solid waste must meet the same requirements under the Regulations.[5]

C. Solid Waste Recycling Plans for Multi-Family Residential Units

The Regulations also require that managers of multi-family residential units submit Plans for the reduction and recycling of solid waste from residential complexes.[6]

The Plan must include: a waste audit; a detailed description of the process by which recyclable materials are to be segregated from waste; and the Plan for the reduction of total waste generated.[7] Managers of multi-unit housing should send a copy of their Plan to the recycling coordinator of the municipality in which the housing is located.[8]

A generator of non-municipal residential solid waste must comply with an approved plan no later than 60 days after approval is issued by the DEM, unless DEM specifies another date for compliance. The owner of multi-unit housing may petition the DEM for an extension of the compliance dates if he can demonstrate an inability to comply with the Regulations because of local zoning or unusual difficulties in providing for segregation and storage facilities. The responsibility for segregating recyclables lies with the owner of the multi-unit housing facility.

D. Solid Waste Management Facilities, Intermediate Processing Facilities, and Materials Recovery Facilities

The Regulations also provide specific requirements for solid waste management facilities, intermediate processing facilities, and materials recovery facilities. All such licensed

[4] *Id.* §8.
[5] *Id.* §9.
[6] *Id.* §10.
[7] *Id.* §10.
[8] *Id.*

facilities must submit a plan for processing recyclables from commercial and non-municipal residential solid waste received at the facility no later than 60 days after obtaining a license. No later than 60 days after approval by DEM, the facility must be in compliance with the Plan. Revisions of the Plan must be submitted to DEM for approval a minimum of 60 days prior to implementation.

No licensed solid waste management facility shall accept, for disposal, commercial solid waste containing greater than 20% recyclables by weight. By March 31 of each year, the facility must report to DEM the total amounts of each material segregated for recycling in the previous year, and the markets for these materials.[9]

E. Approval of Plans

The DEM will notify, in writing, all those who submit a Plan of the acceptance of the Plan, or the DEM will suggest revisions to the Plan.[10] Once a Plan is accepted the business or the manager of the multi-unit housing complex must comply with the Plan within 60 days, unless the DEM has specified otherwise.[11] Once an approved source reduction and recycling program is implemented, the business or government agency must report to the DEM on an annual basis, regarding those materials that have been segregated for recycling during the preceding year.[12]

F. List of Recyclables

Any person has the right to remove a material from the list of recyclables.[13] In removing a material from the list, the person must show that Rhode Island lacks the capacity to recycle the material, that identifying a market for the recyclable is too difficult, and no detrimental impact to the environment will occur if the material is removed from the list.[14]

G. Variances

Any person may request in writing a variance from these Regulations. The request must be submitted to the DEM, signed by the company president and accompanied by a comprehensive waste audit. The DEM will review the request and may enter or inspect any

---

[9] *Id.* §11.
[10] *Id.*
[11] *Id.*
[12] *Id.* §8(A)(3), 9(c).
[13] *Id.* §6.
[14] *Id.*

place the DEM has reason to believe is associated with the generation, segregation, storage, or disposal of solid waste. In addition, the DEM may inspect and copy any records associated with these activities. The DEM may hold a public hearing where substantial questions exist as to the environmental or public health impacts of such a variance. DEM may grant the variance if it is not contrary to the Regulations and serves the purposes of the Regulations by alternative methods.[15]

H. Enforcement

Any person who fails to meet the requirements of the Regulations by not submitting a Plan to the DEM will be subject to a fine of $1,000 for each day the Plan is late or not followed.[16] The DEM is required to send a notice to the alleged violator regarding the violation and penalty.[17] The person receiving the notice of violation must file a written statement within ten days of the receipt of the DEM's notice specifically responding to the allegation and requesting a hearing, if one is desired.[18] If the alleged violator fails to file a response within the ten day period, the alleged violator is considered to have waived his or her right to a hearing and the DEM's assessment of a fine will be final.[19]

---

[15] *Id.* §12
[16]-R.I. Gen. Laws §42-17.6-7.
[17] *Id.* §42-17.6-4(a).
[18] *Id.* §42-17.6-4(a).
[19] *Id.* §42-17.6-4(b).

CHAPTER X:

RIGHT-TO-KNOW ACTS

A. Hazardous Substances Right-To-Know Act

1. Applicability

Under the Hazardous Substances Right-To-Know Act (the "Act"),[1] an employer, who uses, transports, stores, or otherwise exposes its employees to toxic or hazardous substances must obtain, maintain, and make available in each workplace a list of all substances to which employees are or may be exposed. The term "employer" is defined as an individual, partner, association, corporation, business trust or any person or group of persons acting directly or indirectly in the interest of an employer in relation to an employee.[2]

Only employers, however, that use or store more than two gallons or ten pounds of: 1) a designated substance; 2) a mixture containing more than 1% of a designated substance; or 3) a mixture containing a carcinogen, mutagen or teratogen in amounts of 1 part per 10,000 or greater, are regulated by the Act.

The term "designated substance" means any substance that is listed as toxic or hazardous, provided the substance is in quantities exceeding two gallons or ten pounds in the workplace, except in the case of carcinogens, mutagens, or teratogens.[3] The term "hazardous substance" is any chemical substance listed in the latest edition of the chemical data section of the "Fire Protection Guide on Hazardous Materials" as published by the National Fire Protection Association.[4] A "toxic substance" is any chemical substance listed in the latest edition of "Threshold Limit Value For Chemical Substances In The Work Environment" as published by the American Conference of Governmental and Industrial Hygienists and the list of carcinogens as published by the International Agency for Research on Cancer.[5]

There are more than 1100 substances designated as hazardous on the official list maintained by the Rhode Island Department of Labor and Training, Occupational Safety Division, Right-to-Know Unit. Some of the more familiar substances listed are ammonia, carbon

---

[1] R.I. Gen. Laws § 28-21-1 *et seq.*
[2] *Id.* § 28-21-2(6).
[3] *Id.* § 28-21-2(3).
[4] *Id.* § 28-21-2(8).
[5] *Id.* § 28-21-2(13).

dioxide, chlorine, nitrogen, and sulfuric acid. Certain substances are excluded from coverage under the Act, including:

a. Any designated substance that is a food, drug, cosmetic, or tobacco product intended for consumption by employees while in the workplace;

b. Any consumer product and/or food stuff in its finished state packaged for distribution to and intended for retail sale to and use or consumption by the general public;

c. Hazardous or toxic substances being developed or used only in laboratories. "Laboratories" include all laboratories except those laboratories that provide quality control or other support to a manufacturing process, or laboratories that produce products for commercial purposes. However, when such hazardous or toxic substances in laboratories are excluded from coverage under the Act, the employer must still follow certain labeling, training, and informational protocol;

d. Any designated substance being transported by truck where such substances are regulated by the United States Department of Transportation under rules and regulations on hazardous substances;[6] and

e. Any materials removed in trash collection and any substances used in the processing of waste products.[7]

B. Duties of Employer

Every employer regulated under the Act is required to obtain, maintain, and make available in each workplace a list of all designated substances to which employees are or may be exposed. The list of designated substances must be made readily available to employees for examination during all hours of operation. A poster describing the rights of employees under the Act also must be placed in conspicuous locations in each workplace and be readily available to

[6] The United States Department of Transportation's Rules and Regulations on the transportation of hazardous substances are found in the Code of Federal Regulations.
[7] *Id.* § 28-21-11.

employees for examination during all hours of operation. This poster must have the following language: "For further information concerning your rights under the Hazardous Substances Right-to-Know Act, contact the Department of Labor and Training at (401) 462-8558".[8]

1. Chemical Identification List

Each regulated employer is required to obtain and maintain chemical identification lists with the following information on designated chemical substances:

a. The common and trade names of all designated substances present in the workplace in alphabetical order, cross referenced to their chemical names;

b. For mixtures, the list must contain the chemical and/or the trade names of any mixture that contains designated substances in amounts greater than 1% of a volume or more than two gallons or ten pounds within the workplace except in the case of carcinogens, mutagens, or teratogens which must be reported if they are present in amounts of 1 part per 10,000 by volume or greater.[9] The Department of Labor and Training may adopt more stringent standards pursuant to the Administrative Procedures Act.

2. Material Safety Data Sheets

In addition to providing a list of designated substances, employers must obtain a materials safety data sheet for each designated substance or mixture containing the substances.[10] The material safety data sheet is a detailed report of each substance's characteristics and effects and must conform with federal Occupational Safety and Health Administration Regulations.[11] If a manufacturer of a substance does not provide information about that substance to an employer who uses it, the employer may notify the Department of Labor and Training, and the Department of Labor and Training will request the information from the manufacturer. If the manufacturer does not comply with the Department's request for information on this substance within 90 days,

[8] *Id.* § 28-21-1.
[9] *Id.* § 28-21-3(a)
[10] *Id.* § 28-21-3(b)
[11] The Federal Occupational Safety and Health Administration Regulations are found in the Code of Federal Regulations, 29 CFR 1910,1200(g).

the Department of Labor and Training may prohibit the sale or distribution of that substance to any employer in Rhode Island.[12]

3. Training and Education Program

Prior to an employee's initial assignment, the employer must provide employee training and education programs to inform the employee about the designated substances to which he or she may be exposed. The training must include information on the nature of the hazards of the substance, appropriate work practices, protective measures and emergency procedures.[13] The employer must repeat this training annually for each employee. In addition, the employer must provide instructions whenever the employee may be routinely exposed to additional designated substances or to those substances which require special precautions, or whenever the employee's potential for exposure is increased. [Employers, however, do not have to provide training and education to the employees of any subcontractor of the employer. The employer, however, must provide the subcontractor with chemical identification lists and material safety data sheets for those substances to which the subcontractor's employees may be exposed.]

In addition, employers must have, in writing, an outline of their right to know training program, which must be made available, upon request, to employees, the local fire department, employee representatives, treating physicians, and the Department of Labor and Training.[14] The outline should include how the employer will notify employees of chemical hazards, nature of protective measures adopted for the worker's protection, nature of the Rhode Island Right-to-Know Law, and how labeling, lists and the MSDS program works.

4. Fire Safety

Employers must give their local fire department a list of the work areas where designated substances are present. Upon request by the fire department, employers also must provide material safety data sheets for each hazardous or toxic substance present in the workplace.[15] The person responsible for the administration and direction of a fire department in

[12] R.I. Gen. Laws § 28-21-3(c). In the case of a mixture, the manufacturer has 180 days to provide the material safety data sheet.
[13] *Id.* § 28-21-9(b).
[14] *Id.* § 28-21-9(d).
[15] *Id.* § 28-21-5.

a fire district or municipality, including a fire chief or fire administrator or that person's designee, shall maintain the preceding information and shall provide copies of the information 1) to fire suppression and fire inspection divisions within the same jurisdiction, and 2) upon request, to any fire department employee or an employee representative of a fire department employee. Finally, currently conducted fire safety inspections may include, at the discretion of the fire chief or the inspector, compliance with the employer notice requirements as enumerated in the Act.[16]

5. Access to Written Records

Chemical identification lists and/or material safety data sheets must be made available, upon request, to any affected employee within three working days of the request. If the Department of Labor and Training is informed of the failure of an employer to provide the information, the Department of Labor and Training, within seven days, will demand that the employer release the information within 24 hours. Each annual chemical identification list must be kept by the employer for a period of 30 years.[17]

6. Labeling Requirements

a. Generally

The employer must insure that each container of a designated substance in the workplace is labeled, tagged or marked with the following information:

1) Identity of the designated substance;
2) Hazard warnings; and
3) Name and address of the manufacturer or other responsible party who can provide additional information on the designated substance and appropriate emergency procedures, if necessary.

b. Stationary Containers

When stationery containers in a work area have similar contents and hazards, the employer may post signs and placards to convey the required information rather than affix labels to each individual container.

[16] *Id.* § 28-21-5.
[17] *Id.* § 28-21-6.

c. New Labels

The employer does not have to affix new labels to comply with the Act if existing labels already convey the necessary information.[18]

d. Portable Containers

The employer is not required to label portable containers into which designated substances are transferred from labeled containers and which are only intended for the immediate use of the employee who performs the transfer.[19]

e. Incoming Containers

The employer must not move or deface existing labels on incoming containers of designated substances unless the container is immediately marked with the required information.[20]

C. Trade Secrets

An employer may withhold the precise chemical name of a substance if it qualifies as a trade secret. A trade secret is "any formula, plan, pattern, process, production data, information, or compilation of information, which is not patented, which is known only to an employer and certain other individuals, and which is used in the fabrication and production of an article of trade or service, and which gives the employer possessing it a business advantage over competitors who do not possess it."[21] Employers must provide the Department of Labor and Training with basic information about the trade secret's generic chemical classification, properties, and effects, as contained in the material safety data sheet. The exact chemical name of a substance may not be withheld, however, if it is considered a carcinogen, mutagen, or teratogen by the Occupational Safety and Health Administration.[22]

D. Employee Rights

Under the Act, employees have various rights guaranteed to them. For instance, an employee may refuse to work with or be exposed to a designated substance or mixture if the

---

[18] *Id.* § 28-21-18(e).
[19] *Id.* § 28-21-18(f).
[20] *Id.* § 28-21-18(g).
[21] *Id.* § 28-21-10(b).
[22] *Id.* § 28-21-10(a)(2).

employee has requested from his or her other employer information about the designated substance or mixture and does not receive this information from the employer within three working days of the request. However, if the employer has invoked and complied with the procedures set forth in the Act, the time period of three (3) working days, not including weekends or holidays, shall be extended to equal any time period provided to the manufacturer or employer under the Act, or until the information has been received by the employer, whichever is sooner.[23] In addition, an employer may not discharge or otherwise discipline or discriminate against any employee because the employee has exercised his or her rights under the Act. An employer also may not request or require any employee to waive any rights under this Act.

An employee who has been discharged, disciplined, or otherwise discriminated against by his or her employer in violation of the Act may, within 180 days after the violation occurs or 90 days after the employee first obtains knowledge that a violation has occurred, commence an action in an appropriate court, alleging wrongful dismissal and violation of the Act. Furthermore, any employee may commence any action in an appropriate court to enforce an obligation, duty, or responsibility imposed upon him or her or the employer under the Act.[24]

E. Enforcement

Any person who intentionally violates any provision of the Act may be subject to a fine of not more than $5,000 for every day the violation exists. The Department of Labor and Training may impose the fines and enforce the collection of the fines by means of a civil action against the employer. In addition, for any violation of the Act, which is willful and intentional, and which is committed with disregard for the safety of employees, the responsible officer(s) of any offending employer may be guilty of a misdemeanor and may be imprisoned for a period not to exceed one year for each violation.[25]

F. The Hazardous Substances Community Right-To-Know Act

In Rhode Island, there is also a law on community right-to-know, entitled the Hazardous Substances Community Right-To-Know Act,[26] which provides a procedure by which Rhode

[23] *Id.* § 28-21-8(1).
[24] *Id.* § 28-21-8.
[25] *Id.* § 28-21-17.
[26] *Id.* § 23-24.4-1 *et seq.*

Island resident can discover which hazardous substances are used by employers in Rhode Island. Under the Act, any resident of Rhode Island has the right to make a reasonable request to the Department of Labor and Training for copies of lists of designated substances and material safety data sheets.[27] When a request is made, the Department of Labor and Training must request lists of designated substances and/or material safety data sheets from the employer, and the employer must submit such information to the Department of Labor and Training within 30 days of the receipt of the request.[28] An employer, however, is not required to submit information to the Department of Labor and Training if that information qualifies as a trade secret exemption, as discussed above.[29] Once the information is received, the Department of Labor and Training must make the material available to the resident within five days of obtaining the information from the employer and may impose a fee on the resident for each request. Any resident, who makes a reasonable request for data from the employer, and who does not receive the material within 90 days, has the right to take civil action against the employer and the Department of Labor and Training in order to receive that material and any relevant compensatory damages.[30]

Any employer who willfully, knowingly, and intentionally violates the Act is subject to a fine of not more than $100 for every day the violation exists. The Department of Labor and Training may impose fines and enforce the collection of the fines by means of a civil action against the employer and the responsible officers or agents of the employer.[31] Finally, if any provisions or parts of this Act or application thereof to any person or circumstance is held unconstitutional or otherwise invalid, the remaining provisions of the Act and the application of the provisions to other persons or circumstances other than those to which it is held invalid shall not be affected thereby.[32]

---

[27] *Id.* § 23-24.4-4(a).
[28] *Id.* § 23-24.4-5(a).
[29] *Id.* § 23-24.4-6.
[30] *Id.* § 23-24.4-8.
[31] *Id.* § 23-24.4-7.
[32] *Id.* § 23-24.4-9.

CHAPTER XI:

LAND USE REGULATIONS

A. The Coastal Resources Management Act

The Rhode Island General Assembly enacted the Coastal Resources Management Act (the "Act")[1] in 1971 for the purpose of preserving, protecting, developing, and restoring Rhode Island's coastal resources. The Act establishes the Coastal Resources Management Council (the "CRMC"), an independent regulatory agency, which is responsible for developing, implementing, and enforcing the comprehensive long-range programs and regulations for Rhode Island's coastal area.

1. CRMC's Jurisdiction

The CRMC's jurisdiction is defined by the area extending from the territorial sea, which is three miles offshore, to 200 feet inland from any coastal feature, such as coastal beaches, dunes, wetlands, cliffs, bluffs, embankments, rocky shores, and manmade shorelines.[2]

The CRMC regulates any construction project or alteration occurring in and along tidal waters, shoreline features, and the contiguous areas of Rhode Island, including the following:

a. Filling, removal, and grading of shoreline features;
b. Residential and recreational structures;
c. Commercial and industrial structures;
d. Mooring areas;
e. Marinas and launching ramps;
f. Residential docks, piers, and floats;
g. Municipal sewage and treatment facilities;
h. Individual sewage disposal systems;
i. Point source discharges;
j. Shoreline protection facilities;
k. Energy-related activities and structures;

[1] *See* Coastal Resources Management Act, R.I. Gen. Laws §46-23-1 *et seq*. (CRMC enabling legislation).

[2] Complete information concerning the CRMC's jurisdiction and application procedures is available in the State of Rhode Island Coastal Resources Management Program, the "Redbook"-(2002) [hereinafter CRMC Redbook], which is available from the CRMC, Oliver Stedman Government Center, Tower Hill Road, Wakefield, RI 02879.

l. Beach nourishment;

m. Dredging and dredged material disposal;

n. Filling in tidal waters;

o. Aquaculture;

p. Mining;

q. Mosquito control ditching;

r. Construction of public roads, bridges, parking lots, railroad lines, and airports;

s. Maintenance of structures.[3]

The CRMC Redbook (the "Redbook") defines the following six categories of waters which fall within the CRMC's jurisdiction and the actions that may or may not be taken in such waters:

Type 1 waters abut shorelines that are in a natural, undisturbed condition, where alterations, including the construction of docks and any dredging are not permitted;

Type 2 waters are adjacent to predominantly residential areas, where docks are acceptable, but more intense forms of development, such as marinas, are not permitted;

Type 3 waters are dominated by commercial facilities that support recreational boating. In Type 3 waters, marinas, boatyards, and associated activities are permitted, and dredging and shoreline alterations are expected;

Type 4 waters include the open waters of Narragansett Bay and the Sounds, where a balance must be maintained among fishing, recreational boating, and commercial traffic; and

Type 5 and Type 6 waters are those adjacent to ports and industrial waterfronts. In Type 5 waters, a mix of commercial and recreational activities must coexist, and in Type 6 waters, water-dependent industrial and commercial activities take precedence over all other activities.[4]

---

[3] *See CRMC Redbook*, §300 *et seq*. (Activities under Council Jurisdiction).

[4] *Id*. §200.1 *et seq*.

The Redbook also identifies 10 environmentally sensitive areas: tidal waters; beaches and dunes; undeveloped barrier beaches; moderately developed barrier beaches; developed barrier beaches; coastal wetlands, cliffs, bluffs, and coastal headlands; rocky shores, manmade shorelines; and areas of historical or archaeological significance.[5] In addition, the Redbook indicates whether a particular project or activity is prohibited in a designated water type and tidal area or, if the activity is permitted, which type of CRMC assent is required. The Redbook, for example, indicates that a residential structure in Type 1 waters or a conservation area is prohibited unless the area is a developed barrier beach. In developed barrier beach areas, a Category A permit is required for a residential structure.[6]

Inland activities occurring above the mean high water mark, which may impact the coastal region's environment, also fall within the CRMC's Jurisdiction. Examples of these activities include: energy generation; desalination plants; chemical and petroleum processing and storage; sewage treatment and disposal facilities; mineral extraction; shoreline protection facilities; solid waste disposal facilities; and coastal wetlands preservation.[7]

The CRMC also must approve subdivisions of six units or more and facilities requiring one acre or more of parking, which extend onto a shoreline feature or its contiguous area or which are located within the watershed of a poorly flushed estuary.[8] The CRMC also has responsibility for designating all public rights-of-way to the State's tidal areas.[9]

2. CRMC Permitting System

The CRMC must issue an assent, which is basically a permit, for any construction or alteration[10] in the coastal region or tidal waters of Rhode Island if: such work will occur within, above, or beneath the mean high water mark or otherwise within the CRMC's jurisdiction; has a reasonable probability of conflicting with any CRMC regulation; or has the

---

[5] *Id.* §210 *et seq.*, 220.
[6] *Id.* Tbl. 1.
[7] *See* R.I. Gen. Laws §46-236-6(B)(2) (Implementation).
[8] CRMC Redbook §100.3.
[9] *See* R.I. Gen. Laws §46-236-6(5)(E)(1) (rights-of-way). In addition, the CRMC has developed "special area management plans" which provide for more extensive regulation of certain coastal areas in Rhode Island. For example, there is a "special area management plan" for Providence Harbor.
[10] CRMC Redbook §100.1.

potential to make any area unsuitable for use or significantly damage the coastal region's environment. Assents may contain requirements for setbacks and buffer zones.[11]

a. Applying for CRMC Assents

1) Preliminary Determination Forms

A person may complete and submit to the CRMC a preliminary determination form to determine the need for a CRMC assent, as well as to identify the particular type of application required.[12] The CRMC reviews the information on this form to consider whether the project is within its jurisdiction and, if so, whether the application falls into Category A or Category B. These Categories are discussed below. Although not all projects require preliminary determination forms, such forms are helpful because they provide the applicant with guidance for complicated jobs or those in which CRMC's jurisdiction is not immediately clear.

2. Finding of No Significant Impact

Certain construction and alteration activities, such as the construction of attached decks, dormers, porches, second story additions, flag poles, and fences, within 200 feet of the coastal feature, frequently are found to pose little impact or threat to coastal resources and do not warrant full CRMC staff review. After a preliminary review of a proposed activity or upon staff recommendation, the Executive Director of CRMC may determine that the proposed activity will be an insignificant threat to coastal resources and approve such activity. In this case, CRMC will make a finding of no significance impact, inform the applicant of the decision, put limits on authorized work, and set a time frame in which the work is to be completed.[13]

3. Category A Applications

The CRMC assigns an application to one of two categories, depending upon the nature and location of the project. If the proposed project does not qualify for a finding of no significant impact, the project may fall under a Category A Application. Category A projects are routine in nature, meet all CRMC regulations, include proof of compliance with all applicable federal, state and local regulations, and raise no substantive

---

[11] *See* R.I. Gen. Laws §46-23-6(B).
[12] See CRMC's website: http://www.crmc.state.ri.us.
[13] *CRMC Redbook* §11.04.

objections from abutting landowners of those Category A applications sent out to public notice or CRMC personnel, and the Executive Director has not made a determination that the Category A activity in question is more appropriately reviewed as a Category B activity.[14] Category A assents generally do not require review by the full Council and are usually granted more quickly than those in Category B. If substantive objections are raised by abutting landowners or CRMC personnel against a Category A application, review by the full Council and public notice may occur.

4. Category B Applications

The CRMC assigns some applications to Category B, depending upon their size, location with respect to coastal features, commercial nature, or need for a variance or special exception.[15] Category B applications must be reviewed by the full Council, and formal notice of the request is usually provided to all interested parties once completed forms for a Category B application have been filed with CRMC.

b. Application Materials

In addition, all persons applying for a Category B assent are required to describe the boundaries of the coastal waters and land area which will be affected by the proposed project, demonstrate the need for the proposed activity or alteration, and prove compliance with all applicable zoning ordinances, building codes, flood hazard standards, safety codes, fire codes, and any other environmental requirements.[16] Furthermore, a Category B applicant must describe the potential impact of the project on the following: erosion and deposition processes along the shore; abundance and diversity of plant and animal life; water circulation, flushing, turbidity, and sedimentation; public access to the shore; and areas of historical and archaeological significance.[17]

Category B applications also must demonstrate that there will be no significant deterioration of water quality in the immediate vicinity of the proposed project, indicate measures which will be taken to minimize any adverse scenic impacts, and describe potential

---

[14] *Id.* §11.01.
[15] *Id.* §11.02.
[16] *CRMC Redbook* §300.1.
[17] *Id.*

conflicts with water dependent uses, such as recreational boating, fishing, swimming, navigation, and commerce.[18]

c. CRMC Review Process

The CRMC begins its formal review process upon receipt of a completed application.[19] Category A projects are reviewed by the CRMC's Executive Director and staff.

Category B applications also undergo review by the CRMC Executive Director and staff and, then, public notice is sent to interested individuals or groups, municipal offices, the Department of Environmental Management's Division of Water Resources and Office of Environmental Coordination, and any interested federal agencies or other parties. There is a 30 day comment period during which the CRMC staff or any other party may submit reports and comments for review by the full Council.

With respect to a Category B application, a public hearing may be scheduled at the request of four or more members of CRMC, or if any person has one or more substantive objections to the project.

Examples of substantive objections are: the proposed activity threatens direct loss of property, property values, or other tangible assets at the site in question; the proposed activity has the potential for significant adverse impacts on the coastal environment, biological communities, areas of historic and archaeological significance, recreational values, water quality, public access to and along the shore, and flood hazards; or evidence that the proposed activity or alteration does not conform to state or duly adopted municipal development plans, ordinances, regulations, or the CRMC Redbook requirements.[20]

If a substantive objection or request for a hearing is received in regard to a proposed Category B activity, a CRMC subcommittee will hold a hearing. The Council then reviews the hearing record, the subcommittee recommendation, and any new evidence presented to the full Council hearing before issuing or denying an assent. Applicants or objectors may

---

[18] *Id.*

[19] *Id.* Part 1 (Authorities Procedures).

[20] *See CRMC Redbook*, §110.3 (substantive objections).

request judicial review within 30 days after the Council's decision if they disagree with the Council's decision.[21]

d. Variances and Special Exceptions

In addition, the CRMC regulations provide for variances from a CRMC standard if the applicant demonstrates to the Council that the following five criteria are met:

1. The proposed alteration conforms with the goals and policies of the CRMC;

2 The proposed alteration will not result in significant adverse environmental impacts or use conflicts;

3. Due to conditions at the site in question, the standard will cause the applicant undue hardship;

4. The modification requested by the applicant is the minimum necessary to relieve the undue hardship; and

5. The undue hardship is not the result of any prior action of the applicant.[22]

The CRMC regulations also allow special exceptions for prohibited activities that do not conform with the CRMC's goals and policies. There are specific requirements to qualify for a special extension such as: the proposed activity serves a compelling public purpose which provides benefits to the public as a whole, as opposed to individual or private interests, like a utility, energy, communication, or transportation facility; all environmental impacts will be minimized; and there are no reasonable alternatives to the proposed activity. In the case of a special exception, the CRMC will hold a public hearing.[23]

---

[21] CRMC Management procedures §§5-13.
[22] *CRMC Redbook* §120.
[23] *Id.* §130.

3. Enforcement

Any alteration or construction undertaken without a CRMC assent or any activity that is not in conformance with an assent is considered to be a violation of the Act.[24] The CRMC has the authority to issue notices of violation, or cease and desist orders, and to order restoration of the site.[25] The CRMC may file a formal complaint for failure to comply with a CRMC order. There is no statute of limitations on violations and, therefore, a person may be ordered to restore a site months or even years after completion of a project that violates CRMC regulations.

The CRMC may assess fines against any person, who is guilty of a violation, of up to $1,000 for each violation and an additional penalty of not more than $100 for each day during which the violation continues after receipt of a cease and desist order from CRMC.[26] The aggregate penalty can not exceed $5,000. The CRMC must notify the property owner or person committing the violation, by certified mail or personal service, that a penalty is being assessed.[27] The notice must include: a reference to the section of the law, rule, regulation, assent, order, or permit being violated; a concise statement of the facts alleged to constitute the violation; a statement of the amount of the administrative penalty assessed; and a statement of the party's right to an administrative hearing.[28] The party has 21 days from receipt of the notice within which to deliver to the CRMC a written request for a hearing, and such request shall specify the grounds for contesting the notice.[29] If no hearing is requested within the 21 day period, the CRMC will issue a final order assessing the penalty and enforcing the CRMC requirements as specified in the notice.[30]

In addition, any person who knowingly violates any provision of the Act or any CRMC assent, order, or regulation is guilty of a misdemeanor and may be fined up to $500 per day or imprisoned for as long as three months, or both.[31] Each day the violation continues constitutes a separate offense and may be punished as such.[32]

---

[24] *Id.* §170.
[25] *See* R.I. Gen. Laws §46-23-7 (violations).
[26] *See Id.* §46-23-7.1 (administrative penalties).
[27] *Id.*
[28] *Id.*
[29] *Id.*
[30] *Id.*
[31] *See Id.* §46-23-7.3 (criminal penalties).
[32] *Id.*

B. Wetlands Regulation

1. Coastal Wetlands Program

A coastal wetland is a salt marsh bordering on the tidal waters of this state and those uplands directly associated with and contiguous to the wetlands which are necessary to preserve the integrity of the salt marsh.[33] Marshes contain one or more varieties of certain grasses or rushes,[34] and are rich in nutrients, plankton, shellfish, and other marine life. Coastal wetlands provide protection against tidal flooding. One of the purposes of the Coastal Resources Management Council is to preserve, protect, develop, and, where possible, restore the coastal wetlands of this state through comprehensive and coordinated long range planning and management designed to produce the maximum benefit for society.[35]

Responsibility for coastal wetland protection is shared by the Coastal Resources Management Council[36] and the Department of Environmental Management (the "DEM").[37] However, for a complete discussion of the regulation of coastal wetlands, please refer to the previous section on the Coastal Resources Management Council.

2. Freshwater Wetlands Program

A freshwater wetland is a broad term that may include rivers, river banks, floodplains, swamps, ponds, bogs, marshes and surrounding areas.[38] The term freshwater wetland may also include any area that is inundated or saturated by surface or groundwater at a frequency and duration sufficient to support a prevalence of vegetation typically adapted for life in saturated soil conditions.[39] The director of the DEM is authorized to identify and map freshwater wetlands in Rhode Island and forward survey results to individual cities and towns for public inspection.[40]

---

[33] *Id.* §46-23-6(8)(3)(e).
[34] *Id.*
[35] *Id.* §46-23-1(6).
[36] *See* R.I. Gen. Laws §46-23-1 *et seq.*
[37] *Id.* §46-23-10.
[38] Most of these terms carry minimum size and/or vegetation requirements. For example, a "pond" must be at least 1/4 acre in size, and a "marsh" must cover at least one acre and include such plants as cattails, pondweed, water-lilies and phragmites. R.I. Gen. Laws §2-1-20.2.
[39] Rules and Regulations Governing the Administration and Enforcement of the Freshwater Wetlands Act §5.40(b) (the "Rules").
[40] R.I. Gen. Laws §2-1-20.2.

Freshwater wetlands provide rich and diverse habitat for wildlife and are also important areas for recreation and flood control. Thus, the purpose of the freshwater wetlands program is to preserve, protect, and/or restore the purity and integrity of all freshwater wetlands of the State of Rhode Island.[41]

a. Prohibited Areas

Under the Act and the Rules and Regulations Governing the Administration and Enforcement of the Freshwater Wetlands Act (the "Rules"), no person, firm, industry, company, corporation, city, town, municipal or state agency, fire district, club, non profit agency, or other individual or group may excavate; drain, fill; place trash, garbage, sewage, road runoff, drainage ditch effluents, earth, rock, borrow, gravel, sand, clay, peat, or other materials or effluents upon; divert water flows into or out of; dike; dam; divert; clear; grade; construct in; add to or take from or otherwise change the character of any freshwater wetland in any way without first obtaining a permit from the DEM.[42] In addition to those projects or activities proposed either partially or wholly within freshwater wetlands, projects or activities taking place outside of freshwater wetlands which, due to their close proximity to wetlands or due to the size or nature of the project or activity will result in an alteration of the natural character of any freshwater wetland, require a permit from the DEM.[43]

Cities and towns, however, may undertake maintenance projects on existing reservoirs without acquiring a formal permit.[44] Also, normal farming activities, limited cutting or clearing of vegetation, limited maintenance activities, emergency environmental protection activities, site remediation projects, utility emergencies, fish and wildlife management/conservation activities, monitoring and research activities, and the use of temporary recreational structures may be "insignificant alterations" and may be exempt from the permitting provisions of the Act and the Rules.[45] The term "insignificant alteration" means a proposed alteration, limited in scope, area and/or duration, which appears to result in no more than a

[41] Rules §1.01.
[42] R.I. Gen. Laws §2-1-21.
[43] Rules §7.01(B).
[44] R.I. Gen. Laws §2-1-21(4).
[45] Rules §6.00 *et seq.*

minimal change or modification to the natural characteristics, functions, and/or values of any freshwater wetland, and is not random, unnecessary and/or undesirable.[46]

b. Permitting System

1. Preliminary Determination

The first step in the permitting process for a project, which may have even a slight impact on a freshwater wetland, is to file a Request for Preliminary Determination with the DEM.[47] A Request for Preliminary Determination may be submitted to: determine whether or not a specific proposed project constitutes a significant alteration, obtain a permit as an insignificant alteration, or obtain a determination of non jurisdiction. The DEM must make a decision on the Request for Preliminary Determination within 30 days.[48]

A list of requirements is provided with the application package which is available from the Freshwater Wetlands Division of the DEM.[49] Among other things, the Request for Preliminary Determination must contain a brief description of the project and the purpose of the project, along with a detailed site plan which must depict wetland edges, riverbanks, areas of land within 50 feet of any swamp, marsh, bog or pond, and proposed alterations to the property.[50] The DEM also may require site plans to outline floodplain effects, water quality and drainage characteristics. A registered engineer may prepare such plans. In addition, a fee is required with the Request for Preliminary Determination. The appropriate fee is determined as outlined in Rule 8.04 of the Regulations.

2. Permit to Alter a Wetland

If the DEM decides that a proposal represents a "significant alteration" of a wetland, the applicant must file an Application to Alter Freshwater Wetlands.[51] The term "significant alteration" means a proposed project which by its area, scope and/or duration, appears to represent more than a minimal change or modification to the natural characteristics, functions and/or values of any freshwater wetland; may be detrimental to the

46 *Id.* §5.43.
47 R.I. Gen. Laws §2-1-22(a).
48 *Id.*
49 Rules §8.01(A).
50 *Id.* Appendix 5.
51 *Id.* §9.05(A).

basic natural capabilities or values associated with any freshwater wetland; and/or appears to be random, unnecessary and/or undesirable.[52] There is a specific fee schedule for such applications. The fees, range from $300 to $7,500 for the application plus an additional fee per acre as outlined in the regulations, depending on the alteration proposed.[53] The applicant should expect the permit process to require four to six months, or longer, if a public hearing is necessary. Public hearings are generally held when the public raises substantive objections to the proposed alteration.[54]

An application to alter a freshwater wetland must include the overall project proposed or contemplated by the applicant. However, a request for partial review or review of a phase of any overall project may be considered by the DEM when:

a. The DEM has previously reviewed the overall project which allowed the DEM to contemplate full project impacts to freshwater wetlands; and/or

b. The DEM required, as a condition of prior determination, permit, or consent agreement/judgment, separate applications for individual portions of an overall project.[55]

Furthermore, the applicant must demonstrate through plans, evaluations and supporting documentation that the proposed project does not represent a random, unnecessary, and/or

[52] *Id.* §5.79.
[53] *Id.* §8.04.
[54] R.I. Gen. Laws §2-1-22(b).
[55] Rules §9.05(A)(2).

undesirable alteration of any freshwater wetland.[56]

Prior to the public notice of any application to alter, the DEM will review the application to determine whether or not it is a completed application for public notice purposes only. A completed application must include at least the following:

a. The original completed application form, all supporting documentation and appropriate application fee;

b. Where required, written notarized authorization from property owners who owned property containing freshwater wetlands that will be altered as a result of the proposed project;

c. Proof of ownership in the form of a current certified copy of the deed of the subject property;

d. A current list of the property owners whose property lies within two hundred feet (200') of the proposed project. This list must contain the current mailing address of each property owner and must be accompanied by a radius map drawn to scale of not less than one inch to one hundred feet (1"=100') showing the properties, lot numbers, and corresponding owners within two hundred (200') of the proposed wetland alteration;

e. Site Plans which accurately and clearly depict the project and provide, in the opinion of the Director, the correct location and extent of all wetlands within and near the proposed project area;

---

[56] *Id.* §9.05(A)(3). "Random Alteration" means any alteration for which the applicant does not specify in writing through design plans and drawings, the final developed use of the property upon which an application is predicated; or any alteration proposed which is arbitrary or without justification. Rules §5.66 "Undesirable Alteration" means any proposed activity or alteration which is likely to reduce or degrade any freshwater wetland functions and values as set forth in the Regulations. Any activity, alteration or proposed project will be considered "undesirable" unless the applicant shows that she or he has, to the maximum extent possible, mitigated for any damaging effects of the proposed project upon the functions and values provided by an freshwater wetlands. Rules §5.89. "Unnecessary Alteration" means any proposed alteration which is not essential, vital or indispensable to the proposed project and which can be achieved without altering or disturbing freshwater wetlands. Any activity, alteration, or project will be considered "unnecessary", unless the applicant shows that: a) alteration of freshwater wetlands and the function and values they provide have been avoided by exhausting all other non-wetland alternatives; and b) the alterations planned for the wetland functions and values from activities which could otherwise be avoided. Rules §5.90.

f. Following notification from the DEM, the required number of full size and reduced site plans, drawn to scale and legible, which are necessary to provide to the municipality, abutters, and other interested parties;

g. All supporting documents, studies, reports and information upon which the applicant, in his/her opinion, has based the proposed project in order to obtain a permit from the Director; and

h. Sufficient field reference markers and/or points on the property and the site plans which outline the limits of the proposed project area and sufficiently identifies the edge of all wetlands within the proposed project area in order for the DEM to properly complete its evaluation.[57]

Once an application has been determined complete for public notice purposes, no further information may be submitted by the applicant in support of the application unless such information is requested by the DEM.[58]

Within 14 days after the receipt of a completed application, as determined by the DEM, the Director will send a notice of the application to abutting landowners, local city or town representatives, and other interested parties.[59] A 45 day review period is allowed, during which time local governments may deny the permit.[60] Appeals may be brought in the superior court, but the DEM will not overturn a negative decision by the local government.[61] If a substantive objection to the proposal is raised during the 45 day period, a hearing must be scheduled. An applicant who wishes to schedule a hearing must make sure that the DEM receives written authorization and the appropriate fee within 30 days of the receipt of a substantive objection.[62] If written authorization and the appropriate fee are not received within the 30 day window then the DEM will consider the application withdrawn.[63]

---

[57] *Id.* §9.05(B)(1).
[58] *Id.* §9.05(B)(2).
[59] *Id.* §9.05(B)(4).
[60] R.I. Gen. Laws §2-1-21(2).
[61] *Id.*
[62] Rules §9.05(C)(4).

The DEM will then make a final determination on the permit application within six weeks of the close of the review period or the hearing date.[64] In making a final determination on alteration of a wetland, the DEM will consider whether the proposed alteration would result in a random, unnecessary, and/or undesirable alteration of a freshwater wetland.

If the DEM issues to the applicant a permit to alter a freshwater wetland, the applicant must, among other things, only proceed with the approved project in strict compliance with such terms and conditions, including time for completion, as the DEM may require to ensure the protection of freshwater wetlands and the functions and values they provide.[65] If, however, the DEM denies a permit to the applicant, the applicant may appeal the decision.

The applicant has 10 days to appeal the decision from the DEM. A request for an adjudicatory hearing must be in writing, must comply in form and content for such requests as required by the Administrative Rules of Practice and Procedure for the Administrative Adjudication Division (AAD) for Environmental Matters, and must be filed directly with the AAD. A copy of such request must also be forwarded to the Division of Freshwater Wetlands. In addition, a request for an adjudicatory hearing will not be considered timely filed unless accompanied by the full required fee.[66]

c. Compensation Clause

If the DEM or municipality denies a landowner a permit to alter a wetland, the landowner may petition the superior court to have the State or the local municipality acquire the land.[67] If the court determines that the proposed alteration would not injure the natural character of the land or the rights of others, it may direct the State or the municipality to purchase the land at fair market value.[68] If the State or municipality refuses to purchase the land, the landowner may proceed to alter the wetland as proposed.[69]

3. Enforcement

---

[63] *Id.*
[64] R.I. Gen. Laws §2-1-22.
[65] Rules §9.05(E)(3)(a).
[66] *Id.* §9.05(E)(4)(a).
[67] R.I. Gen. Laws §2-1-21(b).
[68] *Id.*
[69] *Id.*

The DEM has considerable power to enforce the provisions of the Act. For example, the DEM is authorized to inspect any site at a reasonable hour, without a warrant, if the DEM believes inspection is necessary to carry out its responsibilities under the Act.[70] In addition, as discussed below, the DEM may impose a variety of penalties on violators of the Act. Private citizens, however, do not have the power to enforce the substantive provisions of the Act.[71]

a. Restoration

Any person who alters a freshwater wetland without a permit may be ordered by the DEM to restore the wetland to its natural state.[72] Restoration orders are recorded in the local city or town in which the wetland is located. Subsequent owners of property with illegally altered wetlands are also subject to the DEM restoration orders.[73] If the restoration work is unsatisfactory, the DEM may hire a new person to complete the job.[74] The violator or subsequent owner will still be held liable for the complete cost of restoration.[75] In addition, the original violator may be fined $1,000.[76]

b. Other Civil and Criminal Penalties

In general, any person who violates the Act or the Rules and refuses to comply with a DEM order, such as a restoration order or a cease and desist order, may be fined up to $500 or imprisoned for up to 30 days, or both for each day the violation continues.[77] In addition, interference with site inspections conducted by DEM personnel carries a maximum fine of $100, or imprisonment of up to 30 days, or both.[78]

---

[70] *Id.* §2-1-10.3(a).
[71] *Citizens for Preservation of Waterman Lake v. Davis*, 420 A. 2d 53, 57 (1980).
[72] R.I. Gen. Laws §2-1-23 and §2-1-24.
[73] *Id.* §2-1-24(a).
[74] *Id.*
[75] *Id.*
[76] *Id.* §2-1-23.
[77] *Id.* §2-1-24(6).
[78] *Id.* §2-1-20.3(b).

CHAPTER XII:

MEDICAL WASTE REGULATIONS

A. Applicability of Regulations

The Rhode Island Department of Environmental Management's Rules and Regulations Governing the Generation, Transportation, Storage, Treatment, Management and Disposal of Regulated Medical Waste (the "Regulations") apply to all people who generate, transport, store, treat, manage and/or dispose of regulated medical waste. Furthermore, regulated medical waste becomes subject to the Regulations at the time and in the location that the material becomes waste, and shall remain subject to the Regulations until such time as the regulated medical waste has been both treated and destroyed.[1]

"Regulated Medical Waste" means a special category of solid waste that includes specific types of medical waste subject to the handling and tracking requirements of the Regulations. A regulated medical waste is any waste generated in the diagnosis (including testing and laboratory analysis), treatment, (e.g. provision of medical services), or immunization of human beings or animals, in research pertaining thereto, or in the preparation of human remains for burial or cremation, or in the production or testing of biologicals, or in the development of pharmaceuticals not otherwise excluded or exempted by the Regulations. Regulated medical wastes mixed with nonhazardous solid wastes shall be considered regulated medical wastes. For purposes of the Regulations, the following categories of medical wastes are regulated medical waste:

1. Cultures and Stocks: Cultures and stocks of infectious agents and associated biologicals, including: cultures from medical and pathological laboratories; cultures and stocks of infectious agents from research and industrial laboratories; wastes from the production of biologicals; discarded live and attenuated vaccines; and culture dishes and devices used to transfer, inoculate, and mix cultures;

2. Pathological Waste: Human pathological wastes, including tissues, organs, and body parts that are removed during surgery or autopsy, or other medical procedures (e.g., obstetrical procedures);

---

[1] The Rules and Regulations Governing the Generation, Transportation, Storage, Treatment, Management and Disposal of Regulated Medical Waste in Rhode Island §§2.02(a), (c).

3. Human Blood, Body Fluids and Blood Products:
    a. Liquid waste human blood or body fluids;
    b. Products of blood;
    c. Items saturated and/or dripping with human blood or body fluids;
    d. Items that were saturated and/or dripping with human blood or body fluids that are caked with dried human blood or body fluids; including, but not limited to, serum, plasma, and other blood components, and their containers (e.g., blood bags and blood vials) and body fluids as defined in Regulations; or
    e. Specimens of body fluids and their containers;

4. Sharps: Sharps that have been used in animal or human patient care or treatment, including sharps generated from the preparation of human and animal remains for burial or cremation, or in medical, research, or industrial laboratories, including but not limited to, hypodermic needles, syringes with or without the attached needle, pasteur pipettes, scalpel blades, blood vials, needles with attached tubing, glass carpules, and glass culture dishes regardless of the presence of infectious agents. Also included are other types of broken or unbroken glassware that have been used in animal or human patient care or treatment, such as used slides and cover slips. For the purposes of the Regulations, disposable syringes and needles are considered regulated medical waste after one use;

5. Animal Waste: Contaminated animal carcasses, body parts, and bedding of animals that were known to have been exposed to infectious agents during research, including veterinary hospitals, production of biologicals, or testing of pharmaceuticals;

6. Isolation Wastes: Biological waste and discarded materials contaminated with blood, excretion, exudates, or secretions from humans who are isolated to protect others from certain highly communicable diseases, or isolated animals known to be infected with highly communicable diseases;

7. Unused Sharps: Unused, discarded sharps as defined above in paragraph 4;

8. Spill/Cleanup Material: Any material collected during or resulting from the cleanup of a spill of regulated medical waste; and

9. Mixtures: Any waste which is a mixture of regulated medical waste and some other type of waste which neither radioactive nor a hazardous waste of a type other than regulated medical waste.[2]

However, medical waste that is mixed with hazardous waste, certain household medical wastes, certain incinerator ash and treatment/destruction residue, certain human remains, certain etiologic and certain enforcement samples are not subject to the Regulations.[3]

B. Identification and Segregation

Any person who generates medical waste within the State must determine if that waste is a regulated medical waste. Any wastes that contain regulated waste mixed with general solid waste shall be managed as regulated medical wastes. However, as mentioned above, any regulated medical wastes which meet the definition of "hazardous waste", or which are mixed with hazardous wastes shall be managed as hazardous waste in accordance with the most current DEM Rules and Regulations for Hazardous Waste Management.[4]

Once it has been determined that certain medical wastes are regulated, generators must then segregate the regulated medical wastes from the general waste stream to the maximum extent practicable to ensure the special handling and treatment required by the regulations. Separation from the general waste stream must occur at the point at which the regulated medical waste is generated. Specifically, generators shall segregate regulated medical wastes into the following groups:

1. Sharps and unused sharps, including sharps containing residual fluid;

2. Fluids in bulk quantities (quantities greater than twenty cubic centimeters (20cm)); and

3. Other regulated medical wastes.

---

[2] *Id.* §2.03.
[3] *Id.* §2.04.
[4] *Id.* §6.02(b).

In addition, regulated medical wastes shall be placed in suitable containers, according to the Packaging and Containment requirements, and if other solid waste is placed in the same container(s) as regulated medical waste, then the entire contents of the container(s) shall be managed as regulated medical waste. However, if a generator manages all solid waste as regulated medical waste, the identification and segregation requirements need not be met.[5] The entire solid waste stream of this generator shall be managed as regulated medical waste and must meet all remaining handling and managing requirements of the Regulations.

C. Packaging and Containment

Regulated medical waste must be properly packaged to assure effective containment throughout the handling, storage, transport and treatment process. In addition to the specific packaging and containment requirements for each category of regulated medical waste, the following general requirements need to be met before transporting or offering for transport such waste off-site or within the generating facility: (1) Generators must ensure that all regulated medical waste is placed in a container or containers that are rigid, leak resistant, impervious to moisture, of a strength sufficient to prevent tearing or bursting under normal conditions of use and handling, and sealed to prevent leakage during transport; (2) Materials for packaging shall be strong enough to remain intact during whatever type of handling, storage, and transport the container(s) may undergo; and (3) Mechanical compaction of regulated medical waste shall not be conducted prior to treatment and/or disposal, unless the mechanical compaction and treatment are part of a single, self contained process that does not place employees or the public at risk of exposure to untreated regulated medical waste.[6] Finally, generators must notify/train their employees involved with packaging and containing regulated medical waste through the use of a medical waste procedure manual and/or through appropriate training materials.

1. Packaging Requirements for Sharps

In addition to the general packaging and containment requirements, all sharps and unused sharps, including sharps with residual fluids, must be packaged in containers that are puncture-resistant. Any sharps placed into such a container cannot be manipulated inside the container and cannot be removed from the container under any circumstances. Furthermore, the sharps shall be placed directly into container without recapping, clipping, bending, or breaking

[5] *Id.* §6.03.
[6] *Id.* §7.01.

unless one of the following criteria are met: (1) The employer can demonstrate that the requirements of this section are not feasible for a specific medical procedure, or (2) such recapping or needle removal is accomplished through the use of a mechanical device or one handed technique specifically approved in writing by the DEM.

Additionally, sharps containers shall be assembled and utilized as intended by the manufacturer at all times while in use. Sharps containers with openings large enough to allow entry of any human hand shall also be subject to any additional physical and/or administrative controls necessary to prevent access by the public during normal conditions of use. Such containers shall be sealable in a manner that prevents spillage of contents during transport, and the container must identify the contents as regulated medical waste by displaying the Universal Biohazard Symbol on the outside of the container.[7]

2. Packaging Requirements for Fluids in Bulk Quantities

In addition to the general packaging and containment requirements for regulated medical wastes, human blood and blood products and body fluids in quantities greater than twenty cubic centimeters (20cm) must be packaged in containers that are break resistant and tightly lidded or stoppered. The container shall also identify the contents as regulated medical waste by displaying the Universal Biohazard Symbol on the outside of the container.[8]

3. Packaging and Containment Requirements for Other Regulated Medical Wastes

In addition to the general packaging and containment requirements, those regulated medical wastes which are not sharps or unused sharps or fluids in bulk quantities, including but not limited to, cultures and stocks, non liquid pathological wastes, non-liquid animal wastes, non liquid isolation wastes and materials saturated with blood, shall be packaged in either rigid containers that are designed to be tightly sealable in plastic bags that meet the following requirements.

a. The plastic bags shall be impervious to moisture and tear-resistant;

---

[7] *Id.* §7.02.
[8] *Id.* §7.03.

b. The plastic bags shall be a distinctive red or orange color, or clear. If a clear bag is used then the Universal Biohazard Symbol shall be appropriately displayed on the bag;

c. In order to allow the use of "single plastic bags", the bags shall be constructed of material of sufficient thickness strength to pass the 165-gram dropped dart impact resistance test as prescribed by the American Society for Testing and Materials Dart Test (ASTM Standard #D-1709-91) and certified by the manufacturer. Otherwise, "double bagging" is required.

d. A container used on-site to hold regulated medical waste shall have either a red or orange plastic bag plainly visible; or if a clear bag is used then the Universal Biohazard Symbol shall be displayed on the container as well as on the bag.[9]

D. Storage of Regulated Medical Wastes

The regulated medical waste shall be stored in a manner that prevents access by, and does not provide a food source for, insects, rodents, or other animals, and all wastes shall be stored in a manner and location which maintains the integrity of the packaging. In addition, on-site storage areas must be restricted to authorized personnel only, and the storage area must be clearly identified as containing regulated medical waste.

The regulations also require that the regulated medical waste be maintained in a nonputrescent state. Except as otherwise authorized, total storage of regulated medical waste cannot exceed fifty (50) pounds or the average quantity of regulated medical waste generated over five (5) consecutive calendar days, whichever condition allows storage for a longer period of time. Additionally, regulated medical waste may not be compacted, undergo grinding, or be subject to violent mechanical stress on-site unless the waste has been treated prior to compaction, grinding, or other mechanical stress; or, unless the compaction, grinding, or other mechanical

[9] *Id.* §7.04.

stress and the treatment are part of single self-contained process that does not place employees or the public at risk of exposure to untreated regulated medical waste.[10]

E. Decontamination Standards for Reusable Containers

Generators, transporters, intermediate handlers, and destination facility owners and operators shall comply with these requirements with respect to reusing containers. Generators shall notify in writing all employees involved with the decontamination of reusable containers for regulated medical wastes of the provisions of these regulations. This training/notification shall be accomplished through the use of a medical waste procedure manual and/or through appropriate training materials.[11]

All non-rigid packaging and inner liners used for packaging of medical waste shall be managed as regulated medical waste and shall not be reused.[12] Any container used for the storage and/or transport of regulated medical waste and designated for reuse once emptied, shall be decontaminated after each use. Decontamination can be accomplished by chemical disinfection, steam sterilization, thermal inactivation, or other suitable process that is suitable for both the type of container to be decontaminated and for the type of contamination present.[13] If any container used for the storage and/or transport of regulated medical waste is for any reason not capable of being rendered free of contamination in accordance with the requirements of these Regulations, the container shall be managed (i.e. labeled and treated and/or disposed of) as regulated medical waste.[14]

F. On-Site Transport of Regulated Medical Wastes

To ensure the safe transport of regulated medical wastes within the generating facility (on-site), generators shall comply with the following requirements:

1. The regulated medical waste shall be properly packaged to ensure containment of the waste and all containers and packages containing regulated medical wastes shall be sealed to prevent leakage or spillage while in transport.

---

[10] *Id.* §8.03.
[11] *Id.* §9.01.
[12] *Id.* §9.02(a).
[13] *Id.* §9.02(b).
[14] *Id.* §9.02(c).

2. The handling, transfer, and loading of packages and containers of regulated medical wastes shall be performed in a manner that does not destroy the integrity of the packaging.

3. Regulated medical waste shall not be subjected to violent mechanical stress during onsite transport.

4. Wheeled carts shall be used for the transport of packages or containers of regulated medical wastes if these packages or containers will be moved more than a short distance or if these containers or packages cannot be easily handled by one person (due to weight, size, shape, bulkiness, etc.) regardless of the distance to be moved.

5. Any regulated medical waste which is contained in plastic bags shall not be moved or transported in mechanical devices, dumbwaiters, or chutes, unless the chutes are designed to prevent accumulation of wastes in corners and edges and are lined with materials which can be easily cleaned (e.g. stainless steel).

6. Carts used for the transport of packages and containers of regulated medical wastes shall be sturdy and shall be routinely cleaned and disinfected, and immediately cleaned and disinfected after use if the cart has been contaminated by medical waste.

7. Items other than regulated medical waste shall not be placed in the same cart with regulated medical waste at any point during on-site transportation.

8. The compaction of packages and containers of regulated medical wastes prior to or during on-site transport is prohibited.

9. Generators will notify in writing all employees involved with the on-site transport of regulated medical wastes of the provisions in these Regulations. The training/notification shall be accomplished through the use of a medical waste procedure manual and/or through appropriate training materials.

G. Labeling and Marking Regulated Medical Waste for Off-Site Transport

All containers used for the packaging and containment of regulated medical wastes shall be labeled with the Universal Biohazard Symbol or shall be labeled as containing regulated medical waste. In addition, all packages or containers which will be transported or offered for transport off-site shall meet the same labeling marking requirements.

Generators must label each package or container of waste with a water-resistant label affixed to or printed on the outside of the container. The label should include the words "Medical Waste", or display the universal biohazard symbol. Red plastic bags used as inner packaging need not display a label.

Furthermore, generators and intermediate handlers must mark each package with indelible lettering on a water resistant identification tag of sufficient dimension and contain the following information: (1) the generator's or intermediate handler's name; (2) the generator's or intermediate handler's address; (3) the transporter's name (if applicable); (4) the transporter's Rhode Island Regulated Medical Waste Transporter Permit number (if applicable); (5) the date of shipment (date of off-site transport); and (6) identification of contents as medical waste. Each subsequent transporter must affix a water-resistant identification tag on the outside of the secondary container. Such tag must be at least three inches by five inches and must not obscure previously affixed identification tags. The new tag must indicate the name, address, business location, and Rhode Island Regulated Medical Waste Transporter Permit number of the transport affixing the tag and the date such transporter accepted the waste. In addition, if the generator has used inner containers, including sharps and fluid containers, each inner container must be marked with indelible ink or imprinted with water-resistant tags. The marking shall contain the following information: (1) generator's or intermediate handler's name; (2) generator's or intermediate handler's address; and (3) identification of the type of contents of container as "medical waste."[15]

H. On-Site Treatment and/or Destruction of Regulated Medical Waste

These requirements apply to generators of regulated medical waste that conduct on-site treatment and/or destruction of regulated medical waste, and to generators that accept regulated

---

[15] *Id.* §11.00 *et seq.*

medical waste for treatment and/or destruction. Generators that accept medical waste from other generators for treatment and/or destruction must apply for a license from the DEM Office of Waste Management. In addition, generators are also subject to the requirements of all applicable State solid waste and air emission regulations.[16] The Regulations also detail recordkeeping and reporting requirements for on-site incineration and they detail on–site steam sterilization standards.[17]Any method or process other than incineration or steam sterilization used by a generator for treatment and/or destruction of regulated medical waste on-site shall be approved by the DEM in accordance with the Regulations.[18]

I. Generator Requirements for Off-Site Transportation of Regulated Medical Waste

Generators who produce fifty (50) pounds or more of medical waste per calendar month must use transporters who have been issued a Rhode Island Regulated Medical Waste Transporter Permit. However, generators that produce less than fifty (50) pounds of regulated medical waste are classified as Small Quantity Generators. Certain Small Quantity Generators need not use a transporter who has been issued a Permit or use a tracking form.[19] In addition, under certain circumstances generators are exempt from the requirement to use transporters that have Rhode Island Regulated Medical Waste Transporter Permits when transporting regulated waste from the original generation point to a central collection point, or between satellite facilities. Furthermore, under certain circumstances, Small Quantity Generators who transport regulated waste (sharps and unused sharps) by the U.S. Postal Service and/or private courier service may be exempt from the requirement to use a transporter who has a Rhode Island Regulated Medical Waste Transporter Permit.[20] Small Quantity Generators who are not required to use Tracking Forms, must, however, maintain shipment logs and submit semi-annual reports to the DEM.[21]

Except as otherwise exempted, a generator that transports or offers for transport regulated medical waste for off-site treatment or disposal shall prepare a tracking form. Samples of the tracking form may be obtained from:

---

[16] *Id.* §12.01(c).
[17] *Id.* §§12.02-12.04.
[18] *Id.* §12.05.
[19] *Id.* §13.02(b)(1)-(3).
[20] *Id.* §13.02(d).
[21] *Id.* §13.07.

Rhode Island Department of Environmental Management
Office of Waste Management
135 Promenade Street
Providence, RI 02908-5767.

A generator is also required to prepare the number of tracking form copies that will provide himself, each transporter(s), and each intermediate handler with one copy, and the owner or operator of the destination facility with two copies. The generator is also required to (1) sign the certification statement on the tracking form by hand; (2) obtain the handwritten signature of the initial transporter and include the date of acceptance on the tracking form; and (3) retain one copy. However, for rail shipments within the United States that originate at the site of generation, the generator shall send at least three dated and signed copies of the tracking form to the next non-rail transporter, if any; or the intermediate handler or destination facility if transported solely by rail; or the last rail transporter to handle the waste in the United States if exported by rail.[22] Generators, including transporters and intermediate handlers that initiate tracking forms, which export regulated medical waste to a foreign country for treatment or destruction, or disposal, shall request the destination facility to provide written confirmation that the waste was received.[23] Each generator must also retain both the original generator receipt (yellow-copy 4) and the completed generator copy (white-copy 1) of each signed tracking form for at least three (3) years from the date the waste was accepted by the initial transporter. Generators that are exempt from using the Medical Waste Tracking Form must maintain a shipment log as required by the Regulations.[24]

In addition, a generator that is required to use a tracking form, or voluntarily initiates a tracking form should contact the owner or operator of the destination facility, transporter(s), and intermediate handler(s), as appropriate, to determine the status of any tracked waste if he does not receive a copy of the completed tracking form with the handwritten signature of the owner or operator of the destination facility within thirty-five (35) days of the date the waste was accepted by the initial transporter (45 days for generators exporting to a foreign country).[25] If the generator has not received a completed copy of the signed tracking form from the destination facility within forty-five (45) days of the date the waste was accepted by the initial transporter

[22] *Id.* §13.03.
[23] *Id.* §13.04.
[24] *Id.* §13.05(b).
[25] *Id.* §13.06(a).

then the generator must submit to the DEM an Exception Report.[26] The generator may also be required to submit a Discrepancy Report to the DEM if there are any discrepancies between the information contained on the original generator receipt and the signed/completed generator copy that are not documented in Block 23 of the Medical Waste Tracking Form.[27] The Regulations detail the requirements for both reports.

The Director of the DEM may also require generators to furnish additional information concerning the quantities and management methods of medical waste as deemed necessary under the Resource Conservation and Recovery Act, Section 11004.[28]

J. Transporter Requirements for Off-Site Transportation of Regulated Medical Waste

No person or legal entity may engage in the transportation of regulated medical waste in or on the land or waters of Rhode Island unless such person or entity has first been issued a permit by the DEM for this purpose.[29] In addition, transporters may not accept medical waste from a generator unless and until the generator has obtained a valid Regulated Medical Waste Generator Registration Number.[30] If the EPA adopts regulations requiring transporters to notify the EPA prior to transporting regulated medical waste, such transporters shall comply with these EPA requirements and obtain an EPA identification number prior to receiving a Rhode Island Medical Waste Transporter Permit, as described in the Regulations.[31]

To obtain a Regulated Medical Waste Transporter Permit, a transporter must submit an application on a form prescribed by the DEM. At a minimum, the application should include the following:

1. Name under which the application is being made;
2. Applicant's business location(s) and mailing address if different from business location(s);
3. Applicant's business phone number;

---

[26] *Id.* §13.06(b).
[27] *Id.* §13.06(c).
[28] *Id.* §13.08.
[29] *Id.* §14.01(a).
[30] *Id.* §14.01(e).
[31] *Id.* §14.02.

4. Name, address and phone number of the owner of the applicant company;

5. The name(s), address(es) and phone number(s) of the applicant's personnel who can be reached in case of an emergency;

6. The name(s) and signature(s) of all company personnel who are authorized to sign medical waste tracking forms;

7. The following information for each vehicle that may be used to transport regulated medical waste:

    a. the manufacturer;
    b. model;
    c. year of manufacture;
    d. vehicle identification number (VIN);
    e. cargo-carrying capacity;
    f. proof of ownership of each vehicle; and
    g. proof of current registration for each vehicle with the appropriate state motor vehicle agency;

8. The address of any transfer station(s) and/or vehicle parking area(s) used by the applicant for storing or parking vehicles;

9. Location(s) to be used for temporary storage of regulated medical waste in vehicles;

10. The specific location(s) and/or person(s) to which the transporter delivers or intends to deliver regulated medical waste, and a signed notarized statement from each person and/or location which certifies that said person/location is in compliance with all applicable licensing/permitting requirements for the jurisdiction(s) to which regulated medical waste will be transported;

11. A copy of the applicant's Spill Management Plan;

12. The permit fee specified by the Regulations;

13. The signature of the applicant or a person duly authorized to act on behalf of the applicant; and

14. Any other information reasonably required by the DEM to demonstrate that the applicant can safely transport regulated medical waste and comply with all applicable provisions of the Regulations.[32]

In addition, a permit fee of one hundred dollars ($100) per vehicle identified on the permit application is required. Furthermore, an annual inspection fee of ($100) per vehicle is required, and the holder of the Permit is required to maintain liability insurance sufficient to provide coverage of one million dollars ($1,000,000) per incident involving the transport of regulated medical waste.[33]

A transporter who has been issued a Regulated Medical Waste Transporter Permit shall notify the DEM in writing of any changes in the information required by the permit application no later than five (5) business days after the effective date of the changes.[34] Requirements of vehicles that will be used to transport regulated medical waste in Rhode Island are listed in the Regulations.[35] Also, each such vehicle shall be inspected by the DEM to demonstrate compliance with all applicable requirements of these Regulations.[36]

Transporters, intermediate handlers and destruction facilities must adopt and adhere to a written procedure developed by the transporter and approved by the DEM, to govern the management and decontamination of regulated medical waste spills. All person required to develop a written procedure must also keep at each site, including each vehicle used to transport medical waste, appropriate equipment and supplies for cleaning up a spill of regulated medical waste.[37]

In the event of a spill of regulated medical waste by the transporter, the transporter shall notify the DEM immediately of the spill. In all cases of spills, the transporter shall immediately take steps to contain and clean up the regulated medical waste. In addition, the transporter must

[32] *Id.* §14.03(b).
[33] *Id.* §14.03(f), (g).
[34] *Id.* §14.03(c).
[35] *Id.* §14.03(d).
[36] *Id.* §14.03(e).
[37] *Id.* §14.08(a), (b).

submit an accident report to the DEM within forty-eight (48) hours of a spill. A copy of the report should be kept on file for a minimum of three (3) years at the same location as the Regulated Medical Waste Transporter Permit. The three (3) year period for retention will start on the date of the report. However, record retention periods may be extended during the course of unresolved litigation, or when so requested by the DEM or by EPA.[38]

The Regulations also contain detailed requirements for vehicles, the accepting of medical waste, the use of a tracking form, rail shipments, reporting, the delivery of medical waste and recordkeeping.

K. Treatment, Destruction and Destination Facilities

A treatment, destruction, or destination facility may not accept regulated medical waste which is not packaged, labeled and marked in accordance with the Regulations and which is unaccompanied by a valid tracking form. In addition, these facilities are required to keep a spill containment and cleanup kit in or near any storage area, loading and unloading area, decontamination area, and treatment area where regulated medical waste is managed. The kit shall consist of at least the following:

(1) absorbent material for spilled liquids with a rated capacity of one gallon per every cubic foot of regulated medical waste normally managed or ten gallons, whichever is less;

(2) one gallon of hospital grade disinfectant in a sprayer, capable of dispersing its charge in a mist and in a stream, and effective against mycobacteria;

(3) fifty red plastic infectious waste bags, sealing tape, and labels as required by the regulations. The bags should be large enough to over pack any box or container ordinarily used to handle regulated medical waste;

(4) two sets of disposable overalls, gloves, boots, caps, and protective eye covering impermeable to liquids; surgical masks and tape for sealing wrists and ankles;

[38] *Id.* §14.08(e).

(5) a first aid kit (unless emergency medical care is available on the premises), fire extinguishers, and other appropriate safety equipment.

In the event of a spill, all treatment, destruction, or destination facilities must implement the following procedures upon the spill's discovery:

1. The cleanup crew must use protective equipment during the spill cleanup operation;
2. Limit access to the spill area only to authorized personnel;
3. Place broken containers and spillage inside over pack bags in the kit;
4. Disinfect the area and take other cleanup steps deemed necessary. Any absorbent materials used to disinfect the area shall be considered regulated medical waste;
5. Clean and disinfect non-disposable items;
6. Remove protective equipment and manage disposal items as regulated medical waste;
7. Take necessary steps to replenish containment and cleanup kit;
8. Call for emergency assistance if necessary;
9. Report immediately to the DEM all regulated medical waste spills or accidents, unless the quantity of such spills is less than one cubic foot of waste;
10. Submit a medical waste spill report to the DEM within forty eight (48) hours, using the spill or accident report form prescribed by the DEM. Any regulated medical waste spill outside the limited access areas must be reported to the DEM. A copy of the report shall be on file at the treatment facility for a minimum of three (3) years. The report shall include, but not be limited to:

    a. name of facility;
    b. name of employer(s) involved;
    c. address of the facility;
    d. date of spill or accident;

e. date of report;

f. short detailed summary of events; and

g. procedure(s) used to clean the spill or accident.

11. All spills should be recorded in a log that is maintained for a minimum of three (3) years from the date of the last entry in the log.[39]

In addition, no regulated medical waste may be stored more than fourteen (14) days and no facility shall store more than seven (7) times its total maximum daily capacity for treatment and/or destruction of regulated medical waste.[40]

The Regulations also contain detailed requirements for recordkeeping, the use of alternative technologies, the use of tracking forms and actual treatment, rail shipments, destruction and/or disposal regulated medical wastes.[41]

L. Registration for Generators of Regulated Medical Waste

No person whose primary business activity is the diagnoses (including testing and laboratory analysis), treatment, or immunization of human beings or animals, in research pertaining thereto, or in the preparation of human remains for burial or cremation, or in the production or testing of biologicals or in the development of pharmaceuticals shall engage in the generation of regulated medical waste unless that person has registered with the DEM in accordance with the Regulations and has been issued a Regulated Medical Waste Generator Registration Number.

A generator is required to apply for a registration number on a form prescribed by the DEM. The application shall include, at a minimum, the following:

1. Name under which the application is being made;

2. Business location(s) used to generate regulated medical waste and mailing address if difference from generation location(s);

[39] *Id.* §15.02(f).
[40] *Id.* §15.02(h).
[41] *Id.*§15.03-15.07.

3. The type[42] of generator facility at each business location;

4. Applicant's business phone number;

5. The name and phone number of the primary contact person for the facility;

6. The approximate amount of regulated medical waste (in pounds) that will be generated per year at each location;

7. If regulated medical waste is to be treated and/or destroyed on-site, provide a description of the treatment/destruction methods;

8. If regulated medical waste is to be transported off-site for treatment and/or destruction, provide the approximate quantity of treated and untreated waste (in pounds), as well as the name(s) and RI Regulated Medical Waste Transporter Permit Number(s) of the transporter(s);

9. The signature of the applicant or a person duly authorized to act on behalf of the applicant; and

10. Any other information reasonably required by the DEM to demonstrate that the applicant can safely generate and manage regulated medical waste in accordance with all applicable provisions of these Regulations.[43]

A Regulated Medical Waste Generator Registration shall expire on December 31 of the year of issuance unless sooner suspended or revoked. However, requests for renewal may be submitted within thirty (30) days of the expiration date of the current registration. The request must contain all of the information required above for new applications.[44] The Regulations also contain requirements for registration of more than one generator at the same site.[45]

The person wishing to obtain a registration number must pay a registration fee according to the following schedule:

---

[42] hospital, laboratory, clinic, physician, dentist, veterinarian, long-term or residential health care facility, blood bank, mortician or other (specify type).
[43] *Id.* §16.01(b).
[44] *Id.* §16.01(c).
[45] *Id.* §16.02.

Generator Category	Waste Generated per Generator per year	Annual Fee for Registration
1	Less than 25 lbs	$30 per generator
2	25 lbs to 100 lbs	$40 per generator
3	101 lbs to 500 lbs	$60 per generator
4	501 lbs to 2,000 lbs	$160 per generator
5	More than 2,000 lbs	$200 per generator[46]

M. Licenses for Storage, Treatment and/or Destruction of Regulated Medical Waste

No person or legal entity may engage in the storage, treatment and/or destruction of regulated medical waste unless that person or entity has obtained a license from the DEM for that purpose. However, the following activities do not constitute practices which require licensure:

1. Storage by the generator before regulated medical waste is treated and/or destroyed on-site, or offered for transport off-site; and

2. Treatment and/or destruction of regulated medical waste by the generator of that waste if the treatment and/or destruction:

    a. is carried out at a generating facility owned and operated by the generator of the regulated medical waste; and

    b. does not include regulated medical waste generated by any other person or legal entity.[47]

A license for the storage, treatment and/or destruction of regulated medical waste shall expire three (3) years from the date of issuance, unless sooner modified, suspended or revoked.[48] The holder of a license must notify DEM within 5 days of any changes in the information provided with the licensure application and in advance whenever possible.

Each application for a license to construct a facility for the storage, treatment and/or destruction of regulated medical waste, or application to renew a license to operate a facility for the storage, treatment and/or destruction of regulated medical waste, shall include a fee in

[46] *Id.* §16.03(a).
[47] *Id.* §17.01(c).
[48] *Id.* §17.01(d).

accordance with the following schedule:

Type of Facility	Application Fee	Renewal Fee
Medical Waste Incinerator	$20,000	$10,000
Treatment, Disinfection And/or Destruction Facility	$15,000	$7,500
Storage/Transfer Station	$10,000	$3,000
Mobile Operation(s)	$15,000	$7,500[49]

Facilities that perform multiple operations as part of a single facility operation are only required to possess the license with the highest fee category applicable to the activities performed at that site. However, two or more independently staffed facilities operating on the same site are each required to obtain a license, as well as pay the appropriate fee.[50]

N. Variances

An application for a variance from the segregation, handling, transportation, storage, or treatment requirements of the medical waste rules and regulations should be made in writing to the DEM. The DEM will then evaluate each request for a variance. A variance may be granted if the DEM finds that such a request will not be contrary to the purposes and policy of the medical waste regulations.[51]

---

[49] *Id.* §17.02(a).
[50] *Id.* §17.02(b).
[51] *Id.* §18.00 et seq.

CHAPTER XIII:

ASBESTOS CONTROL

A. Persons Affected by the Asbestos Act

In 1985, the Rhode Island Legislature passed the Asbestos Abatement Act (the "Act").[1] The Act and the Asbestos Regulations (the "Regulations") regulate contractors, owners, or operators of public or private buildings and residences containing friable asbestos, and all those involved in asbestos abatement.[2] "Friable asbestos" means asbestos containing material which, when dry may be crumbled, pulverized or reduced to power by hand pressure.[3] Flooring, shingles, roofing and any other building materials may become friable during renovation and/or demolition. Asbestos abatement means the repair, enclosure, encapsulation, or removal of friable asbestos in significant quantities.

The Act and the Regulations also regulate manufacturers and retailers by authorizing the director of health to limit or ban the use of asbestos products. In addition, the Act imposes strict liability on those who sell asbestos products that cause injury, death, or damage to any person exposed to our using the asbestos-containing product. Footnote: Id. §23-24.5-10

Furthermore, the Act provides a complaint process through which occupants of a building may request an asbestos inspection from the director of heath or enforcement of an existing asbestos enforcement plan.[4]

B. Asbestos Exposure Standards

The Act prohibits an owner or operator of a structure with friable asbestos, or any person or entity owning or controlling asbestos products in a friable state, from allowing any person to be exposed to asbestos when such an exposed condition violates the Act, any Regulation, an approved abatement plan, or the asbestos exposure standard.[5] Pursuant to the Act the director of health has established asbestos indoor nonoccupational air exposure standards.[6] Any owner of a

---

[1] R.I. Gen. Laws §23-24.5-1 *et seq.*
[2] R.I. Dept. of Health, Rules and Regulations for Asbestos Control §A.2.
[3] R.I. Gen. Laws §23-24.5-2(12).
[4] *Id.* §23-24.5-11.
[5] D. *23-24.5-5(a).*
[6] The standard is 0.01 fibers per cubic centimeter (f/cc) for fibers longer than five microns (or 300 nanograms per cubic meter) as measured by OSHA-NIOSH phase contrast optical microscopic methods and calculated as an eight hour time weighted average.

building with friable asbestos above the air exposure standard level, or any person owning or controlling products with friable asbestos above this level, is in violation of the Act and must remove the friable asbestos.

C. Asbestos Abatement Plans and Licensed Contractors

1. Asbestos Abatement Plans

When the owner of a public or private building containing friable asbestos is required to remove the asbestos, he or she must submit an asbestos abatement plan within 120 days to the Department of Heath and have the asbestos removed by a contractor licensed by the Department of Health. [7] However, if a spot repair or a private residence is involved, the owner need not submit an asbestos abatement plan or hire a licensed contractor. A spot repair is any removal, repair, encapsulation, enclosure or other disturbance which encompasses: (1) up to 10 linear feet of asbestos from piping and/or (2) up to 25 square feet of asbestos from any surfaces other than pipes. Smaller parts of large projects are not spot repairs.[8]

An asbestos abatement plan must include the results of asbestos detection tests, a blueprint of the structure involved, and a detailed program designed to monitor the physical condition of asbestos containing materials, educate those exposed to asbestos, and minimize asbestos release and contamination of humans. [9] The plan also must fully describe the processes to be used for removal, the process by which the licensed contractor was chosen, a time schedule for completion, disposal location and the level of compliance with the exposure standard anticipated.[10] Any person or entity submitting an abatement plan must pay a non-refundable fee to the Department of Health for the review of the plan.[11]

2. Approval of an Asbestos Abatement Plan

---

[7] R.I. Gen. Laws §§23-24.5-6(a). 23-24.5-12 and Rules §§A.4.1 and B.1.1.
[8] Rules §A.1.
[9] R.I. Gen. Laws §23-24.5-6(b).
[10] *Id.* §23-24.5-6(b)(2).
[11] Rules §C.1.6(a)

Under the Act, the Department of Health must either approve, amend, or reject an asbestos abatement plan within 90 days after its submission.[12] Before asbestos removal may proceed, the plan must receive the director of health's approval.[13]

The Department of Health may revoke the approval of any abatement plan which is based on statements that prove to be false or based upon a misrepresentation of fact.[14] The party who submitted the revoked plan may request a hearing by writing to the Department within 10 days of receiving the notice of revocation.[15]

An approved abatement plan will become invalid if the actions under the plan are not commenced within six months after the plan's approval and completed within 12 months after its issuance.[16] One, however, may request, in writing, a 90 day extension.[17] The six-month limit does not apply when the plan has been suspended or ordered abandoned by the court.[18]

3. Operations and Maintenance Program

An interim Operations and Maintenance Program ("O & M Program"), which describes measures to be taken until asbestos abatement begins, must also be provided with the abatement plan.[19] An O & M Program consists of, but is not limited to, actions to be taken when asbestos monitoring reveals the need for abatement; procedures for warning personnel and outsiders of the-asbestos, including signs and labeling; steps to minimize asbestos release monitoring the physical condition of the asbestos containing materials; and steps to minimize human contamination by asbestos.[20]

4. Licensed Asbestos Abatement Contractor

[12] R.I. Gen. Laws §23-24.5-6(c).
[13] Rules §A.4.1(a)
[14] *Id.* §C.1.4(a).
[15] *Id.* C.I.4(b).
[16] *Id.* §C.1.5(a).
[17] R.I. Gen. Laws 23-24.5-6(g) and Rules §C.1.5(b).
[18] R.I. Gen. Laws §23-24.5-6(g) and Rules §C.1.5(c).
[19] Rules §C.1.2(b).
[20] *Id.* §C.1.2(b).

A building owner implementing an approved asbestos abatement plan must first submit to the director of health a certified copy of the license of the asbestos contractor doing the work.[21] Persons performing only spot repairs do not need a license.

5. Penalties

Any person or entity violating the Act with respect to asbestos work or licensure is subject to a fine of up to $25,000 per violation, after a hearing.[22] Each day during which any portion of a violation continues shall constitute a separate offense.

In the case of a notice of violation, the abatement plan must be submitted to the director of heath within 120 days of notice of the violation in order to be relieved of liability for the violation during the abatement process.[23] If the notice of violation states that the evaluation has established an Asbestos Hazard Rating [24] greater than 90, the owner must also submit within 10 days of the notice the immediate corrective actions required by the Department of Health. [25] Failure to comply with an order of abatement issued by the director and to submit an abatement plan may result in a fine, after hearing, of up to $2,500 a day and or the closure of the area in violation.[26] No fine will be assessed to the owner if access to the area in violation is limited to persons certified to enter such areas under the Regulations.[27]

D. Demolition and Emergency Projects

Where a building has been ordered demolished by a municipal official, all friable asbestos must be removed beforehand by a licensed asbestos contractor following an abatement plan previously approved for the demolition of the structure. The licensed asbestos contractor must also provide the Department of Health with all project specific information.

A building owner who finds that he must carry-out an emergency asbestos abatement project is not required to submit an abatement plan, but must contact the director of health in advance for permission to remove the asbestos unless the nature of the emergency requires

[21] R.I. Gen. Laws. §23-24.5-12(b).
[22] *Id.* §23-24.5-26
[23] *Id.* §23-24.5-6(a)
[24] The rating is determined by the Department of Health pursuant to Rules §E.1.
[25] *Id.* §A.4.1(c).
[26] R.I. Gen. Laws §23-24.5-6(e).
[27] *Id.*

immediate action.[28] An emergency asbestos abatement project is "any asbestos abatement project which was not planned but results from a sudden, unexpected event" including non-routine equipment failures.[29] The building owner must notify the director of the health of the emergency abatement project not later than one day after its commencement, and indicate the name and license number of the asbestos contractor performing the work, the amount of asbestos involved, and the expected length of the project.[30] A more detailed report must be submitted to the director of health within 10 days after the emergency project's completion.[31] An emergency abatement project must still be carried out by a licensed contractor, unless it is a spot repair.[32]

E. Building Inspections and Closing

A building owner may face inspections and the closing of his or her building because of asbestos. The Act authorizes the director of health, or his or her designee, to inspect, at a reasonable time and without notice, any building, except a private residence in which a person may be exposed to friable asbestos.[33] The director of health may assess fees for the inspections.[34] Anyone refusing entry to an inspector or obstructuring an inspection ordered by the director of health will be fined $2,500 for each violation.[35]

The director of health is authorized to close any building, or a part thereof, to the public after notice and hearing if the director of health has found friable asbestos in violation of the Act.[36] No building or part thereof may be re-occupied until a re-occupancy permit is issued by the director of health.[37]

Where a building accessible to the public contains friable asbestos in levels greater than the asbestos standard, or where an abatement project or asbestos repair is taking place, a warning sign conforming to the director of health's specifications must be posted.[38] Such warning signs

[28] Rules §A.4.2(b)
[29] *Id.* §A.1.
[30] *Id.* §A.4.2(b).
[31] *Id.*
[32] *Id.* §A.4.2(c)(1).
[33] *Id.* §23-24.5-7(a).
[34] *Id.* §23-24.5-7(d).
[35] *Id.* §23-24.5-7(a).
[36] *Id.* §23-24.5-9(a) and Rules §A.2.4(a).
[37] R.I. Gen. Laws §23-24.5-9(b) and Rules §A.2.4(b).
[38] R.I. Gen. Laws §23-24.5-8(a).

may also be required where there is the possibility of the existence of friable asbestos.[39] In the event of an asbestos violation, notice of the violation will be filed by the director of health in the land evidence records in the city or town where the building is located.[40]

F. Asbestos Abatement Funds

The Act has established an Asbestos and Dangerous Product Abatement Fund ("Fund") within the Rhode Island Department of Administration.[41] The purposes of the Fund are to allow the Department of Health to purchase or lease asbestos testing and removal equipment, to provide grants and low interest loans to qualified persons or entities for asbestos abatement, and to reimburse the Department of Health for the training of persons involved in asbestos abatement.[42]

G. Asbestos Advisory Board

The Department of Health maintains an 11 member asbestos advisory board to oversee implementation of the Act. The board shall monitor all agency activities in the field of asbestos abatement and report to the majority leader on or before March 1 of every year whether changes must be made to the act. The board consists of: the directors of health and administration; the commissioner of elementary and secondary education; two public representatives appointed by the speaker and one by the majority leader; five members appointed by the governor who have asbestos experience (a lawyer, doctor, architect or engineer, a qualified environmental heath expert, and an asbestos contractor).

---

[39] *Id.* §23-24.5-8(b).
[40] *Id.* §23-24.5-8(c).
[41] R.I. Gen. Laws §23-24.5-19(a).
[42] *Id.*

CHAPTER XIV:

MISCELLANEOUS ENVIRONMENTAL LAWS AND REGULATIONS

A. Prohibition of Chlorofluorocarbons

The Rhode Island General Assembly, in response to the mounting concern over chlorofluorocarbons' ("CFCs") harm to the ozone layer, has banned the purchase, use, and manufacture of CFC-11 and CFC-12 processed products in Rhode Island.[1] "CFC-11" and "CFC-12" are members of the fully halogenated chlorofluorocarbons, which are substances containing carbon, fluorine, and chlorine which has no hydrogen atoms and no double bonds.[2] The Rhode Island Department of Environmental Management (the "DEM") may exempt a product from the CFC ban if its producer proves to the DEM that the ban would cause an undue hardship or that the CFC in the product has no effective substitute.[3]

Violators of this ban are subject to fines up to $5000. The DEM may also seek injunctive or equitable relief to enforce the CFC ban.[4]

B. Septage, Industrial Waste, and Waste Oil Pumping, Cleaning, and Transportation

Under the Septage, Industrial Waste, and Waste Oil Pumping, Cleaning, and Transportation Act,[5] no person, firm, corporation, partnership, or association can engage in the business of pumping, cleaning, and/or transporting septage, industrial waste or waste oil, unless he or she obtains a license from the DEM. All licenses are renewable annually, and expire on June 30 of each year unless sooner suspended or revoked by the DEM. Any person who fails to comply with this Act, upon conviction, will be punished by a fine of not more than $100 or by imprisonment for not more than 30 days, or both.

C. Low-Level Radioactive Waste Disposal

Under the Low-Level Radioactive Waste Act,[6] Rhode Island is required to enter into a contract with a low-level radioactive waste compact commission to provide for the disposal of all

---

[1] R.I. Gen. Laws §23-18.10-1 *et seq.*
[2] *Id.* §23-18.10-2(a).
[3] *Id.* §23-18.10-4
[4] *Id.* §23-18.10-6.
[5] *Id.* §23-19.4-1 *et seq.*
[6] *Id.* §23-19.11.1 *et seq.*

low-level radioactive waste generated in Rhode Island. Rhode Island compensates the regional compact commission for providing the disposal of all low-level radioactive waste produced by Rhode Island generators. The term "generators" is defined as all persons who produce or treat low-level radioactive waste in Rhode Island, but do not include persons who only provide a service for the collection, transportation, treatment, storage, or disposal of low-level radioactive waste generated outside the region.[7] The generators of low-level radioactive waste must reimburse the State of Rhode Island for providing the disposal services. All fees for the disposal of low-level radioactive waste will be based on the number of cubic feet of low-level radioactive waste deposited in an approved low-level radioactive waste disposal facility.[8]

D. Used Oil Recycling

The purpose of the Rhode Island Used Oil Recycling Act (the "Act")[9] is to encourage the collection and recycling of used oil. The Act prohibits the collection, transportation, transfer, storage, recycling, use, or disposal of used oil by way of discharge to sewers, drainage systems, surface or groundwater, or by incineration or deposition on land, unless in accordance with the Hazardous Waste Management Facilities Act,[10] the Water Pollution Act,[11] the Clean Air Act,[12] and any of the corresponding regulations.[13]

The term "used oil" means a petroleum-based oil which, after sale to a consumer, has become unsuitable for its original purpose through use, storage, or handling. Used oil constitutes a hazardous waste subject to the Hazardous Waste Management Facilities Act, but, nevertheless, is suitable for recycling.[14]

Under the Act, the Rhode Island Department of Environmental Management (the "DEM") requires persons regularly engaged in the business of selling containerized oil to post and maintain conspicuous signs, which warn consumers of the illegality of the improper disposal of used oil, explain how and where consumers may properly dispose of used oil, and provide

---

[7] *Id.* §23-19.11-1, 2.
[8] *Id.* §23-19.11-4.
[9] *Id.* §23-19.6-1 *et seq.*
[10] *Id.* §§23-19.7-1 *et seq.*
[11] *Id.* §§46-12-1 *et seq.*
[12] *Id.* §§23-23-1 *et seq.*
[13] *Id.* §23-19.6-5.
[14] *Id.* §23-19.6-4(4).

locations and operating hours of conveniently located collection facilities.[15] The DEM also maintains a used oil information center which explains local, state, and federal laws and regulations governing the use and disposal of used oil.[16]

The Act requires the DEM to designate conveniently located state motor vehicle inspection facilities and other appropriate facilities for collecting used oil at no cost to the public.[17] Each designated facility must maintain conspicuous signs that the facility is a used oil disposal location. Each facility must also provide oil collection containers which are properly sheltered and protected to prevent spillage, seepage, or discharge of used oil.[18]

E. Poison Prevention Packaging

The Poison Prevention Packaging Act (the "Act")[19] regulates the special packaging of "household substances" which, by reason of their packaging, are particularly hazardous to children. The term "special packaging" means packaging that is designed or constructed to be significantly difficult for children under five years of age to open or obtain a toxic or harmful amount of the substance contained therein, within a reasonable time and not difficult for normal adults to use properly, but does mean packaging which all small children cannot open or obtain a toxic or harmful amount within a reasonable time.[20]

The Act defines household substances as substances which individuals customarily produce, distribute, or store for consumption or use in or about a household and which constitutes, among other things, hazardous substances, pesticides, food, drugs, cosmetics, or substances intended for use as fuel when stored in portable containers and used in household heating, cooking, or refrigeration systems.[21]

The Act does not regulate any shipping containers or wrappings used solely for the transportation of household substances in bulk or quantity.[22] The Act does not prescribe specific

---

[15] *Id.* §23-19.6-6(1).
[16] *Id.* §23-19.6-6(2)-(3).
[17] *Id.* §23-19.6-7
[18] *Id.*
[19] *Id.* §§23-24.1-1 *et seq.* The Act incorporates by reference the federal Poison Prevention Packaging Act of 1970 15 U.S.C. §§1471-76, but authorizes the adoption of regulations which modify or deviate from the provisions of the federal Act. R.I. Gen. Laws §23-24.1-3.
[20] *Id.* §23-24.1-2(6).
[21] *Id.* §23-24.1-2(3).
[22] *Id.* §23-24.1-2(5).

packaging designs, product content, or package quality. However, in the case of household substances requiring special packaging, the Department of Health (the "DOH") may prohibit the packaging of substances in a way that is unnecessarily attractive to children.[23]

The Act provides an exception for making household substances readily available to elderly or handicapped persons who would be unable to use such substances if packaged in compliance with the required packaging standards.[24] The Act also does not regulate household substances dispensed pursuant to an order of a physician, dentist, or other licensed medical practitioner, when such order authorizes dispensation in a non-complying package or when so requested by the purchaser.[25]

The DOH, which enforces this Act, may enter, examine, or survey at any reasonable time such places as it considers necessary to enforce the provision of the Act.[26] If the DOH has reasonable grounds to believe that there is a violation of the Act, the DOH may give written notice of the alleged violation to the person responsible for the violation. Such notice automatically becomes a compliance order unless the person requests a hearing within ten days after service of the notice.[27] The DOH may issue an immediate compliance order if it determines that the violation may endanger public health, safety, or welfare.[28]

Any person who is convicted of violating any provision of the Act will be fined up to $100 or imprisoned for as long as 30 days, or both. A person convicted of violating a compliance order will be fined up to $300 or imprisoned for as long as 90 days, or both, for each offense, and each day's failure to comply with the order will constitute a separate offense.[29]

F. Battery Deposit and Control Act

The Rhode Island General Assembly enacted the Battery Deposit and Control Act (the "Act")[30] as part of a plan to control the disposal and encourage the recycling of vehicle batteries. A vehicle battery is a battery used in any vehicle, or with a capacity of six volts or more, and

---

[23] *Id.* §23-24.1-3(e).
[24] *Id.* §23-24.1-4(a).
[25] *Id.* §23-24.1-4(b).
[26] *Id.* §23-1-19. Inspection, enforcement, and penalties for violations of the provisions of the Act are governed by R.I. Gen. Laws §§23-1-19 to 23-1-25.
[27] *Id.* §23-1-20; *see* R.I. Gen Laws §23-1-23 (enforcement of compliance orders).
[28] *Id.* §23-1-21.
[29] *Id.* §23-1-25.
[30] R.I. Gen. Laws §23-60-1 *et seq.*

weighing one hundred and fifty pounds or less, and similar batteries for stationary uses. The Act allows dealers to apply a "core charge" to every vehicle battery sold in Rhode Island, paid at the time of sale, except no charge is allowed when the consumer delivers a used vehicle battery in reasonably clean and substantially unbroken conditions to the dealer at the time of purchase.[31] The charge amount will be returned to the consumer when the consumer delivers a used vehicle battery in reasonably clean and substantially unbroken condition to the dealer within seven days of the date of purchase of the new vehicle battery.[32] The dealer must return any used vehicle batteries to the manufacturer or distributor in reasonably clean and substantially unbroken conditions.[33]

The Act also prohibits the disposal of any vehicle battery, except by delivery to a dealer, distributor, manufacturer, the Rhode Island Resource Recovery Corporation, or to a privately operated recycling facility within Rhode Island that is licensed by the Rhode Island DEM or by delivery to an out-of-state recycling facility.[34]

Any person who violates the provision of this Act will be fined up to $1000 for each offense, and each day the violation continues constitutes a separate offense.[35]

G. Vehicle Tire Storage and Recycling Act

The Vehicle Tire Storage and Recycling Act (the "Act")[36] prohibits the disposal of any vehicle tire within Rhode Island, except by delivery of the tire to a tire disposal facility operated by the Rhode Island Resource Recovery Corporation, designated for that purpose or to a privately operated tire storage, recycling, or recovery facility licensed by the Rhode Island Department of Environmental Management (the "DEM") or by delivery to an out-of-state recycling facility.[37]

The Act also prohibits the burning of used tires within Rhode Island as a primary source

[31] *Id.* §23-60-3.
[32] *Id.*
[33] *Id.* §23-60-5.
[34] *Id.* §23-60-6.
[35] *Id.* §23-60-8.
[36] *Id.* §23-63-1 *et seq.*
[37] *Id.* §23-63-2(a).

of fuel and limits the exports of tires for burning outside the state within 30 miles of the Scituate reservoir watershed.[38] The Act permits the export of tires for burning only to a facility that has submitted to the DEM an environmental impact statement conforming to the standards of the United States Environmental Protection Agency and that has been approved by the DEM after a public hearing.[39]

The DEM will license a business as a vehicle tire recycler if the business maintains the proper equipment and facilities for recycling vehicle tire materials and pays the appropriate licensing fee.[40] The Act prohibits a person not licensed by the DEM from storing more than 400 used vehicle tires at any location within Rhode Island.[41]

Any person who violates the provisions of this Act will be fined up to $1,000 per violation, and each day the violation continues shall constitute a separate occurrence.[42]

H. Radon Testing

Under the Radon Testing Act,[43] if the director of health determines that a home should be tested for radon gas, then the property owner must permit access to the property for such testing.[44] The Department of Health must keep records of all radon tests and is further authorized to establish rules and regulations for radon testing.[45] No person may conduct radon tests without proper certification and prior notification to the director.[46]

I. Pesticide Control Act

The Pesticide Control Act[47] and the corresponding rules regulate the labeling, distribution, sale, storage, transportation, use, application, and disposal of pesticides. The term "pesticide" means:

---

[38] *Id.*
[39] *Id.* §23-63-3.
[40] *Id.* §23-63-4.
[41] *Id.* §23-63-2(b).
[42] *Id.* §23-63-5.
[43] R.I. Gen Laws §23-61-1 *et seq.*
[44] *Id.* §23-61-4(3).
[45] Rules and Regulations for Radon Control (as amended 2002).
[46] *Id.* §23-61-5.
[47] R.I. Gen. Laws §23-25-1 *et seq.*

1. Any substance or mixture of substances intended for preventing, destroying, repelling or mitigating any pest; and

2. Any substance or mixture of substances intended for use as a plant regulator, defoliant, or desiccant.[48]

Every pesticide distributed in Rhode Island must be registered with the Rhode Island Department of Environmental Management (the "DEM"). Registrations must be renewed annually prior to January 31. The applicant for registration must file a statement with the DEM which includes:

1. Name and address of the applicant and the name and address of the person whose name will appear on the pesticide's label;

2. The name of the pesticide;

3. Other necessary information required by the DEM;

4. A complete copy of the labeling accompanying the pesticide, including the directions for use and the pesticide's classifications.[49]

When a pesticide is registered, the DEM may require the applicant to submit a complete formula of the pesticide, including its active and inert ingredients. In the case of a renewal registration, a statement is only required with respect to information that is different from that furnished when the pesticide was registered or last re-registered.

Under the Act, no commercial applicator may apply any pesticide classified for general use by the Environmental Protection Agency or by the DEM unless that application is by or under the direct supervision of a person certified as a commercial pesticide applicator. Pesticides may be applied, however, by a person not licensed as a commercial pesticide applicator if the application is on land owned or rented by the applicator or his or her employer.[50]

It is unlawful for any person to act as a pesticide dealer, or advertise as a pesticide dealer without first becoming licensed under the Act. Any person issued a pesticide dealer's license

---

[48] *Id.* §23-25-4(29).
[49] Pesticides are classified under the Federal Insecticide, Fungicide and Rodenticide Act, 7 U.S.C. §136 *et seq.*
[50] R.I. Gen. Laws §§23-25-12, 23-25-13.

under the Act is required by DEM to keep accurate records containing information on the pesticides sold.[51]

The DEM also requires certified applicators to maintain records with respect to applications of "restricted use" and "state limited use" pesticides. All such records must be made available to the DEM at reasonable times to copy.[52]

The DEM may suspend, deny, revoke, or modify any provision on any license, permit, or certificate issued under the Act, if DEM finds that the applicant or holder of a license, permit, or certificate has committed any of the following acts:

1. Made false or fraudulent claims through any medium misrepresenting the effects of pesticides or methods to be utilized;

2. Made a pesticide recommendation or use inconsistent with the labeling with the EPA or state registration for that pesticide, or in violation of the restrictions on the use of that pesticide;

3. Applied known ineffective or improper pesticides;
4. Operated faulty or unsafe equipment;
5. Operated in a faulty, careless, or negligent manner;
6. Neglected or, after notice, refused to comply with the provisions of the Act;
7. Refused or neglected to keep and maintain the records required by the Act;
8. Used or supervised the use of a pesticide by someone not qualified as a certified applicator.

9. Made false or fraudulent records, invoices, or reports;
10. Used fraud or misrepresentation in making an application for, renewal of, a license, permit, or certification;
11. Refused or neglected to comply with any limitations or restrictions on or in a duly license, permit, or certification;

[51] *Id.* §§23-25-15, 23-25-23.
[52] *Id.* §23-25-23.

12. Aided or abetted a licensed or certified, or unlicensed or non-certified, person to evade the Act's provisions, conspired with that person to evade the provisions of the Act, or allowed one's license, permit, or certification to be used by another person;

13. Made false or misleading statements during or after an inspection concerning any infestation or infection of pests found on land;

14. Impersonated any federal, state, county, or city inspector official; or

15. Has been subject to the final imposition of civil or criminal penalties under relevant Federal Laws.[53]

It is unlawful for any person to detach, alter, deface, or destroy, wholly or in part, any label provided for under the Act or to add any substance to, or take any substance from, a pesticide in a manner that may defeat the purpose of the Act. It is also unlawful for any person to handle, transfer, store, display, or distribute pesticides in such a manner as to endanger humans and the environment, or to endanger food, feed, or any other products that may be transported, stored, displayed, or distributed with those pesticides.[54]

Also, no person shall transport, store, or dispose of any pesticide or pesticide containers in such a manner as to cause injury to humans, vegetation, crops, livestock, wildlife, beneficial insects, or to pollute any waterway or water body in a way harmful to any wildlife therein.[55]

The DEM may sample and examine pesticides for the purpose of determining whether they comply with the Act. The DEM is authorized to enter any distributor's premises, including any vehicle of transportation, at all reasonable times in order to have access to pesticides.[56] If the DEM determines that there is a violation of the Act, the DEM will give notice to the alleged violator. Any person so notified has a reasonable time to present his or her views, either orally or in writing, with regard to the alleged violation.

---

[53] *Id.* §23-25-18.
[54] *Id.*
[55] *Id.* §23-25-19.
[56] *Id.* §23-25-20.

When the DEM has reasonable cause to believe a pesticide or device is being distributed, stored, transported or used in violation of the Act, the DEM may issue and serve a written "stop sale, use, or removal" order is made upon the owner or custodian of such pesticide or device.[57] The pesticide or device, then, cannot be sold, used, or removed until the Act is complied with. After service of a "stop sale, use, or removal" order is made upon any person, that person, the registrant, or the DEM may file an action in the appropriate court of Rhode Island for an adjudication of the alleged violation. The court, in such an action, may issue a temporary or permanent injunction, and such other intermediate orders as it deems necessary or advisable. The court also may order condemnation of any pesticide or device which does not meet the requirements of the Act.[58] If the pesticide or device is condemned, it shall, after entry of decree, be disposed of by destruction or sale as the court directs. When a decree of condemnation is entered against the pesticide or device, court costs, fees, storage, and other proper expenses are awarded against the person, if any, appearing as a claimant of the pesticide.[59]

Any person who violates any provision of the Act may be assessed a civil penalty of not more than $10,000 for each offense. In addition to any civil penalty, DEM may ban businesses or commercial applicators from providing pest control services to Rhode Island for a period of up to five years when the DEM finds a business or commercial applicator has violated a provision of the Act with regard to the mixing or application of pesticides. No penalty under the Act will be assessed unless the person charged has been notified and given opportunity for a hearing before the DEM on the charge. In making the assessment, the DEM must consider the size of the business, the ability of the person charged to continue in business, and the gravity of the violation.[60]

Any person who knowingly violates any provision of the Act is guilty of a misdemeanor and shall, on conviction, be fined not more than $25,000 or imprisoned for not more than 60 days, or both. Any person who with intent to defraud, uses or reveals information relative to formulas acquired under the Act, shall be fined not more than $10,000 or imprisoned for not more than 3 years, or both.[61]

---

[57] *Id.* §23-25-21
[58] *Id.* §23-25-22.
[59] *Id.*
[60] *Id.* §23-25-28(a).
[61] *Id.* §23-25-28(b).

J. Lead Poisoning Prevention Rules and Regulations[62]

The Rules and Regulations for Lead Poisoning Prevention were promulgated by the Department of Health ("DOH") for the purpose of establishing environmental lead standards, procedures and intervals for blood lead screening, procedures for laboratory testing and reimbursement by insurers, procedures for conducting environmental lead inspections, procedures for conducting lead hazard reduction activities, and procedures for and licensure/certification of persons conducting environmental lead inspections and/or lead hazard reduction activities.[63]

1. Comprehensive Environmental Lead Inspections

A Comprehensive Environmental Lead Inspection must be conducted for a dwelling, dwelling unit, or premises as follows:

a. The DOH shall conduct Comprehensive Environmental Lead Inspections of the homes of significantly lead poisoned children as part of treatment and follow up;

b. The DOH shall conduct Comprehensive Environmental Lead Inspections of al licensed child care facilities in the State, including licensed preschools, daycares, nursery schools, public and private elementary schools, playgrounds, and shelters and foster homes serving children under seventy-two (72) months of age; and

c. The DOH may elect to conduct Comprehensive Environmental Lead Inspections under any circumstances, which in the Departments judgment, warrant such action or at an owner, tenant, or occupants request.[64]

If after such an inspection, the DOH determines that the premises is not either lead-free or lead-safe, and such premises presents a clear and significant health risk to

[62] Promulgated pursuant to R.I. Gen. Laws §§23-24.6-5, 23-24.6-7, 23-24.6-10, 23-24.6-12, 23- 24.6-14, 23-24.6-17, 23-24.6-20 and 23-24.6-26.

[63] "See also U.S. Department of Housing and Urban Development, 'Guidelines for the Evaluation and Control of Led-Based Paint in Housing,' HUD-006700, June 1995."

[64] The Rules and Regulations for Lead Poisoning Prevention §4.2(a).

occupants then lead hazard reduction to at least the lead-safe level may be required. "Lead-free" premises means a dwelling, dwelling unit, or other premises that either contains no led or contains lead in amounts less than the maximum acceptable environmental lead levels established in the rules and regulations.[65] "Lead-safe" premises means a dwelling, dwelling unit, or other premises that has undergone sufficient lead hazard reduction to ensure that no significant environmental lead hazard is present, and includes, but is not limited to, covering and encapsulation.[66]

2. Lead Hazard Reduction

The inspection report of a Comprehensive Environmental Lead Inspection of any rental unit or of any dwelling, dwelling unit, or premises, occupied by a child under seventy-two (72) months of age in this State which identifies any significant environmental lead hazards and/or the identification of any significant environmental lead hazards during an inspection or a re-inspection conducted pursuant to an Environmental Lead Management Plan shall serve as a notice to abate the lead hazard(s).[67]

The DOH has determined that the following conditions present a clear and significant health risk to occupants and require lead hazard reduction to at least the lead-safe level:

1. Removal of lead-based paint from an interior surface with an area, from which paint is to be removed, of certain sizes specified by the regulations;
2. Any peeling, flaking, chipping, or otherwise damaged (i.e. can be removed with a fingernail or demonstrates evidence of mouthing) lead-based paint on interior or exterior painted surfaces;
3. Lead-based paint that has a visible residue of paint which can be wiped from surface (i.e. chalking), which if therefore considered damaged;
4. Lead-based paint on interior and/or exterior friction surfaces of windows, which is therefore considered damaged;

---

[65] *Id.* §1.0
[66] *Id.*
[67] *Id.* §11-1(c).

5. Lead-based paint on friction surfaces of doors and door jambs, which is therefore considered damaged;

6. Lead in drinking water at concentrations greater than five hundred (500) ug/l for a first-draw sample or greater than fifteen (15) ug/l for a flushed sample from any tap or water source used as a source of water for drinking and/or cooking;

7. Lead in a soil at concentrations greater than one thousand (1000) ppm or lead in exposed bare surface soil at concentrations greater than four hundred (400) ppm;

8. Lead in interior or exterior dust samples at concentrations greater than one thousand (1000) ppm by vacuum sampling, or greater than forty (40) ug/ft^2 on floors and/or greater than five hundred (500) ug/ft^2 in window wells or greater than forty (40) ug/ft^2 on any surface by wipe sampling or lead in interior dust in excess of five thousand (5000) ppm; and

9. Visible dust during renovation of any room(s)/area(s) known to contain lead-based paint.[68]

Lead hazard reduction shall only be performed by Lead Hazard Reduction Contractors, licensed in accordance with the Rules and Regulations for Lead Poisoning Prevention, for the following dwellings, dwelling units, and premises: 1) Residential rental units, as defined in the Regulations, whether occupied or vacant, including common areas; 2) Single family residential dwellings and owner occupied dwelling units in which one or more children under six years of age resides or is expected to reside within the next twelve (12) months 3) Licensed child care facilities whose primary purpose is or will be to care for children under six years of age, including, but not limited to, preschools, daycare facilities, nursery schools, public or private elementary schools, playgrounds, foster homes, and shelters 4) Any

[68] *Id.* §11.1(a).

other property in which a child under six years of age resides or is expected to reside within the next twelve (12) months for fourteen (14) or more days per year.[69]

The Regulations prohibit anyone, however, from using abrasive blasting and/or mechanical removal equipment for interior painted surfaces except as otherwise authorized by the Regulations. In addition, the utilization of a torch or open burning flame, or the utilization of chemical strippers containing methylene chloride for interior work areas, and the dry sweeping of lead-contaminated areas or surfaces is strictly prohibited. Dan-sanding of interior painted surfaces except for "foatheming" of previously treated surface or when conducting mechanical paint remover in accordance with the Regulations is also prohibited.[70]

The Regulations also contain detailed requirements for licensing lead hazard reduction contractors, lead hazard reduction site supervisors and lead hazard reduction workers.[71] Furthermore, the regulations also detail administrative procedures, reporting requirements, enforcement, conflict of interest, and interpretation issues.[72]

---

[69] *Id.* § 2.1, §11.2(a).
[70] *Id.* §11.3.
[71] *Id.* §15.0 *et seq.*
[72] *Id.* §§8.0, 15.0-23.0.

CHAPTER XV:

RHODE ISLAND ENVIRONMENTAL COMMON LAW

Although federal, state and local environmental statutes regulate many environmental cases, the traditional common law theories of nuisance, trespass, and negligence still apply to many environmental issues.

A. Nuisance

The essential element of nuisance action is that persons have suffered harm or have been threatened with injuries they should not bear.[1] Actionable nuisance is classified as either public or private. Although the injury produced by an actionable nuisance may be only threatened, the injury must be real and not fanciful or imaginary.[2] Generally, in Rhode Island nuisance cases,[3] a private nuisance involves an interference with the use and enjoyment of one's property.[4] A public nuisance is an unreasonable interference with a right common to the general public. A public nuisance is behavior that unreasonably interferes with the health, safety, peace, comfort or convenience of the general community.[5]

Perhaps the greatest controversy has arisen over whether a showing of negligence is required for actionable nuisance. Although earlier case law had suggested the necessity to prove negligence, that proposition has been overruled and more recent cases hold that a showing of negligence is not necessary.[6]

B. Negligence

The theory of negligence is that liability should be predicated on fault, whereby the defendant must owe the plaintiff a duty of care. Where there is no duty of care owed, no liability

---

[1] *Weida v. Ferry,* 493 A.2d 824 (R.I. 1985); *Wood v. Picillo*, 443 A.2d 1244 (R.I. 1982); *Citizens for the Preservation of Waterman Lake v. Davis,* 420 A.2d53 (R.I. 1980).

[2] *Blomen v. N. Barstow Co.*, 85 A. 924, 926 (R.I. 1913).

[3] *Weida v. Ferry,* 493 A.2d 824 (R.I. 1985) (odor and files); *Citizens for the Preservation of Waterman Lake v. Davis,* 420 A.2d 53 (R.I. 1980) (water pollution and violation of the Fresh Water Wetlands Act); *Braun v. Ianotti,* 175 A. 656 (R.I. 1934); (contamination of drinking water).

[4] *Weida v. Ferry*, 493 A.2d 824, 826 (R.I. 1985); *Citizens for the Preservation of Waterman Lake v. Davis,* 420 A.2d 53.59 (R.I. 1980) *Infratte v. Ramsden,* 190 A.2d 473 (R.I. 1963).

[5] *Citizens for the Protection of Waterman Lake v. Davis*, 420 A.2d 53, 57 (R.I. 1980); *Radigan v. W.J. Halloran Co.,* 196 A.2d 160, 163 (R.I. 1968).

[6] *Wood v. Picillo,* 443 A.2d 1244 (R.I. 1982); *Braun v. Iannotti,* 175 A. 656, 657 (R.I. 1934.); *Splendorio v. Bilray Demolition Co.,* 682 A.2d 461 (R.I. 1996).

will attach.[7] In a negligence action, the measure of behavior is whether the defendant acted with reasonable care[8] and whether the defendant breached the duty owed to the plaintiff. The burden is then on the plaintiff to establish by a fair preponderance of the evidence that the defendant was negligence and that the negligence was the proximate cause of the plaintiff's damages.[9]

C. Strict Liability

Under the theory of strict liability, defendants are held liable without fault. Strict liability tends to be imposed where public policy considerations outweigh traditional notions of liability predicated on fault. Most cases of strict liability involve dangerous substances, machinery, and other instrumentalities. When dealing with such times, a higher degree of care and vigilance is required than is required in the ordinary affairs of life or business, which usually involve little or no risk of injury to persons or property.[10]

In a case of strict liability, the manufacturer is held responsible for injuries caused by his or her product. One who sells defective products that are dangerous to a person or property is subject to liability for any harm caused to any reasonably foreseeable person or to his or her property, as long as the seller is engaged in the business of selling the dangerous product and the product reaches the person without substantial change in condition. Liability is imposed even though the seller exercised all possible care and preparation in the sale of product.[11]

D. Trespass

Trespass is an activity that causes physical invasion in a tangible manner to a person's possessory interest in land. Some cases have held that a nontangible invasion of a person's property, such as noise or odor, also creates a trespass. Noise alone, however, will most likely not constitute a trespass unless the noise vibrations are so severe as to cause physical damage.

E. Other Theories

A final common law theory used to resolve disputes, especially those involving surface

---

[7] *Vanvooren v. John E. Fogerty Memorial Hospital,* 321 A.2d 100 (R.I. 1974) (water pollution).

[8] *Petella v. Union Carbide Corp.*, 342 F.Supp. 366 (D.R.I. 1964).

[9] *Gagnon v. Laundry, 234 A.2d 674, 676* (R.I. 1967)(Pollution of well from ruptured septic tank).

[10] *Rott v. Blackstone Valley Gas and Electric Company,* 106A.2d 251 (R.I. 1954).

[11] *Ritter v. Narragansett Electric Co.*, 283 A.2d 255 (R.I. 1971); *Klimas v. International Telephone and Telegraph Corp.*, 297 F. Supp. 937 (D.R.I. 1969).

water, is the "rule of reasonable use". Under this rule, the property owner's liability turns on a determination of the reasonableness of his or her actions. The issue of reasonableness is a question of fact to be determined in each case upon consideration of all relevant circumstances. This rule does not rest on negligence, nor does it focus solely on the character of the property owner's action. Instead, it focuses on the results of the action, and the consequent interference with another's use and enjoyment of his or her land – much like the tort of nuisance.[12]

F. Rhode Island Supreme Court Cases

In the last few years the Rhode Island Supreme Court has clarified and ruled on various environmental issues. The following is a summary of some of the more significant decisions:

Splendorio v. Bilray Demolition Co., 682 A.2d 461 (R.I. 1996): Owner of land which adjoined the wrecking yard of a demolition company at which debris from asbestos remediation project on buildings performed by the demolition company had been stored brought an action against an engineering firm which had inspected buildings for asbestos, developed remediation plan, and certified removal of asbestos. The Superior Court granted summary judgment in favor of the engineering firm. On appeal, the Supreme Court held that: (1) a party may be held strictly liable for conduct of an abnormally dangerous activity; (2) actions of the engineering firm did not constitute ultrahazardous or abnormally dangerous activity; and (3) the engineering firm did not owe a duty to the landowner.

Keeney v. Vinagro, 656 A.2d 973 (R.I. 1995): Department of Environmental Management ("DEM") filed a complaint against owners who refused to allow DEM to examine the owners' property after receiving complaints of smoke and odors. The Supreme Court, Providence County, granted Injunctive relief and the owners appealed. The Supreme Court of Rhode Island denied the appeal holding: (1) consent agreement did not preclude the trial court from granting injunctive relief; and (2) the statute authorizing the DEM to make warrantless inspections for violations of Clean Air Act regulations, for sources of air pollution, or for other violations satisfies constitutional requirements for searches.

Hydro-Manufacturing v. Kayser-Roth, 640 A.2d 950 (R.I. 1994): Property owner brought action against successor to parent of corporation which had previously owned land in

[12] *Bulter v. Bruno*, 341 A.2d 735 (R.I. 1975).

order to recover damages for contamination with which property owner had to deal. The Superior Court granted summary judgment in favor of the defendant, and property owner appealed. The Supreme Court held that: (1) statute making person liable for damage caused by groundwater pollution does not apply retroactively; (2) prior owners of property do not own remote purchasers a duty to maintain the property of refrain from activity that will damage it; (3) court would not extend common-law negligence doctrine to create duty running to remote purchaser with respect to contamination; and (4) landowner did not have claim based on private or public nuisance.

Durfee v. Ocean State Steel, Inc., 636 A.2d 698 (R.I. 1994): The Superior Court held air polluter in civil contempt for failure to comply with previous consent decree regarding reduction of air pollution. Appeal was taken. The Supreme court held that: (1) order was not ambiguous, even though it did not provide what would happen in event polluter was unable to meet standards; (2) polluter had not substantially complied with requirements; and (3) closure could be ordered even though there would be substantial adverse impact to local and state economy.

Strafach v. Durfee, 635 A.2d 277 (R.I. 1993): Landowner sought variance to permit location of individual sewage disposal system (ISDS) within 150 feet of ocean in designated erosion-prone areas. The Department of Environmental Management (DEM) denied variance, but the Superior Court reversed. Director of DEM petitioned for certiorari. The Supreme Court held that credible evidence supported the determination by hearing officer that landowners failed to meet burden of proving that requested variance from 1560-foot setback requirement for ISDS in erosion-prone ocean front area would not be contrary to public interest and public health.

Environmental Scientific Corp. v. Durfee, 621 A.2d 200 (R.I. 1993): Applicant seeking to proceed with construction project appealed from final decision of Department of Environmental Management (DEM) which, reversing hearing officer, denied water-quality certificate and application to alter freshwater wetlands. The Superior Court affirmed, and applicant petitioned for writ of certiorari. The Supreme Court held that: (1) DEM's final decision lacked sufficient evidentiary support to overcome deference it had to accord hearing officer's decision; (2) director of DEM should give great deference to hearing officer's findings and conclusions unless clearly wrong; and (3) DEM's rationale in reversing decision of hearing officer must be substantiated by more than mere philosophical differences with officer.

Newbay Corp. v. Sission, 621 A.2d 1250 (R.I. 1993): Corporation sought declaratory judgment on whether it was entitled to a permit from the coastal resource management council (CRMC) for a proposed coal-fired cogeneration facility. The Superior Court granted summary judgment for the corporation and CRMC appealed. The Supreme Court held that the CRMC was required to hold a hearing on the issue of whether the proposed facility would have an impact on the coastal environment, in order to determine whether there was an actual controversy at stake.

Hall v. Nascimento, 594 A.2d 874 (R.I. 1991): Lot owners brought action alleging that they owned land adjacent to their property which was created by dredging the bay. The Superior Court found that lot owners had title to tract of land. Appeal was taken. The Supreme Court held that: (1) considering maps and deeds together, it was clear that boundaries of lot owner's property did not extend to property created by dredging of bay; (2) evidence did not show that common grantor conveyed area of land including high-water mark, and, thus, landowners did not acquire littoral rights; and (3) because property under water was subject to public trust doctrine, property reclaimed by dredging of bay could not be taken by lot owners by means of adverse possession.

Vito v. Dep't of Environmental Management, 589 A.2d 809 (R.I. 1991): Department of Environmental Management (DEM) appealed from order of the Superior Court which directed it to schedule and conduct freshwater-wetlands public hearing within 90 days of denied applicant's request for one. The Supreme Court held that: (1) statute required DEM to schedule hearings within a reasonable time of denied applicant's request for one; (2) failure to schedule the hearings had resulted in denial of due process; and (3) court properly directed that hearings be held within 90 days.

Ratcliffe v. Coastal Resources Management Council, 584 A.2d 1107 (R.I. 1991): Property owners began constructing residence in 1976 after obtaining building permit and sewage disposal permit. Coastal Resources Management Council (CRMC) issued cease and desist order to halt construction. Property owners appealed. The Superior Court vacated CRMC's decision. Environmental advocate sought to intervene. The Superior Court allowed advocate to intervene and dismissed property owner's appeal. CRMC issued second cease and desist order and issued "assent" placing restrictions before construction could be resumed. Property owners petitioned for writ of certiorari. The Supreme Court held that: (1) interests of justice demanded immediate review of assent; (2) assent was invalid; and (3) property owners could continue construction in fashion that was consistent with sewage permit.

Davis v. Wood, 427 A.2d 332 (R.I. 1981): A waste management facility operator who, after being denied a license for violations at his facility, brought suit against the Department of Environmental Management ("DEM") claiming that the licensing power of the DEM was an unconstitutional delegation of legislative power. The trial court found for the operator. On writ of certiorari the Supreme Court held that: (1) the legislative directive that activities relating to management of solid waste be conducted "in an environmentally sound manner" creates a sufficiently intelligible standard for DEM and, hence, provision authorizing licensing of solid waste management facilities does not represent an unconstitutional delegation of legislative power; (2) fact that hearing was aware of DEM's case did not of itself show bias; and (3) hearing officer's questioning of witnesses and inquiry of agency attorney whether certain testimony was forthcoming was merely an attempt at clarification of testimony rather than partisanship to the agency.

PRV1 #94358 v1

Government Institutes Mini-Catalog

PC #	ENVIRONMENTAL TITLES	Pub Date	Price*
949	ABCs of Environmental Regulation, Second Edition	2002	$79
812	Achieving Environmental Excellence	2003	$79
898	Book of Lists for Regulated Hazardous Substances, Tenth Edition	2001	$99
846	Clean Water Handbook, Third Edition	2003	$125
822	Environmental Compliance Auditing & Management Systems (ECAMS)	2001	$1,395
897	EH&S CFR Training Requirements, Fifth Edition	2001	$125
4300	EH&S Daily Federal Register Notification Service (e-mail)	2003	$150
890	Environmental Biotreatment: Technologies for Air, Water, Soil, and Wastes	2002	$149
4045	Environmental, Health & Safety CFRs on CD-ROM, single issue	2003	$450
825	Environmental, Health and Safety Audits, 8th Edition	2001	$115
4900	Environmental Law Expert, CD-ROM	2003	$695
955	Environmental Law Handbook, Seventeenth Edition	2003	$99
688	Environmental Health & Safety Dictionary, Seventh Edition	2000	$95
956	Environmental Statutes, 2003 Edition	2003	$125
957	Fundamentals of Environmental Sampling	2003	$79
689	Fundamentals of Site Remediation	2000	$85
907	Hazardous Materials Transportation Training, Student's Manual	2002	$89
958	Information Technology Solutions for EH&S Professionals	2003	$115
823	Integrating Environmental, Health, and Safety Systems	2001	$495
588	International Environmental Auditing	1998	$179
819	ISO 14001: Positioning Your Organization for Environmental Success	2001	$115
936	Managing Your Hazardous Wastes	2002	$89
830	RCRA CFRs Made Easy	2002	$115
841	Risk Management Planning Handbook, Second Edition	2002	$115
816	Stormwater Discharge Management	2003	$89
946	Wastewater and Biosolids Treatment Technologies	2002	$129

PC #	SAFETY and HEALTH TITLES	Pub Date	Price*
697	Applied Statistics in Occupational Safety and Health	2000	$105
893	Beyond Safety Accountability	2001	$79
894	Building Successful Safety Teams	2001	$79
843	Emergency Preparedness for Facilities	2003	$125
904	Ergonomics: A Risk Manager's Guide	2002	$159
949	Excavation Safety	2003	$85
663	Forklift Safety, Second Edition	1999	$85
814	Fundamentals of Occupational Safety & Health, Third Edition	2003	$79
818	Job Hazard Analysis	2001	$79
888	Keys to Behavior Based Safety	2001	$85
662	Machine Guarding Handbook	1999	$75
838	Managing Chemical Safety	2002	$95
889	Managing Electrical Safety	2001	$69
4800	OSHA Compliance Master CD-ROM	2003	$375
668	Safety Made Easy, Second Edition	1999	$75
947	Safety Metrics	2003	$85
815	So, You're the Safety Director, Third Edition	2003	$89

Government Institutes
4 Research Place, Suite 200 • Rockville, MD 20850-3226
Tel. (301) 921-2323 • FAX (301) 921-0264
Email: giinfo@govinst.com • www.govinst.com

Please call our customer service department at (301) 921-2323 for a free publications catalog.

CFRs now available online. Call (301) 921-2323 for info.

*All prices are subject to change. Please call for current prices and availablity.

Government Institutes Order Form

4 Research Place, Suite 200 • Rockville, MD 20850-3226
Tel (301) 921-2323 • Fax (301) 921-0264
Internet: http://www.govinst.com • E-mail: giinfo@govinst.com

4 EASY WAYS TO ORDER

1. Tel: **(301) 921-2323**
Have your credit card ready when you call.

2. Fax: **(301) 921-0264**
Fax this completed order form with your company purchase order or credit card information.

3. Mail: **Government Institutes Division**
ABS Group Inc.
P.O. Box 846304
Dallas, TX 75284-6304 USA

Mail this completed order form with a check, company purchase order, or credit card information.

4. Online: Visit http://www.govinst.com

PAYMENT OPTIONS

❑ **Check** *(payable in US dollars to* ***ABS Group Inc. Government Institutes Division****)*

❑ **Purchase Order** *(This order form must be attached to your company P.O. Note: All International orders must be prepaid.)*

❑ **Credit Card** ☐ VISA ☐ MasterCard ☐ American Express

Exp. ____ /____

Credit Card No. ______________________________

Signature ______________________________

(Government Institutes' Federal I.D.# is 13-2695912)

CUSTOMER INFORMATION

Ship To: (Please attach your purchase order)

Name ______________________________

GI Account # *(7 digits on mailing label)* ______________

Company/Institution ______________________________

Address ______________________________
(Please supply street address for UPS shipping)

____

City ______________ State/Province ______________

Zip/Postal Code ______________ Country ______________

Tel ( )

Fax ( )

E-mail Address ______________________________

Bill To: (if different from ship-to address)

Name ______________________________

Title/Position ______________________________

Company/Institution ______________________________

Address ______________________________
(Please supply street address for UPS shipping)

____

City ______________ State/Province ______________

Zip/Postal Code ______________ Country ______________

Tel ( )

Fax ( )

E-mail Address ______________________________

Qty.	Product Code	Title	Price

Subtotal __________
MD Residents add 5% Sales Tax __________
Shipping and Handling (see box below) __________
Total Payment Enclosed __________

30 DAY MONEY-BACK GUARANTEE

If you're not completely satisfied with any product, return it undamaged within 30 days for a full and immediate refund on the price of the product.

SOURCE CODE: BP03

Shipping and Handling

Within U.S:
1-4 products: $6/product
5 or more: $4/product

Outside U.S:
Add $15 for each item (Global)

Sales Tax

Maryland 5%
Texas 8.25%
Virginia 4.5%